Peter Hitchcock is a Distinguished Professor of English, Film and Media Cultures, Women's and Gender Studies, and Comparative Literature at the City University of New York (CUNY). He also serves as Associate Director of the Center for Place, Culture, and Politics at the CUNY Graduate Center. His work examines the cultural politics of anti-capitalism and anti-imperialism as they intersect with class, race, gender, and national identity. His books include *Labor in Culture; or, Worker of the World(s)* (2017), *The Long Space* (2009), *Imaginary States* (2003), and *Dialogics of the Oppressed* (1992).

PETER HITCHCOCK

Seriality and Social Change

LONDON NEW YORK CALCUTTA

Sources of images used in the roundels on the cover (from left to right):

Hugo Gellert, Frontispiece in *Karl Marx: "Capital" in Lithographs* (New York: Ray Long and Richard R. Smith, 1934).

Gellert, "Commodities" in *Karl Marx: "Capital" in Lithographs*, p. 21.

Mary M. Talbot and Bryan Talbot, *The Red Virgin and the Vision of Utopia* (Milwaukie, OR: Dark Horse Books, 2016), p. 41.

Gellert, "Law of Capitalist Accumulation" in *Karl Marx: "Capital" in Lithographs*, p. 53.

Karl Marx, *Le Capital,* ISSUE 1 (M. J. Roy trans.) (Paris: Maurice Lachâtre, 1872).

Seagull Books, 2025

First published in volume form by Seagull Books, 2025

ISBN 978 1 80309 583 7

British Library Cataloguing-in-Publication Data

A catalogue record for this book is available from the British Library

Typeset by Seagull Books, Calcutta, India
Cover designed by Sunandini Banerjee, Seagull Books

Contents

PART ONE

A Story of Capital

"Segui il tuo corso, e lascia dir le genti"

This quote, which ends Marx's Foreword to the first German edition (1867) of *Capital* is modified by Marx from Dante's *La Divina Commedia*, so that it reads "follow your own course, and let the people talk." There is an ambivalence here that I read as a provocation. Marx does not say "follow me" as in the original, but take your own path. As for the people, Marx here means public opinion, in contrast to the science of political economy he presents.

But what if taking your own path has a public suasion, or implies a public or popular readership? Does one sacrifice science if one wants to put it in working-class hands? This question will become central to Marx's serial version of *Capital* in French.

WHAT IS SERIALITY?

When Jean-Paul Sartre famously asked "what is literature?" he begins with a reasonable assumption literature exists, it has being and has a category that resolutely denotes it.[1] Sartre will particularize, of course, for this was a time (1948) when literature was secure enough in its designation it required no capital letter to signal universalization from professional interest. Critical claims, like Sartre's penchant for phenomenological realism, were discursive skirmishes within a recognizable field where the seriousness of the question, while hardly rhetorical or only academic, pivoted on an established interpretative community. For their part, Sartre's reader of literature is framed by notions of "induction," "interpolation," and "extrapolation"—all derived from a characterization of the reader's will (yet mediated in no small measure, one should add, by education, language, literacy, and, crucially, time). And what of seriality, something that Sartre also theorized at length? Is this not simply the opposite of literature in its experience? Is it not an everywhere and an everyday (the order of living, industrial and media reproduction, etc.) rather than the vital connotation of the literary as a higher calling and understanding of the way the dynamics of meaning are articulated?[2] To ask "What is seriality?" does not seem to carry a corresponding ontological heft, as if its ubiquity marks less "being toward" and more an inexorable and/or teleological line that means death and suppression without a demonstrable and intricate sense of ending—just a process of perfecting pessimism. The break and continuity of seriality, series, and the serial are at the heart of this study, precisely because the stark opposition read into their logic belies

1 See Jean-Paul Sartre, *Qu'est-ce que la littérature?* (Paris: Gallimard, 1948).

2 For a general definition of seriality, see Shane Denson, "Seriality" in Jeffrey R. Di Leo (ed.), *The Bloomsbury Handbook of Literary and Cultural Theory* (London: Bloomsbury, 2019), pp. 684–85. For an argument detailing a shift in the cultural evaluation of seriality, see also, Shane Denson, "The New Seriality," *Qui Parle* 32(2) (December 2023): 301–39. While there are obvious provocations in Denson's polemic ("the practico-alert") the argument here follows a contrasting genealogy and critique.

not just the literary (the process of novelization, for instance, and serial literature in general) but the role of seriality in social change. Seriality and transformation? Seriality and revolution? The questions necessarily remain questions, with all their attendant contradictions, but reference a central claim, that seriality bears (*Träger*) the power and potential (akin to what C. L. R. James calls "tendencies," or what Sylvia Wynter refers to as "unsettling")[3] of social change in the way it narrates, in how the stories get told.

Seriality is first a list of serialities. It is a social construct. It forges (in more than one sense) collectives. At one point, Sartre describes the nation as "the seriality of serialities."[4] Indeed, for Benedict Anderson the nation is seriality's most dubious and bounded form.[5] Seriality has the air of determinate and determinist structure: in computer science, for instance, serialization can take a data configuration into bits, like sequences into a file. The advent of the qubit in quantum calculation scrambles this, but for now computing is seriality centered, and the universal serial bus (USB) is everywhere a process of ordering "memory." Not surprisingly, the logic of series in mathematics is a basic calculation even though mathematical logic means much more. Seriality is a logic of mediation and as such is a widespread medium of cultural transmission: it is a linchpin of popular cultural studies.[6] Novelization and serialization, as we will later complicate, are not exactly a coincidence. New media announce change in any number

3 Although James does not analyze seriality, I am referring here to the Johnson-Forest Tendency as a political outlook, and "tendency" itself as attendant to the real foundations of Marxist critique. The reference is not about the mid-century factionalism of the American Left but a kind of critical spirit that follows its own course. I read the same tendency in Sylvia Wynter who, by "unsettling" the coloniality of power, also reveals fault lines in Marxist priorities.

4 Jean-Paul Sartre, *Critique of Dialectical Reason, Vol. 1: Theory of Practical Ensembles* (Alan Sheridan-Smith trans.) (London: Verso, 2004), p. 645.

5 See, for instance, Benedict Anderson, *Imagined Communities: Reflections on the Origin and Spread of Nationalism* (London: Verso, 1983). Bound here principally refers to forms of governmentality in the way "nation" is assessed, via rituals, statistics, and modes of subjectivity.

6 See, for instance, Rob Allen and Thijs van den Berg (eds), *Serialization in Popular Culture* (New York: Routledge, 2014).

of ways, including in serial connectivity (as a blockbuster podcast, "Serial," more literally accentuates, but the logic can also be tracked in social media more broadly and in videogaming). Streaming and "feeds" have the aura and agon of seriality. Seriality marks both the schism and intersection of quality and quantity (for Marx, in serial manufacture), of number and measure (at least in Hegel's *Logic*), and of difference and repetition (a Deleuzean philosophy of series and a logic of sense for whatever "counts" as the present). The "one damn thing after another" condition of seriality as social control that we will critique via Sartre reeks of modernity and its burdensome rationality, the prison house of numbering and carcerality in general, but there are many contra-indications, especially if we take seriously labor and desire, the wayward dialectics of affect, or consider the longue durée of, for instance, everyday counter-discourses in oral epics and seasonal observance. Later we will read seriality not just in repetition and recursivity but specifically in replication (an imperative of both the cyborg and AI), where seriality critiques how social change or being human is conceived. The inertial logic, or practico-inert as Sartre calls it, of seriality remains its dominant and dominating feature yet this tends to obscure a more radical dialectical promise, seen in the dynamics of storytelling in all its modalities (in the novels, manga, and anime I discuss but in cultural experience more broadly construed) of revolutions across time. There are crises, or events in Alain Badiou's schema, where what is palpable is more than the immanence of transformation; indeed, part of the polemic here is premised on the idea that seriality, counter-intuitively, undoes the habit of plodding sequence for revelations in division and separation (within and between series). In seriality, knowledge is accumulation by division. It cannot assure radical social change but can keep its measure and a certain measurelessness alive as a contradictory yet affirmative proposition. Seriality does not deduce change syllogistically, but antagonistically. In this way the mass literacy it encourages is something akin to what Marx once described as "mass intellectuality" or "general intellect," but here interpellates a worker in the algebra of social change itself. Methodologically, and announced in his 1857 "Introduction" of *Grundrisse*, Marx continually attempted to strip Hegel's dialectic of its mystical form, while risking its counter-measure in positivism.[7] The honing of *Das Kapital* extends this process and seriality, as much more than the Hegelian afterlife of the *Logic*, informs it.

How can the everydayness of seriality encompass the rupture we associate with revolution? Just as for Sartre the group-in-fusion is not posed simply as the opposite to the practico-inert collectivity of seriality, so here I would emphasize the commonality of seriality bespeaks a dialectical and conflictual openness; that its generalizability across the social means the class contradictions it embodies (in the factory and mechanization, in the queue, in the census, in the digital) cannot consistently sustain the structures otherwise meant to guarantee it. Seriality is not the cause of change but it is operative in what change can become. A series in culture, for instance, may demonstrably confirm the status quo and actively minimize any social struggle that might obtain (a series is hardly outside ideology). The struggle to prevent struggle reveals a Spinozist *conatus* or striving across culture and politics. Any attempt to aestheticize seriality confronts first the dead weight in its omnipresence. Yet even the presentation of basic pleasures and comforts, the calming elixir of apparent non-contradiction, must be constantly negotiated because the context of seriality is necessarily dynamic and the contrast with its content cannot assure an escape from either. On one level, seriality underlines the quotidian as the way things are and justifiably so; on another level, its form extends dissent and is its living-on (*sur-vivre*). The detrimental effects of massification and commodification in the economic, the social, and culture are an incontrovertible part of seriality's story and no one should minimize

---

7 Marx's thoughts on the general intellect appear in his series of notebooks known as *Grundrisse*, with Notebooks Six and Seven taking on a life of their own thanks to their publication under the title, "The Fragment on Machines" ("Frammento sulle machine") by Raniero Panzieri in the 1964 issue of *Quaderni Rossi*. The *Grundrisse* was originally published in Moscow in 1939, and in English in 1973. An analysis of this series will not be taken up here, but I do see "mass intellectuality" itself as germane to Marx's serialization, *Le Capital*, and seriality as "not only in the form of knowledge, but also as immediate organs of social practice, of the real life process"; Karl Marx, *Le Capital* (M. J. Roy trans.) (Paris: Maurice Lachâtre, 1872–75 [published as a single volume in 1875]), p. 706. See Karl Marx, *Grundrisse: Foundations of the Critique of Political Economy* (Martin Nicolaus trans.) (London: Pelican, 1973).

the extent to which positive modes of socialization have been compromised and suppressed by its sway (not least by the necropolitics of mechanized death). It is possible, however, to acknowledge seriality's place in hegemonic discourse, specific languages of state, for instance, while tracking the conditions of its countermands, the measure of seriality unbound (a relation to deleterious binding rather than as binding per se). Obviously, in the current project I do not mean to shift the onus of social change onto, for instance, Marx's work on a serial edition of *Capital* in French 1872–1875, transmogrified in a manga of 2008 in Japan that is itself serialized in a French *bandes dessinées*, as *Le Capital*, in 2011 (which in turn recalls an attempt in France from the mid-nineteen seventies). But what if such texts (across different times and spaces) do not just describe a critical juncture, but participate in its composition and constellation? *Capital* is not a story, a novel, or an epic, yet nevertheless it attempts to narrate and critique a primary relation of existence.[8] When I refer to storytelling here it is not just to recount the many manifestations of Marx's text but it is also to gauge how capital as relation must or can be told. "Telling capital" is an ambivalent phrase, especially because we do not tend to think of capital as an interlocutor (unlike its manifestations, "money talks," etc.). Its perceived absent/presence (the invisible hand for Adam Smith, for instance) and silence are never a void for imagination; indeed, telling capital, telling the story of capital, is a way to come to terms with its apparent ubiquity and the challenge of its supercession. This is how I link telling capital to social change. Who gets to tell revolution, and in what language, also pivots on what may constitute a revolutionary telling in its history. And this is also seriality's measure.

I have already indicated some of the ground to be covered in this study but before returning to those elements in more detail I should also mark what this text is not. First, while it broaches seriality in philosophy it does not pose a philosophical method. My readings here are primarily symptomatic and, although I find some contributions more provocative

8 I see this attention to formal process in conversation with attempts to link form to a specific evolution of capitalism. See, for instance, Fredric Jameson, *The Political Unconscious: Narrative as a Socially Symbolic Act* (Ithaca, NY: Cornell University Press, 1981).

than others, I cleave mostly to a path of materialist substantiation that questions the status of method for seriality. This may be a limit on dialectics but it is simultaneously an opening for narration. Second, and clearly connected to this, the cultural sampling here is relatively narrow and is not meant to represent what is otherwise a massive archive (and the massively non-archived) for critical deliberation. I favor an internal polemic of seriality rather than a theory of popular seriality as such. It may be that unbound seriality necessitates an open series of analysis that, if not commensurate, at least maintains the dynamism at work (which, as Marx found in his critique of political economy, extends well beyond the project projected). Third, and most importantly, the following pages are dedicated to an idea of social transformation that seriality itself struggles mightily to measure. The kinds of change imagined are not realized in text or textuality, yet scales of seriality in these modest examples suggest modes of collective agency (for instance, class informed if not expressed) interested in not just reading this series or that but in making seriality count differently. And this too is a dialectics of becoming.

SERIAL MARX

I begin with some basic questions. What if the very everydayness of the series reveals its transformational capacity in *potentia* and *potestas*, a Spinozist criss-cross of power in potentialities (and *potenza*) minus its theological conundrum?[1] This has something of the sense Harney and Moten invoke when they note, "The preservation of potenza, of what hasn't happened yet; the preservation of the tendency; the conservation of subjunctivity."[2] Could it be that the seriality of the serial keeps alive a logic of revolution (indeed permanent revolution) when the time of revolution itself otherwise appears or is represented as foreclosed? The translations of Marx's *Das Kapital* perform a kind of seriality, but there is one translation in particular that Marx himself took up to extend the meaning of its revolutionary impress. One of the more notable and quoted of Marx's letters was that of March 18, 1872, to Maurice Lachâtre where Marx confirms his enthusiasm for a serial version of *Capital* Volume One to appear in French in instalments: "J'applaudis à votre idée de publier la traduction de *Das Kapital* en livraisons périodiques. Sous cette forme l'ouvrage sera plus accessible à la classe ouvrière et pour moi cette considération l'emporte sur toute autre" ["I applaud your idea of publishing the translation of *Capital* in periodic instalments. In this form the work will be more accessible to the working class, and for me this consideration is more important than any other"].[3] The one-page contract for the project

---

1 Links between Marx and Spinoza necessarily remain controversial, not least because what Spinoza means by power is not simply an immanent expression of capital as power. Here, the power of seriality is not only an economic integer or a mark of cultural domination but their dialectical knot.

2 See Stefano Harney and Fred Moten, *All Incomplete* (New York: Minor Compositions, 2021), p. 157.

3 This letter is reproduced in many places, including the first bound volume of *Le Capital*. I am quoting the reprint in François Gaudin (ed.), *Traduire Le capital: Une correspondance inédite entre Karl Marx, Friedrich Engels et l'éditeur Maurice Lachâtre* (Mont-Saint-Augnan: Presses universitaires de Rouen et du Havre, 2019). A color

underlines the sentiment: "l'auteur exige que l'édition de son livre soit expressément sous une forme et à un prix qui mettent l'ouvrage à la portée des plus petites bourses" ["the author requires that the edition of his book be expressly in form and price one that puts the work within reach of the smallest purses"]. In the same letter above to Lachâtre, however, Marx also doubts the efficacy of the endeavor:

> the method of analysis which I have employed, and which had not previously been applied to economic subjects, makes the reading of the first chapters rather arduous, and it is to be feared that the French public, always impatient to come to a conclusion, eager to know the connection between general principles and the immediate questions that have aroused their passions, may be disheartened because they will be unable to move on at once. That is a disadvantage I am powerless to overcome.

An acknowledgment of the fickle reader, particularly a French one (!), might seem reasonable, although this is a fairly basic rationalization and defense of the difficult nature of Marx's text. The ideas and concepts of the first two chapters are some of the most complex in Marx's oeuvre and any reader in any language is quickly disabused of a "royal road to science" in favor of the "fatiguing climb of its steep paths" that Marx also invokes in this famous missive. Without laboring the point, Marx is convinced that serialization in a "cheap popular edition" (Marx to Lafargue, December 18, 1871),[4] will help disseminate his critique of political economy to a working-class readership otherwise priced out of its polemic, but at the same time he realizes it is the very nature of the text, rather than its price, that would tend to exclude those readers whose class interests would be well served by the knowledge and analysis it provides. Seriality is not just about conformity but dialogicity; that is, opening text to a new context. Here we track not the form of appearance of value in Marx's work (*Erscheinungsform*), but specifically the form of appearance of *Capital*, the work.

---

reproduction of the original letter appears on page 90. Note: Lachâtre's name is sometimes rendered La Châtre, but I have retained the former for consistency. Unless otherwise stated, all translations are mine.

4 Karl Marx and Friedrich Engels, *Collected Works, Volume 44: Letters 1870–1873* (London: Lawrence and Wishart, 2010), p. 283.

Marx's oeuvre was still relatively unknown in France (by the mid-1860s, as Eric Hobsbawm reminds us, almost nothing that Marx had written was still available in print), although discussion was ongoing among French socialists and economists alike, especially in relation to German socialism. Recognition began to change, of course, with the 1867 publication of *Das Kapital* (Marx wrote that the publication of his book was, "without question, the most terrible missile that has yet been hurled at the heads of the bourgeoisie") and this renewed interest in the *Communist Manifesto* in various editions and translations (one should note the *Manifesto* initially appeared in 1848 in several forms, including a serialized version in the *Deutsche Londoner Zeitung*—the first English translation of *Das Kapital* [Third Edition] would also be serialized, in the monthly *To-Day*, beginning October 1885). Marx's involvement with the International Working Men's Association certainly raised his profile, as did his writings on the Paris Commune ("The Civil War in France") so it was hoped he could extend that familiarity and build on French worker discontent, particularly in light of the crisis signaled by the Commune. On the whole, however, Marx could not assume a large French audience and even among socialists he was not considered a major figure (in Manon's 1872 book on French socialism Marx gets only a few sentences).[5] Even so, it is true serialization was enjoying broad popular appeal at the time, not just in fiction (Hugo and Balzac, both discussed in *Capital*, were available in serialization—this key genre of seriality will be discussed in Part Two) but in tracts and in excerpts from non-fiction works. This is why Lachâtre would suggest the same format used for his papal history: an eight-page, two-column "livraison" priced at 10 centimes per issue, which in the case of *Le Capital* would be noted as 44 instalments for a work that was approximately 351 pages in total. With a widely accepted place in reading culture, the *livraison periodique* was in some ways an optimal platform for *Capital* (although not just for popularity, a point to which I will return). The press envisaged a print run of 10,000 copies per issue with 100 copies going to Marx (initially in lieu of payment) for circulation to interested reviewers and "des groupes d'ouvriers et d'ouvrières" (male and female

5 K. Steven Vincent, *Between Marxism and Anarchism* (Berkeley: University of California Press, 1993), p. 71.

workers—there is no extant record the latter distribution occurred). After the first 10,000 copies Marx would receive a princely half centime per livraison, and overall to cover the costs of the project the press would need to sell around 10,000 copies of the complete series. With these details the questions begin to multiply. A book that theorizes the serial production of commodities is itself commodified in series for a readership hardly outside the discourse of fetishism and alienation it details. The very form of the text is a heuristic about the relations of production it otherwise challenges (there is pre-capitalist seriality but in mass production it assumes a specific form). As we will see, seriality is a scene of antinomy, but never more so than in a work that demonstrates the conditions of its very possibility. This is not to fault the desire for serialization but is to remark upon the nature of its business (there is no neat equivalence between the logic of valorization and the logic of serialization yet they do exist in productive stress).

Popular publications at the time like *Petit Journal* could sell over 300,000 copies per issue and even more modest endeavors like the *L'Intransigeant* could muster sales of 70,000 on a regular basis. Despite the inherent difficulty of the text, success for *Le Capital* as a serial did not in principle seem far-fetched, although a stand-alone publication was a harder sell. There were, however, significant problems, not least of which was that *Capital* as a whole was still in progress (Volume Two in particular) and Marx was also working on revisions for what had already been published (there was a new Appendix to the 1867 edition and other changes would be evident in the 1872 edition—one should note that in addition to all of his other writing projects, Marx had also just overseen a Russian translation of Volume One). Marx saw the French translation of the text as an opportunity for further revisions and, as is well known, *Le Capital* would end up being the version that Marx rewrote and edited the most. Without doubt, Marx sought precision in his concepts and analyses, and this desire was not necessarily fulfilled by the publication of an individual work or edition, despite a paradoxical desire of some critics to isolate the moment of precision from the demonstrably unfinished process of revision in which it is enmeshed (this is not to fault the desire for an authoritative text but is to note how the dynamism of the text in production and circulation might frustrate such desire). The work on the project began just five months after the massacre that ended the Paris Commune, with historical repercussions that would mediate discussion of Marx's text, as well as spur Marx's direct commentary on what is a key event in the history of communism.[6]

Other pertinent factors that would affect the progress of the French edition include the poor state of Marx's health. In addition to his joint pain and vision problems, Marx continued to suffer from carbuncles that produced discomfort ranging from annoying to excruciating. Bouts of depression were routinely disruptive and harmfully reinforcing, since the depression itself was linked to Marx's disappointment at not being able to complete adequately all of the tasks he set before himself. Interestingly, in his biography of Marx, Gareth Stedman Jones suggests "It seems clear that it was not so much lack of physical exercise, but rather the need to confront theoretical difficulty that brought on headache attacks, insomnia and liver disease."[7] If theoretical difficulty made even Marx ill, the French working-class reader might be forgiven for relative discomfort before Marx's text. There are those, of course, who roundly assert such biographical, physiological, and psychological conditions have little or nothing to do with *Capital*'s real arguments and a defense can certainly be made, yet to excise simply such context is not exactly a creative materialist maneuver, still less a resolutely Marxist one. To free Marx's text from its very possibility is not only to misread how capital works, but also to misconstrue why we still read *Capital* today, where its real arguments are rewritten under the sign of specific contradictions. Meanwhile, the logistics of the French edition could not but be a source of continuing frustration. Livraisons would be published when they were ready but any deadlines had to account for the fact that Marx was in London, the publishing house was in Paris,

---

6 Kenneth Hemmerechts and Nohemi Jocabeth Echeverría Vicente have published a pertinent article on this juncture. See Kenneth Hemmerechts and Nohemi Jocabeth Echeverría Vicente, "The Paris Commune and Karl Marx's *Le Capital*," *Modern Intellectual History* (2022): 1–21. Obviously, the current work will pay close attention to the Commune, but in a different key.

7 See Gareth Stedman Jones, *Karl Marx: Greatness and Illusion* (Cambridge, MA: Harvard University Press, 2016), p. 537. Although Stedman Jones's book is far from hagiographic, he deeply appreciates the conceptual weight that attends Marx's life so that the ideas live with the body, however debilitating that could be.

the publisher was in exile (Spain, Belgium, then Switzerland), and the translator was in Bordeaux. Manuscript and letters seem to fly in all directions and, while the momentum of the project was initially quite admirable, it was impossible to issue the series with any regularity (important to note because an element of expectation was another founding rationale of serialization). Unlike the mass serialization of Eugène Sue, who Lachâtre also published, the suspense was not in the story, but in the logistics of delivery. At the end of 1872 Marx sent the printer proofs of issues 8, 9, 10, and 16, which showed progress but obviously the sequence had to wait on further editing and translation. The latter, in particular, commanded Marx's attention, and appreciably so (Marx, of course, was fluent in French).

Initially, it was thought that Charles Keller would translate the German text, although, as he indicated in letters, he was neither a friend of Marx's ideas nor particularly drawn to the style of his language. For his part, Marx favored Joseph Roy, who had previously translated Feuerbach. The problem with rendering *Capital* in French was that, according to Marx, Roy "often translated too literally" and so Marx decided to "rewrite whole passages in French, to make them more palatable to the French public" (Marx to Danielson, May 28, 1872).[8] Marx was certainly not advocating a dumbed-down version of the critique of political economy, although in a letter he admits he had "sometimes been obliged—principally in the first chapter—to smooth or simplify [*aplatir*] the matter" (Marx to Danielson, November 15, 1878).[9] Translation is serial, not literal, and Marx dialogically engages the materiality of the process which signifies the actual concreteness of *Capital*'s circulation. The more Marx read Roy's translation, the more he corrected and re-translated himself. If Marx felt the French working-class reader might be impatient with his writing style, Marx's own impatience with Roy meant that he spent many working days of his busy schedule re-translating pages at a time. Meanwhile, the process of production was also delayed by specific requests by Lachâtre for the edition, including a signed image of Marx, and a separate biography to more-fully

8 Marx and Engels, *Collected Works*, VOL. 44, p. 385.

9 Karl Marx and Friedrich Engels, *Collected Works, Volume 45: Letters 1874–1879* (Moscow: Progress Publishers, 1991), p. 343.

acquaint French readers with the author. At one point, Marx wrote to Paul Lafargue (March 21, 1872) in frustration and called Lachâtre "un charlatan abominable. Il fait perdre le temps par des choses absurdes" ("he wastes time over absurd things"—clearly, the biography could wait, but Marx is also referring to Lachâtre's idea of including a response to Marx's letter to the reader in the first issue, which eventually was included).[10] Meanwhile, Roy defended his translation from German to French by suggesting French and the French reader were less tolerant of what he politely calls "repetition" or a minimal variation in the prose; to be fair to Marx, he is aiming for a consistency adequate to at least some of the procedures of science. It should be underlined that the French translation of *Capital* that would become so influential in subsequent language versions (Spanish and Italian translations drew directly from the French, and the extent of the French empire meant a central work of Marx was now also available for anti-colonial critique that would be spurred by the chapter at the end of Volume One) was Roy's translation as "thoroughly revised" by Marx and, while Engels was often critical of *Le Capital*, he incorporated important elements of it into the German fourth edition. Still, with the combination of serialization, translation, the French reader, and Marx's mode of exegesis, from the outset Marx was hesitant about this version's prospects. He wrote to Lachâtre,

> The method is quite different from that applied by the French socialists and others. I do not take as my point of departure general ideas such as equality etc., but I begin, on the contrary, with the objective analysis of economic relations as they are and that is why the revolutionary spirit of the book only reveals itself gradually. What I fear, on the contrary, is that the dryness of the first analyses will put off the French reader. (March 7, 1872)

A French serial puts pressure on the language and abstraction of Marx's polemic and how a revolutionary spirit (l'esprit révolutionnaire) is not

---

10 Marx and Engels, *Collected Works*, VOL. 44, p. 346–47. Quoted in Alix Bouffard and Alexandre Feron (eds.), *L'édition française du Capital, une oeuvre originale*: *Le Capital, Livre I*: *Présentation, Commentaires et Documents* (Paris: Les Éditions sociales, 2018), p. 80.

only produced but maintained for a projected audience with a more recent intimate experience of the conditions of class war.

Editing his text of the French edition, Marx continually reflects on how he presents his critique as an intellectual project and whether it can be understood as a much broader social intervention. Again, he writes to Lachâtre: "Il y a ici un malentendu. Je n'expose pas ma méthode, mais je l'applique dès le commencement, mais son application, dans les premiers chapitres, à l'analyse de la "marchandise," "la valeur," "l'argent" est par la nature de la chose elle-même un peu difficile à suivre" ("There is a misunderstanding here. I do not reveal my method, but I apply it from the start, yet its application, in the first chapters, in the analysis of 'commodity,' 'value,' 'money' is by nature of the thing itself a little difficult to follow"; March 20, 1872).[11] The worry for Marx is the method will not be picked up intuitively in those early chapters or livraisons and that he will effectively lose his reader. The serial does not always depend on initial commitment—there are serials that permit entry at different points in their narrative—but in this form and given the plan derived from the German edition, Marx the creator faces the challenge of serial engagement. If, unlike French socialists, Marx does not begin his intervention with a discussion of common themes like equality, but instead presents the reader with objective economic relations, can reader interest be maintained and understanding be achieved? Nevertheless, by August 1872 Marx had completed his editing and retranslation of the first six issues. Five of these went on sale in September, and by October Lachâtre reported that they had sold 576 copies, about twenty a day—a respectable number, he noted, given that there had been no advance notices or advertisements about the publication (the sales compare favorably with other editions of *Capital*, although obviously this is a relatively small portion of the whole text). Lachâtre was prudent about marketing *Le Capital*, especially against the backdrop of state anti-socialism and associated prohibitions that emerged in the aftermath of the Paris Commune. Lachâtre told Lafargue it was more important the text appeared at all rather than sold, although this would seem to contradict the initial intention of the project: to get Marx's thinking in proletarian hands.[12]

---

11 Gaudin (ed.), *Traduire Le capital*, p. 90.

The first issue of the serial *Le Capital* is grandly illustrated with a cover featuring a bare-breasted Marianne (a figure popular from the French Revolution on), with a mélange of heraldic insignia flanked by cherubs (such imaging and ornamentation is hardly beyond question but familiarity with the symbols and decoration was obviously felt to be comforting in advance of the analysis itself, which immediately defamiliarizes the most basic assumptions about commodities, value, and money). Marx's "terrible missile" is launched for the planned price of ten centimes (the price and number of the livraison appear on the title page). In a letter to Marx, Lachâtre explains the price: "les pauvres ne pouvant payer la science qu'avec l'obole"—"the poor being able to pay for science only with a small contribution."[13] The pages are dense with text although this is not unusual for such publications of the period (most serials enhance their revenue through advertising and subscription, however, and it is important to underline that Marx's French serial stands alone, not as part of a periodical, like the first English edition of *Capital*). The main reason I have to imagine reading *Capital* in series is primarily because those who do comment on the publication of *Le Capital* at the time do not register this experience directly.[14] *La Patrie*, for instance, a paper formerly of Bonarpartist fame,

12 There is some confusion about sales of the series *Le Capital*, especially in light of Lachatre's letter of December 24, 1873, when he notes: "La vente est nulle sur votre livre"; Gaudin (ed.), *Traduire Le capital*, p. 152. Given that sales of the issues of the project were compiled and reported by him earlier and the series is not complete at the time of this letter, the sense here is either of a book that is not yet for sale or of a remark on the current issue within the series, stalled by what are called "inevitable interruptions" (the complex process of translation/editing/production/distribution noted above, plus the aura of state repression, which is demonstrable). This has not stopped rare book sellers, for example, quoting the letter and others to the effect that the French edition was a sales disaster (while pricing the 1875 first edition in the thousands of dollars!). Clearly, the concept of surplus value does not die with Marx's *Capital, Volume One* (as *Volume Four* attests).

13 Lachâtre in Marx, *Le Capital*, p. 8.

14 Jean-Numa Ducange and Jean Quétier usefully assemble a smattering of responses to the series, which in the main reveal a hostility to Marx and his analysis, sometimes, as Marx notes in a letter to Lachatre, without reading the text (September 18, 1874; Gaudin (ed.), *Traduire Le capital*, p. 158). See "Selected Correspondence on the French Translation of *Capital*" in Marcello Musto (ed.), *Marx and "Le Capital": Evaluation,*

KARL MARX

PARIS

ÉDITEURS, MAURICE LACHATRE ET CIE

38, BOULEVARD DE SÉBASTOPOL, 38

Prix de la Livraison : **DIX centimes** 1re Livraison

FIGURE 1. Karl Marx, *Le Capital*, VOL. 1 (M. J. Roy trans.) (Paris: Maurice Lachâtre, 1872).

offers a series of critiques of Marx's work, with expected keywords like "ignorant" and "infantile." *Le Capital* is described as replete with "gross economic error." *La Patrie* distributes its summaries and adumbrations of *Le Capital* to an audience greater than that for the serial of *Le Capital* itself. Most "true" Marxists stuck to the German editions of *Capital* available (and detractors to Marx's approach generally did the same, like Maurice Block, who classed Marx's work among "*doctrines excentrique*")[15] and it is otherwise difficult to gauge how many French workers in Paris (the primary place of distribution) actually gave their ten centimes worth of reply (a point to which I must return). The mode of publication itself is hardly here, as elsewhere in this project, some formal guarantee that a rationale for social change is being adequately disseminated and is actively participating in the implications of its polemic. Marx did not believe that accessibility in itself was some social catalyst on a par with consciousness or seizing the means of production. Yet, as a popular mode in periodicals and newspapers, serialization held a promise that critique might reach those who would benefit most from changing the world based on reading its substance. This is a small point, but the picture of Marx accompanying the publication has him looking away from the reader, as if his most quoted letter to Maurice Lachâtre (that of March 18, 1872, above) does not quite believe in the power of *livraisons periodique*. By February 1873 the next five issues are available, constituting around 80 pages of the work to that point. From the correspondence, it appears batches were published according to the editing process rather than for reading impact, as Marx attempted to maintain all of his other commitments and struggled with his health (during this period Engels' doctor recommended Marx work no more than two hours a day while his body healed).

History, Reception (London: Routledge, 2022), pp. 227–66; Jean-Numa Ducange and Jean Quétier, "The Contradictory Reception of the French Edition of *Capital*" in Musto (ed.), *Marx and Le Capital*, pp. 175–88. Like Gaudin's book, this collection is essential in an understanding of *Le Capital*. Musto's introduction, for instance, is very perceptive on the influence of the French edition, as are several contributions. While the collection does address the series, however, it does not consider *Le Capital* as a series.

15 Gaudin (ed.), *Traduire Le capital*, pp. 17–18.

The following year, as censorship and book bans intensified in France, Lachâtre (still in exile) managed to get notifications out regarding the project: "*Le Capital*, by Karl Marx. 10 centimes per issue. Complete work: about 50 issues. Each series of 5 issues: 50 centimes. This work of the great philosopher, called by free-thinkers the Bible of workers, must be in all hands and serve as a guide to those who want to work for the triumph of social ideas. 'To each his share in the common good.'"[16] By January 1875 Marx is editing issues 33–35 with a recommendation by Lachâtre to remove "Germanisms" left by the translator.[17] Much to Marx's frustration, he adds, "Your book continues to lead the reader into spheres above the intellect of common people. I note it—with real sorrow, the French workers, less educated than the German workers, will not be able to assimilate anything of your work." In light of these criticisms and others, Marx wrote a note to the reader, which he sent to Lachâtre in April:[18]

> Advice to the reader—M. J. Roy had undertaken to give a translation as exact and even as literal as possible; he scrupulously fulfilled his task. But his very scruples forced me to modify the wording, in order to make it more accessible to the reader. These changes made day by day, since the book was published in issues, were executed with uneven attention and had to produce stylistic discrepancies. Having once undertaken this work of revision, I was led to apply it also at the end of the original text (the second German edition [also published in instalments—nine—July 1872 through March 1873]), to simplify some developments, to complete others, to provide materials, additional histories or statistics, to add critical overviews, etc. Whatever the literary imperfections of this French edition, it has a scientific value independent of the original and must be consulted even by readers familiar with the German language. I give below the parts of the afterword of the second German edition, which relate to the development of political economy in Germany and the method used in this work.

16 Gaudin (ed.), *Traduire Le capital*, p. 44.

17 Gaudin (ed.), *Traduire Le capital*, p. 46.

18 Gaudin (ed.), *Traduire Le capital*, p. 47.

Lachâtre will include this extensive note in the last issue of *Le Capital* (number 44), along with extracts from the Afterword of the second German edition, errata, and a table of contents. Marx writes to Wilhelm Bracke on May 5, 1875,[19] that the project is basically complete, although French authorities still attempt to prohibit the printing of the final issues (approximately 1000 copies) and the distribution/sale of the over 100,000 issues that remained in stock (a not inconsiderable number).

Letters indicate sales of the serial continued informally, in bundles of five rather than single issues, but it is clear that, even if we set aside all of the problems Marx confronted with the text itself in serial form, state repression severely limited its readership. At one point, Lachâtre suggests that *Le Capital* could be sold as a bonus for subscribing to the newspaper, *La Revolution*, a tie-in he thought could sell 10 to 20 thousand copies (this idea was not pursued but might have changed the impact of the serial). By the time Lachâtre returns to France from exile in 1879, only around 600 copies of the last numbers of *Le Capital* had been sold (over a period of six years). Economically, the publication was not a success, but its contribution to the dissemination of Marxism in France at the time was substantial. This is in part the political unconscious of the project imbued in the logic of seriality itself, which must include not just the copies in circulation but also its reappearance in other forms (including the single volume text from 1875 on) as well as its basis for further translations and edited versions and the conversations these engendered. Seriality is a movement infrastructure, a catalyst not of consciousness-raising per se, but of its potential. As a narrative mode it offers the prospect of sequence, if not of order, but in practice it is replete with formal contradiction (something that Marx clearly appreciated). In part, this is because it tracks in itself the conditions of its own materialization: it is symptomatically suffused with the competing claims of cultural, social, and economic logic, whatever the manifest content of its expression. "Serial Marx" does not define the vexed relationship of the revolutionary idea as a law of social exchange, yet *Le Capital*, even in this short reflection on its emergence, elaborates a founding tension in promulgating radical social change. Contra Marx's invocation of Dante at the end of the preface to the first edition of *Capital* (that

19 Gaudin (ed.), *Traduire Le capital*, p. 48.

constitutes my epigraph) the tongue-wagging popular is where seriality lives its socialization most acutely and contradictorily. Even the royal road to science is flecked with its material inconsistencies. And for Marx, the tension between his ideas and their impact is never outside "Le mouvement contradictoire de la société capitaliste." Seriality is indeed a space for its examination and metacommentary.

The place of *Le Capital* continues to be one of disputation. In general, the point here is not to favor the French text merely on the basis of Marx's extensive close attention to translating, editing, and rewriting in its production, although most scholars of the edition acknowledge the importance of Marx's labor in this regard (including his ongoing desire to de-Hegelianize the first German edition of his magnum opus). Even as Marx was already revisiting *Capital* as a project some of the edits Marx made in the French version appear pronounced if not indisputable. Raya Dunayevskaya, for instance, notes the shift from the fantastic to the necessary form of the appearance of production relations in the exchange of things. The fetishism of commodities looks different in the materialization of crisis where the fantastic bends beneath the needs of social contradiction. This is less a question of translation choices and more, again, a reflection of the impact of the Paris Commune on Marx's thinking.[20] If the fault of Roy's French translation was a tendency to literalism, one that Marx strenuously attempted to revise, an adjacent paradoxical inclination is to emphasize the best word for translation without elaborating the extent to which writing and rewriting are context specific: the edition is the sediment of more than intention and technical skill—we might say for the edition that, here as elsewhere, social being determines its consciousness. The fact that Engels incorporated this element of *Le Capital* in the fourth German edition is consistent with the aims of Marx's broader project, so Marx's labor was hardly lost for future translations, into English in particular (of course, what Engels leaves out or otherwise elides remains germane). If *Capital* invites a dialectical understanding of political economy,

20 See, for instance, Raya Dunayevskaya, "The Paris Commune Illuminates and Deepens the Content of *Capital*" in *Marxism and Freedom* (New York: Bookman, 1958), pp. 92–102. See also Raya Dunayevskaya, "*Capital*: Significance of the 1875 French Edition of Volume I" in *Rosa Luxemburg, Women's Liberation, and Marx's Philosophy of Revolution* (New Jersey and Sussex: Harvester, 1982), pp. 132–52.

its editing and translation is not outside the process defined. This does not diminish Marx's desire and expertise in authoring *Le Capital* but does not cede all authority to text in that regard. Because of Marx's extensive editing of the text, some have claimed *Le Capital* to be the definitive text of *Capital* (Kevin Anderson, for instance, has argued as much)[21] but *Das Kapital* is not a stone tablet and its materialism has no problem with the idea of authority as dialectically always already overdetermined if not overwritten. What if translation, however, also exists at the level of form? If, as noted, Marx assigned a specific scientific value to the French edition he worked on, what of the formal value? Is it possible to assess how the interpretation of *Le Capital* is affected in its division?

Here the value is theoretical rather than definitive, speculative rather than empirical. Marx's assumptions about publishing *Le Capital* as a serial are not unfounded, but for reasons explained above, specific conditions of serialization were not and could not be met. One of the suppositions in recounting Marx's adventure in *Capital* as serial is that there is a possibility in its form that exists beyond the event of the publication Marx was alive to witness (part of the power of seriality exists not only in expectation, but in latency). Yet here we face a somewhat stark realization, perhaps already indicated in the comments so far. Marx resists the process of serialization at every step because the argument of *Capital* exceeds the capacity of serialization to capture its conceived totality, which clearly pre exists Lachâtre's bold suggestion. Marx was never able to square his desire to reach the French working class with the actual demands of his critique of political economy. When he attempts to "smooth" the text for his French audience this is not a condescending move to the proletarian (despite Lachâtre's comment about a French lack of comprehension vis-à-vis the reading skills of German workers): he is struggling more with the dialectical impress of his critique. Engels, who was predominantly averse to the French edition, warned Marx on several occasions that the French language was diminishing the power of his polemic. In one letter (November 29, 1873), Engels notes:

---

21 Kevin Anderson, "On the MEGA and the French Edition of *Capital*, Vol. I: An Appreciation and a Critique," *Beiträge zur Marx-Engels-Forschung Neue Folge* (1997): 131–36.

> Yesterday I read the chapter on factory legislation in the French translation. With all due respect for the skill with which this chapter has been rendered into elegant French, I still felt regret at what had been lost from the beautiful chapter. Its vigor and vitality and life have gone to the devil. The chance for an ordinary writer to express himself with a certain elegance has been purchased by castrating the language. It is becoming increasingly impossible to think originally in the straitjacket of modern French.[22]

The fate of the French edition for reading *Capital*, especially after Marx's death, pivots not inconsequentially on Engels' reservations about the capacity of the French language to carry the critical weight of Marx's project. The fourth German edition of *Capital*, central to Marxism and Marxology, would reflect Engels' doubts, even though, as noted, Marx had explicitly asserted "the scientific value of the French edition, independent of the original." Again, translation appears to trump form, but it is clear from the exchanges that give rise to *Le Capital* as a serial, division reorganizes the emphases of the text.

Serial exigency in this case does not mean that Marx specifically tailored chapters to fit a two column, eight-page format, but very long sections, like that on primitive or original accumulation, were split up and would appear as separate chapters (Chapter Four in the German edition, for instance, becomes three separate chapters in the French edition). The chapters themselves, even the opening ones, appear less intimidating in division, although publishing five issues together at a time might permit a reader to skip Marx's difficult opening (Louis Althusser, in his introduction to the 1969 edition of *Le Capital—1*, implores readers to skip Chapter One, with all of its Hegelianisms and talk of fetishism—Althusser's collective project of *Reading Capital* itself gives us a dialectic of reading by not reading).[23] Most reader guides to *Capital*, from Harvey to Heinrich,

22 Rodrigo Maiolini Rebello Pinho, "The Originality of Marx's French Edition of *Capital*: An Historical Analysis" (Naomi J. Sutcliffe de Moraes trans.), *The International Marxist-Humanist* (September 2021): 5. See also Michael R. Krätke, "An Unfinished Project: Marx's Last Works on *Capital*" in Musto (ed.), *Marx and "Le Capital"*, p. 149.

23 Althusser's preface is extremely important to the representation and interpretation of *Capital* in French. In addition to the warnings about Hegelian conceptual issues,

maintain a Marxological fidelity to the chapter sequence of the book edition because Marx, especially in Volume One, meant it that way. One could say the conformity in expertise has an air of seriality about it but seriality itself is not beyond questioning authorial intent. Marx is no Scheherazade, but in committing to serial form he must have understood that his book, in the process of its division, could not be read whole in French. The invitation is to partiality (in more than one sense), which obviously does not exclude sequence but this is not held, in one's hands or in one's head, as a book (if we say the book is the point of the project, we should be careful to register what its serialization means). The French working-class reader, however continually phantomatic to those critics of *Le Capital* who can only imagine the wholeness of the first book edition of 1875, takes up the text first as a serial, a use value in exchange for ten centimes. Surely the process in which Marx engages (and described above) is not outside the condition of seriality, which has its own readerly demands and expectations? Reading habits are disruptive, as Emma Bovary teaches us in another serialized work in French. The idea is not to conjure the reader or the response but is to consider the impress of seriality in the critical consciousness desired. Seriality is not popularity, although no doubt Marx would have appreciated a larger readership than the modest sales figures indicate (this is in part the potential in *potentia*).

Althusser directly takes on the problem of readership which, as we have learned from Marx on *Le Capital*, is not a minor concern in disseminating a critique of capital. Althusser does, however, make assumptions, e.g. "proletarians or wage-labourers in direct production [. . .] have no ideologico-political difficulty in understanding *Capital* since it is a straightforward discussion of their concrete lives." Of course, since Althusser recommends putting aside the beginning of *Le Capital* initially, the issue of "straightforwardness" is at once vexed. One could add that the nuances of symptomatic reading, developed by Althusser and the "Reading Capital" project also seem to mitigate and mediate the prospect of working-class apprehension of the text, despite direct experience of its subject. Much of the desire in serialization here rests on "tout bonnement" or "quite simply" as a reading practice, which does not mean simple and certainly does not mean "straightforward." Louis Althusser, "Preface to *Capital, Volume One* (March 1969)" in *Lenin and Philosophy and Other Essays* (Ben Brewster trans.) (New York: Monthly Review Press, 1971), pp. 71–101. See also Louis Althusser et al., *Reading Capital—The Complete Edition* (Ben Brewster and David Fernbach trans) (New York: Verso, 2015).

In the practice of smoothing, Marx is perhaps thinking serial exigency and even the immanent measure of his text. The title of the French edition is simply *Le Capital*, without reference to a critique of political economy (an intimidating subtitle to be sure—Heinrich, among many others, only thinks of *Das Kapital* with its subtitle and not what happens or is possible without it). In *Le Capital* Marx does not water down concepts but sometimes they are reaccentuated by modulation. For instance, in the justly famous opening chapter on the commodity, once Marx has invited us to consider the exchange value of the commodity more closely, he offers that a quarter of wheat has many exchange values and gives us the example of x boot-polish, y silk, and z gold. The magnitude and replaceable character of their exchange values for a quarter of wheat express something equal but then, "exchange-value cannot be anything other than the mode of expression, the 'form of appearance,' of a content distinguishable from it" (in the form of appearance, or manifestation—*Erscheinungsform*—Marx suggests a philosophical distinction as an economic relation, in contrast to Hegel). The French, however, reads: "Elle doit donc avoir un contenu distinct de ces expressions diverses" ("It must therefore have a content distinct from these various expressions").[24] We seem to have lost the impress of philosophy while emphasizing the expression of exchange value in its distinct content. The abstraction remains, but not necessarily the abstractness (part of the project of the Jean-Pierre Lefebvre translation of 1983 was to move the French version closer to the available German editions and away from not just Roy's literalism but also to some extent Marx's own efforts of "smoothing"). The challenge of *Capital* in French becomes for Marx not just one of conceptual translation but of dialogicity itself, which includes projecting a reader whose context provides another dimension of "distinct content."

On one level, then, we have Marx's dedication to an expanded readership, one that might prove *Capital*, for all of its complexity, can be learned as more than a Marxological exercise or textualist conundrum. On another level, Marx finds this task daunting and distracting, and he cannot rest easy with a translation of *Capital* that would in any way miscommunicate the critique essential to the work's intervention. For

24 Marx, *Le Capital*, p. 14.

many workers, the experience of capitalism itself is a knowledge adequate to understand its logic of exploitation. Explaining capitalism as process and living it are not mutually exclusive and Marx saw serialization as an opening to negotiate the point. If the serial itself did not in fact do this, the principle of seriality within it carries (*Träger*, again) the relation, dialectically. This is not a solution, however, to the dilemma *Le Capital* represents, nor is it, in itself, obviously the linchpin in the ongoing sublation of capitalism more broadly construed. Here I want to say more about the condition of seriality in and for *Le Capital* before addressing "serial Marx" and social change as a cultural problematic.

In Chapter Fourteen of *Le Capital* (that putatively begins in Livraison number 19) we are introduced to the relationship of the division of labor to manufacturing. Manufacturing, and indeed the factory, organizes labor differently. Marx wants to show a de-skilling peculiar to capitalism, in which the nature of craft is transmogrified, and with it the worker's relationship to work. Work is initially combined but then compartmentalized so that production may be maximized in one place across the production process. The worker no longer makes a complete commodity but participates only in its partial production, alongside workers who are also engaged in this activity. The consequences of such organization are pronounced: "Mais quel que soit son point de départ, sa forme définitive est la même: un organisme de production dont les membres sont des hommes" ("But whatever its point of departure, its final form is the same: an organism of production whose parts are humans")[25]—the French is Roy's rendering of "ein Produktionsmechanismus, dessen Organe Menschen sind" where the German more forcefully stresses that humans have become organs for a mechanism, a different sense of organic manufacture and one consistent with Marx's idea that the factory itself is an automaton and also a social order). In the next section of the chapter Marx goes into more detail about what this degree of specialization does to the worker. The manufacturing process reduces the work practices, described as series, available to the worker and produces a one-sidedness in labor through the repetition of a narrowly-defined act (among the things that manufacture makes is, paradoxically, decomposition). Labor

25 Marx, *Le Capital*, p. 147.

abstraction or its congealed residue may be difficult to fathom, but this experience of work itself would have been all too familiar to the French working class in manufacture at this time. The clarity of Marx's explanation is pronounced, although the juxtaposition of two forms of series or the replacement of one by another is perhaps a more complex process to comprehend.

The skill of the worker is not elided but is repositioned and repurposed within serial production. Again, the German text accentuates that the worker is transformed into an organ of the productive process: "Eben weil das handwerksmäßige Geschick so die Grundlage des Produktionsprocesses bleibt, wird jeder Arbeiter ausschließlich einer Theilfunktion angeeignet und seine Arbeitskraft in das lebenslängliche Organ dieser Theilfunktion verwandelt."[26] The partial or piecemeal function of the skilled worker is exclusively appropriated as a lifelong organ of the machine they operate. If one series for the skilled worker represents an intensity and flow wrought by the difference in activity and the tools for its conduct, the other series is marked by a kind of flattening in repetition, a seamlessness, of course, that permits the extraction of surplus to continue apace (later we will revisit the concept of series between difference and repetition). The French translation balks once more at the "becoming organ" of living labor (even though this trope of nature runs throughout Chapter Fourteen): "Précisément parce que l'habileté de métier reste le fondement de la manufacture, chaque ouvrier y est approprié à une fonction parcellaire pour toute sa vie." One wonders whether this is less a concession to the French (in its, or Roy's, resistance to Marx's German metaphoricity) but one to its assumed reader who may not see themselves as the machine's extension? In fact, of course, Marx rekindles the idea from the German text in the very next paragraph, minus the previous explanation and introduction: "Il est d'abord évident que l'ouvrier parcellaire transforme son corps tout entier en organe exclusif et automatique de la seule et même opération simple."[27] The difference between appropriation and automation is salutary, yet again the reader who is assumed to perform this function may be more hesitant about living its mechanistic impress.

26 Karl Marx, *Das Kapital: Kritik der politischen Ökonomie* (Hamburg: Otto Meissner, 1890 [MEGA2 2.10]; Berlin: Dieter Verlag, 1991), p. 305.

27 Marx, *Le Capital*, p. 147.

The next section of Chapter Fourteen (still Livraison 19) deepens the distinction in two forms of series—the first dedicated to "heterogeneous manufacture," the second to "organic manufacture." The latter in Roy's translation is rendered as "manufacture sérielle"—the German is "organische Manufaktur," which might suggest Roy is not being literal enough (!) but the process here is manufacturing through series so one could register organic as organized manufacture, but once more lose that aspect of the human/machine. Interestingly, the end of the opening paragraph in the German edition lends some consistency to the French version: "Es wird entweder gebildet durch bloß mechanische Zusammensetzung selbstständiger Theilprodukte oder verdankt seine fertige Gestalt einer Reihenfolge zusammenhängender Processe und Manipulationen";[28] and in *Le Capital*: "Ce double caractère provient de la nature du produit qui doit sa forme définitive ou à un simple ajustement mécanique de produits partiels indépendants, ou bien à une série de procédés et de manipulations connexes."[29] Here the series of connected processes and manipulations is common to both. The distinctiveness of "organic" remains, but as a serial relation ("Reihenfolge"). The key here, as David Harvey points out, is "the space-time organization of production and the efficiencies that can be gained through spatiotemporal reconstruction of the labor process as a whole."[30] In effect, one witnesses a chronotopic rationale that cleaves to sequence as utilitarian, a kind of production queue that Sartre would find profoundly alienating. One should note the deep irony that Marx recognizes the efficiencies of seriality in one mode while suspending such a possibility in his French publishing project. These are different series to be sure; nevertheless, the effulgence of mass serial publication itself is not outside the meaning of seriality for manufacture (they are co-present within industrialization). The question is whether the series helps claim a seriality against its hegemonic form; whether, indeed, the specification of serial processes in what is also a series reveals that such a claim is possible, and necessary.

28 Marx, *Das Kapital*, p. 308.

29 Marx, *Le Capital*, p. 143.

30 David Harvey, *A Companion to Marx's Capital* (London: Verso, 2010), p. 178. The immense value of Harvey's reading of Marx is also a reminder the French worker did not have this communal luxury as they perused this *livraison* of *Le Capital*.

Beyond the organizational and publication constraints flagged above, is there also a dialogue on revolution between *Le Capital* as critique and its serialization for a French working-class readership? In his critique of *Capital* from a "multilinear, peripheral angle" (a workable definition of seriality) Kevin Anderson argues ideas of revolution are explicit and implicit in Marx's intervention. Anderson's point is to reject the notion *Capital* is dry scholarship for the brainy and bookish, over and above the barricade-builder. This approach also permits Anderson to extend his argument for the pivotal importance of *Le Capital* (referred to as the 1872–1875 French edition).[31] Chapter 32 (indicated in Livraison 43) focuses on the historical tendencies of capitalist accumulation, ones which result in the revolt of the working class and the "expropriation of the expropriators." While the language of revolt peppers the discourse of *Capital* as a whole, this chapter, for a French working-class reader, provides a rationale for the hundreds of pages that precede it. Anderson tracks other intimations of revolution in Marx's discussion of Irish agrarian uprising and the racial capitalism mediating the US civil war and its aftermath. The extensive work on primitive or original accumulation yields a different version of revolutionary futurity in *Le Capital* so that its potential is extended beyond its specificity in the English example:

> Elle ne s'est encore accomplie d'une manière radicale qu'en Angleterre: ce pays jouera donc nécessairement le premier rôle dans notre esquisse. Mais tous les autres pays de l'Europe occidentale parcourent le même mouvement, bien que selon le milieu il change de couleur locale, ou se resserre dans un cercle plus étroit, ou présente un caractère moins fortement prononcé, ou suive un ordre de succession different.[32]

This modification will be important not just to the Russian radicals with whom Marx was in contact at this time but clearly to the emergent discourses of combined and uneven development eventually used to read

31 Kevin B. Anderson, "Marx's French Edition of *Capital* as Unexplored Territory" in Musto (ed.), *Marx and "Le Capital"*, pp. 41–59. See also Kevin B. Anderson, "The 'Unknown' Marx's *Capital*, Volume I: The French Edition of 1872–75, 100 Years Later," *Review of Radical Political Economics* 15(4) (1983): 71–80.

32 Marx, *Le Capital*, p. 315.

the Russian Revolution of 1917 and the revolutionary movements of the Global South. As Anderson points out, Marx does not address the potential of the village commune in this text, but it is clear he is going deeper into revolutionary possibility based on his analysis. Importantly, Anderson flags the profound influence of the Paris Commune on the revisions of *Le Capital*, and for me, as will be clear from a subsequent case study, there is a serial logic and radical concreteness in play.[33] The desire for freely associated labor in the Paris Commune, remarked upon by Marx in the *Civil War in France* text, inexorably feeds Marx's project for the French worker. The desire necessitates an abolition of a certain form of the state, one which the Commune, for both obvious and complex reasons, was not able to achieve. The lived reality of the Paris Commune was therefore for Marx a "possible Communism."[34] The serialization of this desire in *Le Capital* refracts not just the possibility of revolution, but also the necessary conditions of impossibility in what is, between 1872–1875, *an impossible series*. As a preamble to the next section on the theorization of seriality, "serial Marx" must clarify the substance of this impossibility.

With all that is latent and immanent to the idea of *Capital* as a serial indicated in these notes, Marx's project in *Le Capital* stands as a warning about serial desire. Like an artisan of the popular, Marx works very hard on *Le Capital* as a series, but the idea as it is forged exists mostly in its futurity. Marxists always and everywhere refer to *Le Capital* as a serial, 1872–1875 but the text considered is that which is collated into the book of 1875. Both the BNF (Bibliotheque Nationale de France) and the MEGA² (Marx-Engels-Gesamtausgabe), central archives for the present study, use the same year range yet reproduce the book of 1875. There are some technical arguments (and more) why we should maintain the difference of the *livraisons periodique* from the book. The most important reason and, to quote again from Marx, the "considération l'emporte sur toute autre," is that the book is not intended for the working-class readership that Marx envisaged. But surely, this does not matter if the book reproduces the text of the serial and maintains the faith of Marx's revisions? I cannot stress enough how wrong-headed this is. *Le Capital*, the book, has become

33 Anderson, "Marx's French Edition of *Capital*," p. 41.

34 Karl Marx, *The Civil War in France* (Peking: Foreign Languages Press, 1970), p. 68.

an alibi for not addressing its seriality. To focus on the book as if it is a serial (the book, as archived in and outside Marxism) is precisely to miss the internal polemic of its intervention. Over and over again, and to the present (including the most recent publications on *Le Capital*),[35] Marx's project is almost literally "bookmarked"—the text, its meaning, assiduously and expertly dissected as if the question of the series exists only in its absence (my discussion here is not simply outside such positioning). We have the publication process of *Le Capital* in minute and extensive detail, yet the project itself exists as a future conditional, like that famous hobgoblin stalking Europe at the beginning of the *Communist Manifesto*. First, of course, and despite the confident dependence on the series, we have no reflection by a French worker on the serialization of *Capital*. We have the sales but not the sense of them. We have figures for the print run, but not where the print runs. Frank Kelleter notes that in "serial storytelling [. . .] reception and production are typically intertwined in a feedback loop,"[36] but this is not the story *Le Capital* traditionally tells. Solemn allusions to this text as not only definitive based on Marx's intense editing/translation, but as unique in its intention for the workers, do not address its primary readership but get straight on to arguing at length among specialists who can now download the book version in an instant. There are lots of reasons the working-class reader disappears (who asks them about "l'abstraction de la valuer usage"?). This is not simply the result of condescension or of

35 There are literally dozens of texts that ritually refer to the book of 1875 as the serial 1872–1875 yet, beyond the citation of occasional letters between Lachâtre and Marx, do not consider its production and distribution as a serial. In addition to the recent Musto collection, see also Kenneth Hemmerechts and Nohemi Jocabeth Echeverría Vicente, *Publishing Karl Marx's "Le Capital" (1871–1875)* (London: Brill, 2024). To be fair, the scholarship is expertly concerned with the process of the *Le Capital* project, not the implications of its form and Marx's belief in it. The latter, for me, constitutes a transformational desire that lives on with the project.

36 Frank Kelleter, "From Recursive Progression to Systemic Self-Observation: Elements of a Theory of Seriality," *The Velvet Light Trap* 79 (Spring 2017): 100. While this piece paints in broad strokes it usefully delineates several genealogical strands of conceptualization around seriality. Kelleter's own position allows us to think of the reader as an agent in the continuing life of a serial, even if not represented as such. This is something of the presence of the worker's absence in the serialization of *Le Capital*.

the rigorously informed banter of German-reading French socialists at the time. Part of the issue here, and by all means it is a serial issue, is that scholars of this text do not appear to have access to the series itself.

How is this possible? The text of the series is reproduced in the book, *Le Capital*, and textual scholarship clearly shows that this is the work of Marx editing/translating Roy's version of *Das Kapital*. The problem is that the division of the text is not necessarily respected or corroborated. If the scholar were to confront the series, they would be addressing text in 8-page divisions (basically, a double folio) that, because each livraison is sold, logically would include a cover page that notes which issue of the series it is and its price. The price and number of a serial issue cannot be intuited. If the series was in fact sold in batches of five livraisons then the page total would be 40, one of which would have to be a title page that signaled to the purchaser the price of 50 centimes. These arrangements are noted variously in letters, in the contract, and in the advertising or notice copy provided by Lachâtre and are available in the archive. Yet the evidence of this form is effectively erased from the series. The book version of *Le Capital* reproduces the cover from the first livraison, as described above, but to date this is the only cover, one out of 44 apparently, available. If it was sold in batches of five there would be nine covers to reflect this division, but none, it appears, are extant. Because the first cover is reproduced, critique more easily adopts the position the text is serial. Should we speculate on these missing covers? Are the sales and stock figures quoted above inventions? The book version of the serial, while reproducing the text, does not acknowledge the question of division. The BNF facsimile edition of *Le Capital* copies the text of the 1875 book and includes the first cover. No more covers appear, but the copy purports to show the eight-page divisions of the livraisons by marking the issue with a number appearing in the bottom right corner of the page. If this is Marx's serial, according to the contract and letters, then those divisions must be false or at least in need of qualification. There are two possibilities. The cover page with title and price does not have to be paginated, but for the printer it still counts as a physical page (as the cover of the first issue clearly shows); that is, the easiest process for the printer is to take two sheets, print on them, then fold them to make eight pages or two folios. In this scenario, the maximum number of printed pages for each issue of *Le*

Capital is therefore 7 pages or 39 pages if published in batches of five (strictly speaking, the latter form contradicts Marx's intentions, since 10 centimes periodically is easier than 50 centimes in one go). This is a conundrum. Using the 8-page division of the book suggests that some livraisons begin in the middle of a chapter with no title or price indicated (there is magic in the commodity as Marx suggests, but this example would require sorcery of a different kind), yet using these divisions does yield 44 parts in the book (the first livraison, even with its front matter, seems only to have six pages, but blank pages are not a problem for a printer, just loose ones). One of Lachâtre's notices (mentioned above) does refer to 50 livraisons, which is close to what the divisions would be if covers were included (this plan was still being announced as late as 1874), but scholarship on *Le Capital* overwhelmingly accepts the division of the text without an infrastructure for its sale (again, ironically, this would be an elision of the analysis of commodities and pricing explored within the text). That Marx sent chunks of the project, sometimes in forty-page batches to friends and colleagues accords with the book version but not with the serial per se. Even Marx's papers deposited with the British Library contain no covers for the serial. Could it be they do not exist?[37]

The second scenario offers less incredulity yet a corresponding measure of impossibility. What if a loose sheet was inserted that then permitted the printing of a cover page with price and issue number? There is some discussion in letters about attaching covers to extra copies of *Le Capital* for the book version, yet no concern is extant about adding a cover page

---

37 Correspondence with several key researchers on *Le Capital*, including Kevin B. Anderson, Kenneth Hemmerechts and Nohemi Jocabeth Echeverría Vicente, and François Gaudin, all of whom have written extensively on the production of *Le Capital*, has not revealed a single cover beyond that of the first issue. While the archive clearly supports evidence of 44 issues (particularly in the letters between Marx and Lachâtre), the distribution of the text as a series (for sale to French workers) remains a mystery. Gaudin notes, "Je connais des livraisons d'Eugène Sue éditées par Lachâtre, avec des couvertures particulières et des publicités," but of *Le Capital*? They must have been destroyed. He adds, in jest, "Sans doute faisaient-elles partie des documents stockés par les héritiers dans une grange où des chevaux pouvaient entrer." If the workers could not have them, the horses could!

for the periodical issues after the first one. The insertion of a loose half sheet might seem to free the issue for more text but problems remain. Would the title page be printed on the original two sheets? If it is integral to the publication that would make its disappearance more problematic. An additional half sheet would mean two pages for a total of ten, again requiring some explanation for its function and integration. As Lachâtre details the form of the publication and the costs of production no mention is made of a cover page as a wrinkle in the appearance of the series. If we are to accept the eventual publication of 44 livraisons in 8-page segments, adding cover pages should appear somewhere in the accounting. They are a cost of production. The circle is still broken, not squared. Our narrative around the manufacture of the serial suggests the serial is manufactured, and paradoxically so.

I do not believe Marx is disingenuous in his desire for his magnum opus to reach a French working-class reader in a form, if not content, with which they were familiar. Seriality in this instance is a utopian desire. Marx seeks an adequate notion over the adequacy of its form in the hope that both will be realized together. In light of Marx's political convictions and with respect to his understanding of the Paris Commune and its violent denouement, the serial project of *Le Capital* has a vitality and prescience deeply resonant for anti-capitalist praxis and socialist organization of various kinds. Marx did seek to reach a French working-class audience on other occasions. In my book on *Labor in Culture*, I explore the phenomenon of the worker inquiry, initiated for Marx by a request from *La Revue socialiste* in 1880 to put together a questionnaire that would help socialist organizers to understand the political constituency and needs of French workers.[38] As with this serial, there is no record of worker responses to Marx's entreaty (he posed 101 questions) but I trace the genealogy of the idea to the present (with all of its problems about verifiability and the checking off of working-class attributes). In both examples, *Le Capital* and "L'Enquête ouvrière," the worker is something of a doubled or divided subject in Jacques Rancière's sense, not quite a fiction

38 See Peter Hitchcock, *Labor in Culture, or, Worker of the World(s)* (New York: Palgrave, 2017), pp. 3–36.

but certainly not beyond projection.[39] Perhaps the circumstances of publication on the project thwart its completion. Marx signed a contract to a series but could not commit himself to seriality as such, as if his prodigious intellectual capacities could not take the time that seriality takes. This is a temporality of sequence and division that has no obvious consonance with the translation of a German text marked by theoretical heft over the demands of wider and popular circulation. The contrast is not absolute (as later examples will underline) yet serial Marx lives on in other series than the one Marx so enthusiastically embraced. A dialectics of seriality maintains the possibility of praxis in Marx's series for the present. To call *Le Capital* an impossible series is not to denounce it: it is quite clear the project passionately attempted to address a political need. Seriality as a problematic is within the text of *Le Capital*, and in the concrete relations of its sale and distribution. Would it be less "impossible" if complete livraisons, with their covers, subsequently appeared? It would certainly lend credence to the representation of *Le Capital* as a serial, but because of Marx's specific intentions and belief in this publishing project, possibility already resides in the articulation, even when phantomatic, of a working-class reader. The impossibility is a present conjunction, not a foreclosure of radical dialogicity (this is, in part, the substance of Marx's reading of the Paris Commune immediately preceding *Le Capital*). The serial does not provide a formula for cultural or political reflection; it is, rather, the disjecta membra of praxis here bound by a narratological compulsion that the working-class reader exists for social change (but not alone, or under conditions of their own choosing, to borrow from Marx).

There are, of course, political ramifications to what appears a missed opportunity. Rather than reproduce the series as an exculpation for a letter,

39 Rancière explores a variation of this notion in several works. See, for instance, Jacques Rancière, *La Nuit des prolétaires: Archives du rêve ouvrier* (Paris: Fayard, 1981), translated as *Proletarian Nights: The Workers' Dream in Nineteenth-Century France* (David Fernbach trans.) (New York: Verso, 2012); *Le Philosophe et ses pauvres* (Paris: Fayard, 1983), translated as *The Philosopher and His Poor* (Andrew Parker trans.) (Durham, NC: Duke University Press, 2004); and *Staging the People* (David Fernbach trans.) (New York: Verso, 2011). Rancière maintains a belief in the worker writing as a veritable demystification of doubling, yet what authenticates the reading?

as it were, that was not received, let us pursue the serial symptom in Marx's project as a challenge for seriality and social change itself. That seriality appears in *Le Capital* without its serialization is more a limit of the text as Marx translated and revised it than it is a block on the prospect of serialization itself. The political force of seriality is sensitively dependent on a concrete chronotopicity, by which I mean that although seriality assumes a general outline in modernity (as a quotidian symptom of narration in production and circulation) it is highly responsive to crisis and the immediacy of adequate articulation. In the case of *Le Capital*, its event as serial is linked to the Paris Commune and its impasse is inflected by the reactionary pall that hung over its aftermath. For those of the organized French Left who were neither in prison nor in exile, political appeals to industrial workers were generally hushed. In France, formal participation in the International was illegal and restrictions on the press would remain in effect until 1881. Constraints on worker association and indeed any activism that might favor worker rights were severe. Because of the Commune, there was a general suspicion of worker political agency and many French people, particularly those of the middle classes, favored the new regime's imposition of order. This did not stop worker associations from re-emerging, nor did it close off all avenues for the publication of radical thought, but the aura of repression mediates the publication and distribution of *Le Capital* and sanctions to a degree Lachâtre's reaction above to modest sales—that it was more important the text appeared at all than sold. The time/space of crisis overdetermines the political efficacy of Marx's project, yet this insistence must inflect subsequent critique about the meaning of *Le Capital* in its moment. The serial will return in due course, but what of the theory of seriality in which it is enmeshed but also shapes?

SARTRE AND SERIALITY

From Marx's analysis of manufacture we know that seriality is a productive force. Does it enjoin a theoretical discussion that is itself productive? For Sartre, what is manufactured in seriality is conceptually its greatest weakness for philosophy.[1] Lining up anything (Sartre's principal example is the queue) is just "one damn thing after another" and more likely to produce torpor than transformation. Marx too resists such a notion of seriality in his critique of manufacture and, as we have seen, this may extend to the production of *Le Capital* as serial itself. What Sartre reads in seriality, of course, stands in sharp contrast to the process analyzed so far. For Sartre, seriality is a condition of political stasis, and expresses all that is inert in the practico-inert—the weight of the past as a block on viable and transformative political constituency—the latter Sartre terms the "group-in-fusion." The worked matter of the practico-inert directs activity but flattens socialization: it can order subjectivity and ideologically overdetermine various forms of subjectivation (for example, in patriarchy, race supremacy, and bourgeois hegemony). You are in the queue yet its community is a restricted and restricting imaginary: it is a structural function not a communal imperative, a collective marked by indifference, not the reciprocity of will in common revealed in radical collectivities of race, gender, and class.[2] Seriality here is founded on ontological distinctions,

---

1 The following commentary will refer principally to Sartre's *Critique of Dialectical Reason*. See Jean-Paul Sartre, *Critique of Dialectical Reason, Vol. 1: Theory of Practical Ensembles* (Alan Sheridan-Smith trans.) (New York: Verso, 2004); *Critique of Dialectical Reason, Vol. 2: The Intelligibility of History* (Arlette Elkaïm-Sartre ed., Quintin Hoare trans.) (New York: Verso, 2006).

2 Beginning from Sartre's concept of seriality, Iris Marion Young makes some categorical distinctions in which a particular use value for seriality emerges. By posing "woman" as a serial collective, a bound seriality, Young usefully separates the group from essentializing tendencies and frees various forms of feminist politics to pursue specific collectivities. While I argue such concrete possibilities exist *within* the series, Young's critique nevertheless underlines that in seriality a politics is always at stake. Amanda Gouws uses this lesson from Young to make a similar point about the category of race,

some of which bear on Sartre's earlier *Being and Nothingness*.[3] To be next in line in the queue is less about social cohesion as it is about social control—one's being is defined by the order of agglomeration and not by being together as a mark of deeper recognition and co-participation (one can sense at once how this power might undermine viable politics of race, class, gender, or sexuality). The form of seriality in this example places no direct demand on the variables of imagination or on a self-consciousness with collective consequences. Like Fordism, Sartre's seriality is predicated on an extraction of purpose rather than a concrete realization of human praxis. It represents a (dis)comforting uniformity and an expectation of representation itself as a formal guarantee, as an essentialist prescription. Puncturing the perceived passivity of seriality requires an active yet contingent ontological relation in the mutual recognition of an external threat of an Other as a third presence, as that which would otherwise seek to preserve consensual inertia. For Sartre, such activity is the kind of fusion that predicates the storming of the Bastille, an eventness of change bound by the conditions of actually-existing class struggle. Yet, since Sartre's project is about the dialectical force of conceptualization, what exists in seriality as a countermand to its assumptions on plodding regularity and a being united primarily by an abstract and debilitating consent?

Much depends on how far one reads seriality as a linear imperative, as an absolute limit on self actualization. When Sartre examines radio culture, he sees seriality at its most obdurate and stultifying. To understand why, one must come to terms with how Sartre elucidates "collectivity" within social relations. Chapter Four of Volume One of Sartre's *Critique* begins by suggesting that both interior and exterior relations of collectivity, or being in relation to the Other, can be combined in the practico-inert such that contradiction in the realm of the Other is transformed into seriality. Seriality in this sense is the supercession of antinomy, a negation

race as series, in higher education admissions processes. Iris Marion Young, "Gender as Seriality: Thinking about Women as a Social Collective," *Signs: Journal of Women in Culture and Society* 19(3) (1994): 713–38. See also Amanda Gouws, "Race as seriality: A response to David Benatar and Zimitri Erasmus," *South African Journal of Higher Education* 24(2) (2010): 313–17.

3 Jean-Paul Sartre, *Being and Nothingness* (Sarah Richmond trans.) (New York: Routledge, 2020).

of collective crisis or crisis for the collective. Inertia is a dynamic, but one that appears to subtend creative forms of collective praxis. Seriality acknowledges the Other but only to the extent it confirms a radical indifference, an "interpenetration of individuals" subject to the "new rule of series."[4] How can culture in series be anything but negative for the worker who participates in it (to draw from the story of *Le Capital*)? The series, or in Sartre's main example, the queue, is a massification of the social ensemble. It reveals its indifference in the interchangeability and instrumentality of a collective formed by convention or the law of lining up. To be sure, the order of the queue is not wholly inconvenient. Did Sartre muscle to the front of the line for his train ticket, theater ticket, or plane ticket? Admonishing fellow customers that they were given over to the practico-inert may not have sustained his privilege. Perhaps the lived experience of the line informs Sartre's abstraction? In her book on Beauvoir and Sartre, *A Dangerous Liaison*, Carole Seymour-Jones notes:

> Beauvoir no longer queued, but went out with her friends to restaurants, which were divided into four classes. For 250 francs a reasonable meal could be had at a second- or third-class restaurant; she could afford to boycott the fourth-class, where rutabagas and artichokes were on the menu. Sartre continued to lunch with his mother, who kept a bourgeois table, thanks to the black market, at her elegant apartment, 23 avenue de Lamballe, at Passy, and sent her maid to stand in the queues.[5]

Sartre's class position does not negate the theorization of seriality in play but it is not simply beyond its materialization. Class struggle is sometimes signed by the absence of one of its actors. The point is in the logic of the ensemble not in the light of practical exigency in this example or that. What Sartre is marking is a certain isolation in reciprocity, which is by all means an ontological scission, as if the intimacy of the Other is suspended in this collective.

---

4 Sartre, *Critique of Dialectical Reason, Vol. 1*, pp. 255–56.

5 Carole Seymour-Jones, *A Dangerous Liaison* (New York: Overlook Press, 2009), p. 263.

Sartre is also demystifying being in convention, the order in the everyday, the quotidian as a brake on radical collective consciousness. The abstraction of the bus queue is not a remark on character but on what overdetermines the nature of the worker taking the bus. Public transportation is a service, yet it is not about who is being serviced (the worker as commuter) but what is being serviced. The queue is therefore a functional extension of the place of work, a space where serial division will be replicated. For Sartre, the series is a condition of "abstract generality." The order of the bus line preempts disruption by assigning access. In this sense of the series the tendency is not towards dissemination but it instead pivots on regimentation: it structures being in the cause of reproducing it. If the individuality of the commuter remains, it is only to the extent that the worker's experience is interchangeable with any other person in the queue. To borrow from Hegel, we might say the quantity represented by the queue occludes the quality of each person being in it. Sartre continues: "There can be no concept of a series, for every member is serial by virtue of his place in the order, and therefore by virtue of his alterity in so far as it is posited as irreducible."[6] I will return to this assertion regarding a reappraisal of "serial Marx" below, but here let us assess whether this rubric actually describes the experience of the queue or indeed the cultural correlative Sartre reads into the radio show.

In the queue the worker is situated but they are not, in Sartre's reading, in a situation, or enacting a freedom to break ritualized action. The line necessitates passivity and consent but does this exhaust the worker's situatedness? As Sartre asks in "What is Literature?," "What are we to think about a worker?"[7] What if the worker is taking the bus to a strike or a picket line or to a veritable storming of the Bastille? Is the integrity of seriality for ruling class interest or the state maintained? One is reminded of this cut across seriality in a poem by Philip Levine, "What work is": "We stand in the rain in a long line/waiting at Ford Highland Park. For work./You know what work is—if you're/old enough to read this you know what/work is, although you may not do it./Forget you. This is about

---

6 Sartre, *Critique of Dialectical Reason, Vol. 1*, p. 262.

7 Jean-Paul Sartre, *What is Literature? And Other Essays* (Bernard Frechtman et al. trans) (Cambridge, MA: Harvard University Press, 1988), p. 28.

FIGURE 2. Hugo Gellert, "Law of Capitalist Accumulation" in *Karl Marx: "Capital" in Lithographs* (New York: Ray Long and Richard R. Smith, 1934), p. 53.

waiting,/shifting from one foot to another."[8] The circumstances of the line are overdetermined by labor as relation and the worker's necessity to secure a position in the tight labor market of the US car industry at the time. Levine writes this out not as a sociological note, however, but by voicing the thoughts of a worker in that queue (perhaps Levine himself) which deepens its phenomenological event: "You love your brother,/now suddenly you can hardly stand/the love flooding you for your brother,/who's not beside you or behind or/ahead because he's home trying to/sleep off a miserable night shift/at Cadillac so he can get up/before noon to study his German./Works eight hours a night so he can sing/Wagner, the opera you hate most,/the worst music ever invented."[9] The lightness of touch in this sibling intimacy defies the reality of the line in its form and substance. And the brother sings Wagner when reading *Das Kapital* (serialized or not) would be an obvious choice, a story of shifting work in shift work. Of course, in Sartre's procedure, seriality exists in its abstraction as the order of things, yet it remains possible to maintain the nuance of "totalization" in Sartre's thought (admittedly a thankless task of Sisyphean propensity for some today) and reassert his dialectical concern, that human praxis not be reduced or the human objectified by the abstractions of existence. Thus, even the phenomenological structure of the queue for seriality cannot cancel in itself the capacity for contra-indications. The process of negation contains its negation, itself a lot more than a footnote in Sartre's dialectics. Neither praxis nor passivity are given in the form of their appearance. The queue remains a hypostatized collectivity but cannot contain every measure of its intended totalization. Choosing to line up does not preempt decision. The situatedness of the worker in the queue is a space of mediation. Not only does seriality not escape its mediation but, contra Sartre yet in the spirit of his dialectics, it is itself a mediatory mode that foregrounds the contingency of sequence and, yes, "situation" even when or precisely because it orders reality. The queue is also a space where force decides. One thinks of Gillo Pontecorvo's *Battle of Algiers*, where the *porteuses de feu* line up and use social convention to pass through checkpoints.[10]

8 Philip Levine, *What Work Is* (New York: Knopf, 1991), p. 32.

9 Levine, *What Work Is*, p. 33.

10 *The Battle of Algiers*, directed by Gillo Pontecorvo (Allied Artists, 1966).

Anti-colonialism exploits order to its own ends. Could Sartre's series, the ten volumes of *Situations*, be ordered differently? What of the periodical he edited, *Les Temps Modernes*? Perhaps, but, as with *Le Capital*, it is more interesting to consider the conditions of situatedness and procedure. Clearly, there is catachresis in play between seriality, series, and serial but we could still refuse their practical inertia, not to collapse distinctions between existential structure and cultural expressivity, but to assert the prescience of their intermingling in how social change is composed.

In effect, Sartre dialectizes the anti-dialectics redolent in seriality in his comments on radio, where the cultural logic of series mitigates the passive activity the radio is otherwise read to instantiate, even as Sartre himself adumbrates the meaning of such technology. Like the queue, the radio broadcast individuates the listener in a relation of indifference and anonymity. Interpellated by the broadcast, the listener works on their passivity and pacification in the guise of attention or "being before." On the one hand, the scene of the broadcast, if not its situation, is the product of an infrastructure that has been made: every element of this collective possibility, a microphone, a broadcast tower, and the radio itself, contains stored or congealed labor for and in exchange. On the other hand, the listener appears commodified by this chain of production, as an inactive participant of messaging (this is radio before the call-in or on-air response, but even then, specific protocols obtain—the on/off switch is of a different order between the broadcaster and the listener). One element appears to be an effect of the other (indeed, as an Other), yet again this is not the totality of seriality's instantiation. The simultaneity in listening, its "meanwhile," has the negative connotation of bound seriality that Benedict Anderson reads into the nation form as determinate structure.[11] For Sartre, the broadcast is little more than a cultural diktat:

---

11 See Anderson, *Imagined Communities*. In *The Long Space* I suggest "Serialization is [. . .] time's writing system of nation" in part by triangulating "meanwhile" between Eric Auerbach, Walter Benjamin and Anderson. Peter Hitchcock, *The Long Space: Transnationalism and Postcolonial Form* (Palo Alto, CA: Stanford University Press, 2010), see especially Chapter One. The serial production of "nation" not only illuminates the importance of print media (in Anderson's key examples) but also a specific logic and politics of temporality.

> the mere fact of listening to the radio, that is to say, of listening to a particular broadcast at a particular time, establishes a serial relation of absence between the different listeners. In this way, the practico-inert object not only produces a unity of individuals outside themselves in inorganic matter, but also determines them in separation and, in so far as they are separate, ensures their communication through alterity (and the same applies to all 'mass media').[12]

This is a sweeping judgment (Jameson calls it "the only genuine philosophy of the media"[13] which is equally an overstatement) whose implication makes of radio a propaganda machine—which of course it can be. Here one might recall another dialectician, both a radio presenter and a theorist of the form, Walter Benjamin. Benjamin would certainly agree with Sartre on the question of individuation through absenting—that listeners are united by their shared abstraction. Like Sartre, and more sharply Adorno and Horkheimer, Benjamin bemoans the downside of massification where the listener, rather than expecting openness and access among speakers, finds praxis reduced to the act of turning off the device. Yet Benjamin goes further and notes, for instance, the radio broadcast is like a visiting guest and the listener, passive as they may seem, monitors the appropriateness of the radio's presence. In addition, Benjamin considers the radio play alongside the theater, not as an equivalent but as a form not beyond instruction and complexity (the liveliness of knowledge is also a philosophical disposition).[14] Indeed, this reminds us that Sartre invokes seriality in culture without need of a corresponding sociology of culture (or, in Benjamin's example by contrast, an audience sociology). The scheduling of a radio show, like the issue of a *livraison periodique*, is not a small matter and affects how leisure time, down time, family time are conceived and realized.

---

12 Sartre, *Critique of Dialectical Reason, Vol. 1*, p. 271.

13 Fredric Jameson, Foreword to Sartre, *Critique of Dialectical Reason, Vol. 1, xxviii.*

14 See Walter Benjamin, *Radio Benjamin* (Lecia Rosenthal ed., Jonathan Lutes et al. trans) (New York: Verso, 2014), especially the essays in Part Four. While the podcast has taken up much of radio's serial relation between broadcaster and listener it offers a pertinent provocation for intermedial critique.

A close reader of Sartre, Frantz Fanon reveals other elements of *potentia* in the radio, particularly its role in anti-colonialism and consciousness-building in Algeria. In *A Dying Colonialism* (*L'An Cinq, de La Revolution Algerienne*) published the year before Sartre's *Critique*, Fanon devotes a chapter to the radio, "This the Voice of Algeria," which at the very least proffers the implication that at the intersection of structure and culture Sartre's understanding of seriality is a materialist ground of social contradiction in modernity.[15] Fanon notes how the French colonial, in his example, the petty-bourgeois, sees in radio ownership a sign of cultural prestige and this is hardly a blank confirmation of the practico-inert:

> It [. . .] gives him the feeling that colonial society is a living and palpitating reality. with its festivities, its traditions eager to establish themselves, its progress, its taking root. But especially, in the hinterland, in the so-called colonization centers, it is the only link with the cities, with Algiers, with the metropolis, with the world of the civilized. It is one of the means of escaping the inert, passive, and sterilizing pressure of the "native" environment.[16]

If the radio is a medium of seriality, for the colonial it is precisely a means to separate themselves from the "inert, passive" world of the colonized. Between the settler and the colonized the meanings of the radio are not technological absolutes, but Fanon is clear that even when the deployment of the radio symbolizes French presence and colonial occupation, counter-narratives and practices can be and are articulated. To oppose the "truth" of the oppressor, as Fanon describes it, did not signify absenting oneself from forms of communication, but occupying them. This had been occurring in the press prior to the Algerian war but certainly intensified during it. The war of the press is conducted between the street and the kiosk as local and imported papers struggle over the war's conduct. Eventually, Fanon notes, "The acquisition of a radio set in Algeria, in 1955,

---

15 Frantz Fanon, "This Is the Voice of Algeria" in *A Dying Colonialism* (Haakon Chevalier trans.) (New York: Grove Press, 1965), pp. 69–98. See also Ian Baucom, "Frantz Fanon's Radio: Solidarity, Diaspora, and the Tactics of Listening," *Contemporary Literature* 42(1) (Spring 2001): 15–49.

16 Fanon, "This Is the Voice of Algeria," p. 71.

represented the sole means of obtaining news of the Revolution from non-French sources."[17] By 1956, with the launch of the Voice of Free Algeria, the radio became the "only means of entering into communication with the Revolution, of living with it."[18] Indeed, the role of radio in anti-colonial praxis is long established (the stories of Radio Cairo in Egypt and Radio Rebelde in Cuba, for instance, are pertinent in this regard) and reveals a dimensionality to radio that is not outside the claims of seriality itself.[19] If Marx sees a revolutionary potential for *Le Capital*, the series, that is not realized in his lifetime, Sartre roots such an impasse in the logic of series itself as if participation is submission, and sequency and frequency are unidirectional and monologic.

Sartre has an answer to this disjuncture in the uses of radio literacy, of course, which is that even if the anti-colonialist or a counter-hegemonic party deploys radio broadcasting (including propaganda against propaganda) the negative inclinations of seriality remain, and the listener listens in the absence of Others listening in the same way, "the structure of exteriority which has been interiorized in knowledge."[20] Yet one can acknowledge the fact of exteriority in the form while challenging how the medium might be mediated in its moment. Whatever authority is established by the radio voice, its experience is fundamentally overdetermined. No listener listens from a zero degree of experience or cultural articulation and the voice is never heard in isolation, even when a particular event of listening is individuated. For every voice there is the potential of double-voicing; for every utterance, there is a context in which its expression is dialogized. Perhaps the monologic is held in common, but the listener is not its guarantee. Sartre follows the process but is convinced it lulls the listener into "unawareness." It is "doubly a collective" even though "reciprocity has been destroyed." It is my contention seriality

---

17 Fanon, "This Is the Voice of Algeria," p. 82.

18 Fanon, "This Is the Voice of Algeria," p. 83.

19 See, for instance, Howard H. Frederick, *Cuban-American Radio Wars: Ideology in International Telecommunications* (Ann Arbor, MI: University of Michigan Press, 1986); Simon J. Potter et al. *The Wireless World: Global Histories of International Radio Broadcasting* (Oxford: Oxford University Press, 2022).

20 Sartre, *Critique of Dialectical Reason, Vol. 1*, p. 274.

in fact negates this negation and that its force for change lies in conditions of narration against the inauthentic and enclosed Otherness of individuation. Seriality affirms commodity consumption in common, but this commoning does not exhaust what may be held in common, which the recursive logic of seriality attempts to remedy yet in fact preserves.

Volume One of Sartre's *Critique* offers a methodology for a subject elsewhere, specifically a philosophy of "history" in Volume Two, again a serial connection distinctive and yet active in the seriality conveyed. The meaning of praxis in one is only authorized by the philosophical exegesis of the other; side by side, perhaps, but also collectively in fusion. This trope is *not* analogic: the sequence of texts does not simply correspond to the relationship of speaker and listener with the radio. Nor does it mean that the individuated introjection of otherness represented by the person in a queue, lines up with published issues of a manga in my critique, for instance, or the periodical parts of *Le Capital*. Instead, the event of series, in the collocation of subjects and objects, is a dialogic dynamic, one where division and divisibility are radically situated and compose the very possibility of narration—the story, as it were, of relation itself. Sartre elucidates the social condition of seriality without the variables of its formation and thus the praxis of the group in fusion is read as what seriality is not. The person in the queue is not only Other to themselves, but disjunct to what seriality is held to determine. The serial conditions of culture can certainly be read as expressions of the ontology of impotence Sartre decries, but as culture are not univocally so. Indeed, even when the divisions of narrative connote the production efficiencies of capitalism, they do not simply confirm the accumulation axioms of capital as relation. The consumer may find convenience in division yet also meaning in connection, even if the event of conjunction cannot be seriality's alone. The aim is to emphasize being otherwise in seriality rather than reaffirm being seriality's Other. One lives with the othering of seriality in order to other it.

A DIALECTICS OF SERIALITY

As we noted above, Marx's theorization of capital also attends to the logic of seriality and we return to this understanding to emphasize the dynamic at stake in my comments on Sartre. Like Sartre, Marx sees in seriality a structural power (specifically in ordering manufacture) but links this less to a division between inauthenticity and the authentic (where Sartre adds existentialism to Heideggerian phenomenology) but to the problem of measure between quantity and quality. Division remains operable and vital, of course, especially given what Marx will analyze as the division of labor, but it is the tension in measure that constellates the barbarism of commodification as such. If, for Hegel, measure is the abstract. unification of quality and quantity; for Marx the commodity measures the transformation of one into the other. For his part, Hegel will further differentiate measure into specifying measure, that which measures an instance of measure, and real measure, which is the measure between measures, the relation of measures.[1] Once Hegel has examined the internalization of the latter, he is ready to calculate essence, the space of subjective logic. Yet the logic of series seems to stop there in that determinateness does not follow a process of comprehension but instead clings to Hegel's earlier discussion of qualitative leaps or interruptions of a succession of merely indifferent relations. Perhaps not surprisingly, it is this condition of break, or the series as constellated interruption, that materialist dialecticians, including Sartre, find more formidable. It is true Marx's calculations and modes of measurement often depended on forms of mathematics that Hegel otherwise decried (witness Marx's extensive mathematical notebooks[2], the *Grund*, as it were, for the calculations

---

1 See Georg Wilhelm Friedrich Hegel, *The Science of Logic* (George di Giovanni trans. and ed.) (Cambridge: Cambridge University Press, 2010), especially Book One, Section Three.

2 Partially translated as Karl Marx, *Mathematical Manuscripts* (C. Aronson and M. Meo trans) (London: New Park, 1983). Marx's notebooks on mathematics total over a

provoked by *Das Kapital*), but this is only to underline the qualitative leap a critique of political economy required in the face of the emergence of statistics with the state, the conditions of its own limitations (in the specific example of nineteenth century British industrialism) and in its relationship to a philosophy of number. Almost all the measure Hegel places at the service of spirit Marx transforms into another matter of the human, labor (the link exists in the notion of *Geist* as collective). The struggle over the notion of number itself becomes the scene of antagonism in social measure, value, and the ways in which a human represents themself to themself, socially.

What Sartre sees in the queue as a semblance of a group, Marx discerns in the experience of factory work, whereby the worker, divided in the segmentation of the act of labor, is submerged in the process and removed from the notion of its totalization (like fetishism, this aspect of alienation in Marx's work is easily misconstrued). If the worker's experience of seriality is to be unbound or delinked the semblance of the group must be overreached by the concreteness of collective situation, a break in the order of commodified being and the realization of labor power. In the "Poverty of Philosophy" (1847) Marx will provide a sustained critique of Proudhon in which divisibility normalizes value extraction.[3] If the question of division in seriality is decisive yet literally divisive (the place of stipulation *and* controversion), so in production Marx seizes on division as that which also sets living labor apart. Unlike Proudhon, Marx sees labor division as historically concrete, as embedded in the struggle of labor and capital. As above, we are thinking here with seriality not as categoric but as an agon in logic. If the capitalist mode of production, as evidenced by serial manufacture, imposes a distinct and exploitative division of labor it only appears as a law but is in fact a contestable condition of labor's production and reproduction. In Marx's disputes with Proudhon over matters like labor division another division ensues, between Marxist and anarchist

---

thousand pages and accentuate his desire to hone the scientificity of his critique. True to his multi-tasking, these investigations began while he was working on the serialization of *Le Capital*.

3 See Karl Marx, *The Poverty of Philosophy* in Karl Marx and Friedrich Engels, *Collected Works, Volume 6: 1845–1848* (New York: International Publishers, 1976).

elements of the International Working-Men's Association at that time. Marx's "Poverty of Philosophy" is unbending but although not every part of the division discussed is unwarranted there are still common provocations among socialist thinkers, like the idea of worker councils in relation to the commune. The division of labor articulated in *Capital* is more complex, and perhaps more difficult still in the *Grundrisse*, where the labor force not only suffers its division but learns from it. Understanding the full development of productive forces is both an extension of knowledge and a realization of "the universality of [the worker's] real and ideal relations."[4] Learning from labor in its division is itself a process, one that conjoins the real of experience in production with the imagination of its universalization as a material force. The space of division becomes a heuristic and seriality itself, unbounded, a teaching machine.

Of course, there are all kinds of reasons that learning the division of labor does not necessarily sublate its foundations in capitalism. For instance, state education, as Marx well knew, was not primed to enhance worker knowledge but programmatically assign places within existing relations of production, and the place of work itself resolutely reinforced the division of who does what and when and for how long. Still, it is important to note the relay Marx establishes between the division of labor in manufacture and the social division of labor. One division is not simply the mirror of the other but they are mutually reinforcing and are active in political economy as a whole. The enslavement of Africans was not a by-product of capitalist development but was essential to its emergence. The social construction of racial difference catalyzed and overdetermined production processes just as imperial conquest and colonization codified racism as rational accumulation. It is said that capitalism has long since departed the barbarism of hierarchization based on racial and ethnic division, but while the institutional infrastructure of enslavement may seem to have abated in absolute terms, the *ratio* of its social division casts a long shadow to the present, not least over the Global South where massive proletarianization often pivots on accumulation axioms elsewhere (the territorial division of labor, as Marx called it, is globalized). Marx reads the division of labor and social division as braided but specific in their

4 Karl Marx, *Grundrisse* (David McLellan trans.) (London: Macmillan, 1980), p. 130.

entanglement according to the development of productive forces. Marx reminds us that specialization in the factory means the worker does not actually produce a commodity but only a fragment of one, although such fragmentation is not mechanistically correlated socially, even as social need itself is divided by productive capacities and choices. Nevertheless, the divisions of one cannot be alien to the other, as Marx's painstaking analysis of the working day in *Capital* makes clear. As with seriality, the division of labor pre-exists capitalism but the capitalist must consider market exigencies before any conciliatory adaptation. The hegemonic mode of production sets the terms of goods and values, and will find a seriality in which the conditions of production and reproduction are putatively optimized. Again, division is not absolute but seeks an adequate composition of socio-economic process. A dialectics of seriality is always about the adequacy of division because even at its most regular it can neither expunge economic inconstancy (the market) nor social volatility (social justice demands contest false or oppressive division). A second order of contradiction exists in the genre of series: there are divisions of seriality but also divisions within seriality. For all of the emphasis I may place on seriality and cultural expressivity such work does not stand in for social division tout court or its contestation. Yes, there are metaphorical missiles at stake, as Marx points out, but the hard work of decomposing detrimental modes of seriality clearly does not rest on the cultural dynamics of a new series or a timely serialization (a remark, obviously, on my primary case studies).

But why a dialectics of seriality? Just as Ngũgĩ takes on the challenge of Hegel's dialectic of master and slave in the cause of its global sublation (the term he uses is globalectics, a dialectics of nurture and nature),[5] so we can subject seriality's subjection, from "bounded" nations to statistical profiles, through contradictory omens that are immanent to its logic. One could think of this alongside what Marx and Engels believe produces world literature (a dialectical promise even for those who privilege the global literary in more rarified air):

5 Ngũgĩ wa Thiong'o, *Globalectics: Theory and the Politics of Knowing* (New York: Columbia University Press, 2012).

> In place of the old wants, satisfied by the productions of the country, we find new wants, requiring for their satisfaction the products of distant lands and climes. In place of the old local and national seclusion and self-sufficiency, we have intercourse in every direction, universal inter-dependence of nations. And as in material, so also in intellectual production. The intellectual creations of individual nations become common property. National one-sidedness and narrow-mindedness become more and more impossible, and from the numerous national and local literatures, there arises a world literature.[6]

If seriality helps to articulate nation, nationalism, and "national one-sidedness and narrow-mindedness" it yet popularizes and disseminates modes of intellectual production that call into question this very bordered and secluded imaginary, even when it might do this specifically for a nation or the idea of nation itself. World literature, from this perspective, is both a serial projection of nation identity (as it was in a sense for Goethe, from whom Marx and Engels borrow) and a medium of its impasse. Worlding does not always undo a national agenda (as imperialism is wont to remind us) but it extends the field of contradiction, as if seriality participates in a commoning it cannot ultimately legislate. No doubt such tension can be examined non-dialectically, post-critically, or as the basis for cultural description (seriality certainly favors description, whereas social change embodies explication and articulation). Clearly, it is also the case the dialectic, as an analytical mode, is hardly uniform and can be dialectized accordingly (which is part, a least, of the achievement of Marx's engagement with Hegel). Basically, a dialectics of seriality challenges the reification processes of the latter, not as an unveiling or revelation of a hidden truth in Hegel, but as a means to figure the contradictory totalization of Hegelian logic. This may be glimpsed or grasped in seriality's forms of narration, yet the point is always to concretize individual instances in relation to a dialectical totality, here examined as a constellation in contestation. The problem of seriality persists in a kind of anodyne version

6 Karl Marx and Friedrich Engels, *The Communist Manifesto* (London: Vintage, 2018), pp. 27–28.

of *Verstand*, or understanding in Hegel's schema, whereby its very everydayness renders the present as inexorable, a dynamism paradoxically in the service of what Fukuyama once extravagantly proposed as an "end of history."[7]

A dialectics of seriality is not just attentive to bound and unbound versions of community or collectives but is also vigilant within those oppositions and across seriality's other—a realm of the speculative and utopian yearning. The latter resists a metaphysical ground or a Hegelian path to the Absolute but is instead a materialist injunction about what seriality looks to foreclose—a story in which seriality's institutional infrastructure is itself dissolved. What appears to arrest in seriality, its phenomenological stasis in Sartre's sense, is simultaneously a dynamic in its telling and where the movement in cognition of dialectics is challenging for a politics of culture and more. What seems old or irretrievably sedimented in forms of seriality is subject to a dialectical frisson where content wants to recompose or transform formal assumptions in their history. It is not the case that when seriality reflects on a will to conformity the latter is at once sublated: reflexivity alone does not overcome what is inert in its structure. Yet the form of reflection can, and particularly in moments of crisis, draw on the conditions of historical impasse and submit the finitude of *Verstand* to the exactitude of other imperatives. And in this a new quality of measure is articulated.

To be clear, the continuing struggles against racism, neo-colonialism, and late or global capitalism, for instance, are not outside seriality's sway (which is part of their own continuity) but the logic in division challenges cognitive claims regarding the meaning and effects of ongoing socialization. Environmental struggle, legitimately fought against the most pointed of existential crises, both performs and resists seriality's impress. One dimension imbues a logic of mass education and consciousness-raising in dissemination; another is determined by a recognition of institutional inertia, particularly in support of the fossil fuel industry and carbon-centered subjectivity. Again, several dialectical antinomies are at stake

---

7 See Francis Fukuyama, *The End of History and the Last Man* (New York: Free Press, 1992). A paean to liberal triumphalism at the end of the Cold War, Fukuyama's thesis engendered much critique, eventually from Fukuyama himself.

even when or precisely because social actors cleave to a status quo and/or see their force in not using it. The intimacy and imbrication with seriality might seem to be the cognitive limit of dialectical materialism, an analytic ultimately ill-equipped to fathom a real *coupure* with the way of the world. In this view, for instance, Marx failed to catalyze worker consciousness with his serial not because of his editing decisions or his misunderstanding of basic principles of serialization, but because he believed seriality would work with revolutionary desire. This is not my position (which is closer to the idea seriality is embroiled in *Vergesellschaftung* or processes of constituting the social) but I will further address the concern below in a discussion of Deleuze and series. Here we should stress that the contribution of dialectics is not watered down by some sociological impress or philosophically-adjacent sociocritique. The analysis of seriality stages in its own way a symptom of cognitive crisis refracted in the limits of social change. The political challenge is not reduced by attention to telling better stories unless of course the limits are explained away or, as it were, re-individuated in the manner Sartre bemoans. This would be a moment when critique obviates the political for a form of mysticism and a negation of rupture for its own sake. The divisibility in seriality is at its most prescient when it questions individuation as its highest form and foregrounds the social conditions of its production and reproduction.

A dialectics of seriality attends to seriality's contradictory will to universalism in understanding by presenting the latter as a rational order of being. What in division is supposed to reaffirm that logic can be subverted by examining division's meaning. The ordinary sense of seriality's data is problematized theoretically but concretized in crisis, where what counts for living can no longer adequately measure the possibilities in living together. If seriality, like modernity, is historical then its tendency to counter-discourse might be read to signal the conditions of its expiration. While seriality is not outside history, it is relatively easy to imagine its logic of measure beyond a history that is human (dystopian versions of AI draw directly from such non-human extension). Dialectics tarries with the negative of seriality perhaps in the vain hope human agency decides seriality's creative path or scope. Seriality in its own way is like Hegel's positing of forms where the belief is not always adequate to the practice

(*Le Capital*, once more). The ordering of practice fosters unruly praxis so it would be mistaken to view seriality as simply the ground of stability. The shortfall is not in itself the scene of measurelessness but marks a crisis in division that is historical, a long division if you will, one putting pressure on narrative convention as unalloyed social distillation. Perhaps, in Hegelian fashion, we could say that what seriality presents as understanding can offer a reason beyond itself, a level of indeterminacy in which a collective articulates a new reason to be. This I would read as the positive Hegelian impulse in thinkers like C. L. R. James and Fanon, and as a dialectic subject to further "tremulous thought" in the work of Édouard Glissant and Sylvia Wynter. But what if seriality is simply the wrong name for series and their contradictions? What if what is inadequate in dialectical thinking are its limits before the true knot of seriality: difference and repetition?

DELEUZE, IN SERIES

If dialectics opens critique to the differences between seriality, serialization, serial, and series (serialization names a process drawn from the philosophical term, seriality, with serial and series being examples of the forms that it can take), it is often read to obsess over the impasse it identifies to the point of merely reproducing it. Thinking the negative is appropriate to the seriality outlined above, and the praxis indicated should not be reduced to the thought itself (this is something of a parallax in Zizek's elaboration of the dialectic).[1] In discussing the problem of seriality in the articulation of a serial (Marx's in particular), the cultural mode of serialization appears to underline the limits to each term in their relation (serialization cannot overcome the norming that structures seriality, and an individual serial can be broken by that obligation). Even if a dialectics of seriality is other than Sartre's conceptualization, it remains the case the most pointed rethinking of seriality after Sartre is in the work of Deleuze, whose philosophy of series is not tied to the impasse announced by seriality's negation, in part because it begins from a very different notion of what constitutes an event (politically, culturally, linguistically).[2] In what follows I do not offer a gloss or commentary on Deleuze's oeuvre or especially *Logic of Sense* and *Difference and Repetition*.[3] Here, I am primarily

---

1 See Slavoj Žižek, *The Parallax View* (Cambridge: MIT Press, 2009). The parallax emphasizes a dialectic mediated by a materialist shift in perspective.

2 Although I will refer principally to Deleuze's texts in what follows, clearly Henri Bergson's thoughts on duration and the continuous flow of time influence Deleuze's position. Although Bergson's idea of multiplicity has a kind of serial unconscious that we could read into Deleuzean repetition, the question of difference (or in my reading, division) resonates more in Deleuze's representation of Bergsonism. See Gilles Deleuze, *Bergsonism* (Hugh Tomlinson and Barbara Habberjam trans) (New York: Zone Books, 1988).

3 The central texts here are Gilles Deleuze, *Difference and Repetition* (Paul Patton trans.) (New York: Columbia University Press, 1994[1968]); *The Logic of Sense* (Mark Lester trans.) (London: Athlone, 1990[1969]).

interested in the implications of Deleuzean thinking for a materialist elaboration of seriality and social change, a Sisyphean task to be sure, but not simply outside or antithetical to the politics pursued.[4]

To restrict these comments still further, what if Deleuze's interpretative mode, the interpretation of an interpretation (interpretation for Deleuze is immanent to the "thing" interpreted) comes across the politics of Marx's serial as event? Part of the challenge, as it was for Marx, is interpretation as translation. Marx, for instance, offers a serial in which organic manufacture (serial manufacture) is intricately detailed in terms of production and value. In the vitalist slide from, say, assembly to assemblage the real of production is virtualized. True, virtual is not the opposite of real in Deleuze's terms but it is a field of potential to be actualized (this is a Spinozist thread I have already invoked), yet taken as a whole seriality and series have a contrasting working relation in Deleuze's philosophy. *Logic of Sense* is a collocation of series in reciprocal relations, which is to say Deleuze conceives series as multiple series in relation. The "minor" figures he presents (minor being another multivalent term that even extends in *A Thousand Plateaus* to "the proletariat")[5] only make sense in their series' relation to one another, although this is a philosophical presentation of how logic works. One element of seriality I have examined so far is the political link between a serial project and seriality's constraints on the social (the queue, the census, the order of being). In "sense," Deleuze's series undo such order not because of the struggle over the political but because the political is functionally everywhere. The concreteness of antagonism and contradiction which I have located, for instance, in division and extension seems to evaporate before the act of interpretation itself

4 There are many examples of theory attempting to imbricate Marxian and Deleuzean thought—two series, perhaps, unassimilable to one another. The aim here is not to read Deleuze as a "minor Marxist" but is to think with Deleuze in tension with a materialist theorization of seriality. For a much broader text on the Marx/Deleuze conjunction, see Nicholas Thoburn, *Deleuze, Marx, and Politics* (London: Routledge, 2003).

5 Gilles Deleuze and Félix Guattari, *A Thousand Plateaus: Capitalism and Schizophrenia* (Brian Massumi trans.) (Minneapolis, MN: University of Minnesota Press, 1987), p. 472.

(one is reminded here of Marx's Eleventh Thesis on Feuerbach). Yet this irreconcilability is not unproductive. The difficulty rests on the sense of event in series and how an event is prioritized (is it a biographical moment, a conceptual instance, a social crisis, a publishing sequence, language, any and all events internal to a narrative?). The eventness of a series or serial is no small matter, not just because it embodies kinds of change but because it provokes or is active in specific forms of it. My use of "social change" marks this specificity against a backdrop of change in general. For Deleuze, by contrast, events prescribe substance, and the point of agency, signaled by "social," cannot assume such generality. It is entirely symptomatic Deleuze's conceptualization begins in *Logic of Sense* with a literary text, and Lewis Carroll's *Alice*, for it is hard to think of writing better equipped to imaginatively displace the conventions of event than the allusion, elusion, and illusion of Dodgson/Carroll's sentences (the author of *Alice's Adventures in Wonderland* was not only a word-monger but a noted mathematician—witness his *Symbolic Logic*—which provides another route to the subject of series here and, tangentially, the deliciously obscure locutions of Deleuze's style). Seriality, in this example, does not lock in sense but unbinds it, not just towards nonsense (Carroll's humor) but extra-sense, an event of multiple layers and the asynchronic. Part of seriality's lure is expectation, it maintains surprise—the issue is expected, the contents may contravene. In Deleuze's series in *Logic of Sense* (chapters that are resolutely not chapters) he emphasizes connections but not sequence, or at least not sequence alone since the aim is to challenge the order (of things). The complexity of the reading practice required is immense and reminds us of what reading *Capital* demands, a kind of thinking beside itself (or a concept of intuition that itself has to be intuited). The main difference is not just between philosophy and political economy but in laying out the terms of social being. If Marx's text is less playful (he is, however, the better humorist, despite Deleuze's "Nineteenth Series") its hook is in taking the social relations of production as a political horizon and radical heuristic. Deleuze shares much of this vision (he was not beyond describing himself as a Marxist in this regard, as well as a "pure metaphysician," and his last planned work was said to be "The Grandeur of Marx" which perhaps compounds the ambivalence, yet like *Le Capital*, the series, is a missed opportunity) but he theorizes paradox over dialectical contradiction, and always becoming over sublation (although I hold these here in tension). The question rests to some extent on how one views creative engagement over invention as its own reward. Deleuze's immense conceptual generation is itself a confrontation with seriality's will to conformism and pushes the very idea of series onto a different plane, of immanence and more besides (interestingly if not ironically, the desire for concepts is a feature of the early Marx of the philosophical manuscripts). One could argue that by relating the series in Deleuze's work the task of creation is actually the reader's own and such an impetus, for both philosophical and political reasons, is to be appreciated. Like the French worker perusing Marx's exegesis of the fetishism of commodities, however, the reader of *Logic of Sense* might still wonder how far a refusal of work extends to the work of reading. As an example of series, Deleuze's book is a critique of its form and formal logic. True to its theorization of event, we could say its event has already happened in Victorian serialization, even in the work of Dodgson himself. Since Deleuze uses the term *mise en series* (or "seriation") a difference is at work, especially in the idea of the necessity for inclusion in a series. Again, because of seriality's ubiquity such necessity seems suspended in advance, but thinking about Marx's desire for *Capital*'s publication in French, Deleuze's point can be taken to ask whether the necessity for *Le Capital* as a serial has been established?

Deleuze's series cleave close to a philosophical disposition at some remove from social collectivity (class, group-in-fusion, etc.) even as they unpick serial assumptions in their play. The philosophical gainsay in the juxtaposition of the Stoics, Leibniz, Lautman and Simondon is in its challenge for sense, but the politics implied remain doggedly diffuse. The series stretches "great politics" to singularities "which are neither general nor individual, neither personal nor universal. All of this is traversed by circulations, echoes, and events which produce more sense, more freedom, and more strength than man has ever dreamed of, or God ever conceived."[6] One of the paradoxes of series for Deleuze is the production of political singularity without affiliation. A reader is interpellated to do the work of series, in essence, to establish connections, but that praxis is unique and

6 Deleuze, *Logic of Sense*, p. 254.

virtually incommunicable in its individuation. We might say, as Sartre notes of seriality, that Deleuze's series is both sensed and queued, divided in its othering from a material collective with an Other. It is difficult to prioritize this event as political without negating its substance. Because Deleuze has an explanation for "alogical incompatabilities" one could easily argue the opposite, that political immanence is foregrounded precisely by what the series fails to achieve and this itself necessitates the reconceptualization of sense beyond the sensate and certainly a history of the human in the formation of the five senses to which Marx alludes in *The Economic and Political Manuscripts of 1844*.[7] Yet again, the question of division is provocative—in *Le Capital*, 44 livraisons (at least), in *Logique du Sens*, 37 series (where, albeit oddly, Deleuze is more methodological in division than Marx, which reminds one of how Spinoza counted affect). Division is elaborated in the appendices to Deleuze's book rather than in its series, with reference to Plato and dialectics, and this reflects back on our discussion so far. He notes, "The purpose of division then is not at all to divide a genus into species, but, more profoundly, to select lineages: to distinguish pretenders; to distinguish the pure from the impure, the authentic from the inauthentic."[8] Indeed, referring to the *Phaedrus*, Deleuze asserts "the Platonic dialectic is neither a dialectic of contradiction nor of contrariety, but a dialectic of rivalry (amphisbetesis), a dialectic of rivals and suitors." One could argue the rivals in the *Phaedrus* are contradictory and contrarian but Deleuze's point is "The essence of division does not appear in its breadth, in the determination of the species of a genus, but in its depth, in the selection of the lineage." Even if this represents the nature of division for Plato, one wonders if this extends to Deleuze's series, one where, rather than following numerical order, the reader is asked to select, to make connections, across the exegesis articulated? As Deleuze says of the *Phaedrus*, the text appears to renounce its task of division, letting itself be carried a long by a myth of circulation (of souls), but "myth interrupts nothing." He continues, "The characteristic of division is to surmount the duality of myth and dialectic, and to reunite in itself dialectical and mythical

7 Karl Marx, *Economic and Political Manuscripts of 1844* (Martin Milligan trans.) (Moscow: Progress Publishers, 1959).

8 Deleuze, *Logic of Sense*, pp. 72–73.

power. Myth, with its always circular structure, is indeed the story of a foundation."[9] No doubt this narrative of division does not map unproblematically onto seriality, or even the tension of myth and dialectic, yet it remains a productive antinomy, not just in questioning the role of dialectics in division (again, for Hegel, measure between quality and quantity), but also in reflecting on Deleuze's own sense of series, where his acts of division themselves are not beyond a certain myth-making. From Deleuze's reading of Leibniz we could say that rather than circularity, seriality stages "compossibility," an individuation that may, within certain conditions and constraints, facilitate being together or beyond the division posed. Could this be the positive power of seriality's simulation (the composition of possibility), that in its will to power and division it frames the "story of a foundation" the series struggles to contain? Perhaps such staging can be clarified by reference to a contemporaneous work of Deleuze, *Difference and Repetition*.

To the extent that much of what has been offered on seriality so far hinges on notions of representation, it fails to provide an escape or line of flight from the norms of subject/object relations. *Difference and Repetition* can be read as an answer to such a limit (of structure and structuralism), and especially in relation to what characterizes series in *Logic of Sense*. Indeed, the latter helps to explain the odd array of the former's intervention where few clues are provided for why one chapter follows another (the book has the feel of a Bergsonian-inspired drip painting as a "space of succession"). The difference in series can be registered by the difference in difference Deleuze examines (conceptual difference, non-conceptual difference—experience, for instance—and interior difference, singular and non-assimilable). These versions of difference do not exclude representation or identity and identification but pick away at the truths of representation. To recall organic manufacture once more, its seriality depends not just on sequence and division but on flexibility, the ability to change a production cycle according to market demands. This, we might say, is a conceptual difference in representation, and the commodity "represents" such a logic. Both management and labor are capable of non-conceptual difference, at least in their experience of what works in the space of production, another

9 Deleuze, *Logic of Sense*, pp. 254–55.

sense of productive capacity. Singular difference, however, is less easy to accommodate within this materialist version of seriality. It may not be acted upon or be represented but exists as an unspoken or measureless demand. It is not a ghost in the machine of production yet seems to interiorize an externality as a spectral indifference to division (of labor, in series). Any invocation of the collective, in or against serial manifestations, would tend to draw difference back to a representational core. It would also be well served by a dialectical understanding of this challenge. Nevertheless, the point here is that dimensions of difference destabilize constellations of series without rendering the difference of representation itself a fetish of seriality as a whole. Much more could be said about the instability or absence of representation's ground (what would this tell us about an assumed democratic structure, for instance?) but at the very least it complicates any representational relay between seriality as concept and social change as a condition of praxis.

Difference, like division, does not mean contradiction but in series expresses the instability (or "indiscernibles") of continuity and limit. This space of compossibility may not define social change yet the latter is immanent to it and so one can imagine a dialectics of difference even in a series meant to overcome it. Of course, this is not the focus of Deleuzean difference in *Difference and Repetition*, which is a means to attend to a very specific genealogy of philosophical thought, say from Aristotle through to Duns Scotus, Spinoza, and Nietzsche (with a round on Leibniz and Hegel on the question of representation). Even if this constituted a series, seriality itself appears adjacent not central to its concern. Yet *Difference and Repetition* is replete with a sense of series as troublingly connective, and this has implications even for the quotidian materializations of seriality that are my chief concern. A limit to culture, for instance, "difference must be shown differing,"[10] is simultaneously a critique of series within a condition of seriality. In works by Mallarmé and Joyce, Deleuze sees objects dissolving in divergent series, a reminder that series are subject to difference and differentiation, and the specification of an individual series does not necessarily do the work of series in difference even as its simulacrum. When Deleuze contrasts difference *in* itself from repetition *for* itself both

10 Deleuze, *Difference and Repetition*, p. 57.

terms are changed in combination. Seriality might be said to permit the repetition of habit and memory, but for Deleuze repetition is also a mode or condition of refusal which is repeatable (between two series): of a content of repetition drawing from difference, and of a form of repetition which includes difference in the cause of a thought and a production of the "absolutely different."[11] Seriality can only be a reduction (rather than, to borrow from Deleuze, an intensity) of this realm of difference but it can usefully be elaborated as a condition of series for such philosophical investigation. Thus, when Deleuze discusses Bergson on "real series" and a "series of real objects" we are reminded of seriality in its reality effects—the many ways in which it signals not just the real time of its reader, for instance, but the virtuality of time in that experience (its "meanwhile" in relation).[12] Although I do not use "real series" as concept in the seriality I explore (even at the level of character, as Deleuze does in his comments on Proust's *In Search of Lost Time*), I have some interest in the production of the Real in the Lacanian sense, and a necessary unrepresentability in that regard which may in its own way be a difference in the repetition of Deleuze.

One of the many provocations on series in *Difference and Repetition* is the idea repetition exists in the alignment/non-alignment of two series arrayed in difference. True, for the most part Deleuze considers "verbal series" within a single work rather than examining a work in series. *Le Capital* is a series (or at least a projection of one) in itself, but clearly links to the production of *Das Kapital* in editions (a key focus of Marxist scholarship) and other series serialized (the second German edition, the first English edition, etc.). Seriality extends the text but also reconfigures its meanings not simply as a function of context but as a living mediation of the limits of its idea. The modesty of such series belies their social impress in discourses of change. Deleuze, not surprisingly, quickly jumps scales to maximize disparate series, "all the divergent series of the cosmos," glimpsed through "linguistic dark precursors."[13] The metaphysical poetry of this move should not be underestimated or lack criticism, but other

11 Deleuze, *Difference and Repetition*, p. 94.

12 Deleuze, *Difference and Repetition*, p. 102.

13 Deleuze, *Difference and Repetition*, p. 121.

dynamics are at stake that explicate the impress of series; for instance, in a dialectic of over-representation and under-theorization. Deleuze's point is about the specificity of the series over abstraction from it which is not an either/or between metaphysics and materialization. While here we tend to favor resistance as more than singularity, and contradiction over the play of paradox, without doubt series after Deleuze hardly makes of seriality in culture an innocent philosophical process (thus, a series of the Sixties that questions the present). Perhaps, in keeping with Deleuze on "indefinite regression" we might say serialization ensures redefinition and a certain disequilibrium between series.[14] In his close attention to manifestations of signifier and signified, Deleuze places series at the heart of signifying practices in general. This is one way that the signification of *Le Capital* is active in the idea of serial manufacture and also in its own series of iterative materializations. The relative displacement of series does not directly produce absolute transformation but fosters the conditions of its possibility. It is never the only narrative of seriality, yet it is one that permits an understanding of the role of the everyday in one that is not.

14 Deleuze, *Logic of Sense*, p. 36.

We have not and will not offer a compendium of "Marx, the series" (even in the appreciable enormity of labor producing the MEGA^2, the horizon of series recedes). The focus is on the initial conditions of Marx's *Capital* (from, yet despite nineteenth century British industrialism, and cultural phenomena like Victorian serialization) and how labor and other readers might learn from it in translation and popular rearticulation/dissemination. The series, from Deleuze on numbers, symbols, and words, appears to order but inconsistently so, evincing both centrifugal attributes and a recursive desire for stability. Its dynamic accumulates originally but intensifies in exchange (with other series and components of itself). A Deleuzean sense would yield a universal contingency in the capacity of series, a notion like Gödel's on systemic inconsistency. The capitalist must have variables in series because any magnitude in accumulation can only be secured through difference (in price, in costs of production, etc.). Marx's critique of Hegel starts by accounting for such difference dialectically without resort to pure contingency.[1] Of course, the labor theory of value can be philosophically relativized, from within and without a series of materialist ideas, but the persistence of Marx's *Capital* is not in the happenstance of applicability in series but because of material imperatives in serial engagement. The compulsiveness of historically concrete crisis continues to find a critique of political economy. What dissolves capitalism is also what renders *Capital* superfluous, if not an archival curiosity. It would then live on in series, but not one primarily bound to capitalist crisis itself. I have indicated multiple series so far, including one specifically dedicated to the effulgence of Marx's texts, in order to accentuate the critical valence of seriality in confronting and/or constructing an algebra

1 This is evident even in the early text from 1843 (unpublished in his lifetime), Karl Marx, *Critique of Hegel's Philosophy of Right* (Annette Jolin and Joseph O'Malley trans) (Cambridge: Cambridge University Press, 1970). Again, this is more groundwork than elaboration but the aim remains to disengage critique from dialectical idealism.

of social change. Although there are not ideal forms of serial engagement (the aim is not to distill a typology of serial discourse), there are genres of cultural expression that seem simultaneously to banalize and to bolster the relationship of critique to more radical socialization. Reading *Capital* is an industry, sometimes in the service of not reading it (most introductions, however, whatever the summary or beginner aspects, require cross-referencing to substantiate their claims). For the most part, this is *aplatir* in the negative sense as "simplify" rather than smooth. Plenty of introductions, companions, illustrated editions, guides, and handbooks go much further than simplification, and interrogate as well as explicate Marx's *Capital*, consciously or not extending and providing new meaning in a process that is serial and *Capital* in series. These texts, including their translations and reissues, number in the hundreds, and obviously this is before accounting for the thousands of narratives that take up *Capital* explicitly in their worldview (cultural production that flourished towards and in "actually existing socialism"). Some publications, like a new translation of *Capital*, are events in themselves, but together they constitute the eventness of Marx's critique and translatability, as much part of the archive as his original writings. Marxism has certainly benefited from variegations in the secondary literature and from the forms of its publication and distribution. Having investigated key elements of the conceptual difficulty in seriality and its necessary limitations for change more broadly construed, I now want to return to *Le Capital*/*Capital* to provide examples of its series and to elaborate how they extend and qualify the series Marx intended. These iterations are not simply produced by socio-economic crisis alone but they participate in how crisis of this kind can be understood. They are a dialogic inscription of praxis—symptoms of change they cannot in themselves enforce (precisely the dilemma implicated in Marx's letter to Lachâtre quoted above). Is the living-on of *Capital* (as serial, in series) adequate to the change it implies or does ever-late capitalism confirm that such change is not so much a specter as it is a zombie, and one apposite only with a deathly entertainment that *Capital* in series dutifully and repeatedly performs? Does the prospect of "manga Marx" merely mangle Marx and permit further finger-wagging about dialectical dilution and the elitist and distasteful horror of Marxism for morons? Engels' reactions to *Le Capital* already indicate a fear of vernacular Marx, the idea that popularizing *Capital* in series guts the Marxism and makes the event of its text little more than anti-intellectual froth (and in French, no less, worries Engels). Does unbinding the text in seriality loosen the terms of critique to the point of easy, relaxed, or lifestyle acculturation? Is the immense intellectual force of the text irredeemably compromised by serialization, or could the latter meet the remit of change actually taking place?

Marx believed it was possible to maintain the integrity of his text in translation (linguistically, formally), and Marxist scholars appreciate the attempt while reserving the right to a definitive edition relatively free from adaptation and abridgement (an authenticity in Marx perhaps unavailable in Marxism). Clearly, if the question was merely can Marx be multiplied (and/or commodified) there would be little debate. Similarly, if the point was just popular culture versions of Marx matter, it could be made in understated terms without recourse to any event of form through politics, philosophy, or aesthetics. If, however, the everydayness of capitalist critique embodies the potential of rupture then the division in series, for instance, signifies at other levels and is especially prescient in events of crisis where form struggles with content as content seeks to exceed the forms given to it. Seriality, from this perspective, not only signals an understanding of an individual series, but offers genealogical links in series that elaborate how the possibility of dispute is preserved as a historical impasse to be confronted. Seriality finds a logic of necessity in socio-economic contradiction.

GELLERT, OR LITHOGRAPHIC CAPITAL

Hugo Gellert (1892–1985) is a renowned Hungarian-American graphic artist and muralist of the twentieth century whose worker artistry takes Marx at his word.[1] In one of his justifiably revered projects, (Karl Marx's) *Capital in Lithographs* (also known as *Capital in Pictures*, 1934), Gellert restates and revises the renowned letter to Lachâtre: "*Das Kapital* is our guide. Like the X-ray, it discloses the depths below the surface. It is my hope that in this abbreviated form the immortal work of Karl Marx will become accessible to the Masses" (November 7, 1933). Gellert's work within American socialism and communism was already well known and his art was available in radical journals like *The Masses*, *The Liberator/The Workers Monthly*, and *The New Masses*, and he was a founder of *Art Front* (which began in the same year his *Capital* was published. The *Daily Worker*, *New Yorker* and the *New York Times* also recognized his timely and artistic talents). In addition to his activism in the New York socialist/artist Popular Front network (with links to the John Reed Club and Artists Union), his output as a visual artist in portraits, caricatures, and cartoons was immense, and his murals, while not of the influence and revolutionary ardor of the Mexican anti-fascist muralists of the time ("los tres grandes," Diego Rivera, David Alfaro Siqueiros, and José Clemente Orozco most prominently), continue to resonate. Gellert's other books of the period, including *The Mirrors of Wall Street* (a who is who of American capitalism), the wildly satirical *Comrade Gulliver*, and the classicist revision *Aesop Said So*, would require much more space than here, but they are of a piece with his aesthetic and political commitments. *Capital in Lithographs* is another genre again and is a work in and out of time around series and the material conditions of seriality. The form of the book juxtaposes key passages from Marx's text

1 A brief biography and assessment published not long after Gellert's death can be found in Zoltan Deak (ed.), *Hugo Gellert, 1892–1985: People's Artist* (New York: Hugo Gellert Memorial Committee, 1986). A useful collection of Hugo Gellert papers have been gathered by the Smithsonian's Archive of American Art and can be found online: rebrand.ly/e65198 (last accessed: August 26, 2025).

with an explanatory or dialogical image of its ideas. Basically, we have a series of *Capital* in excerpts alongside a second series of graphic reconceptualizations/reflections. These series exist in a dialogic and independently. The concern is less whether they do justice to their sources but what happens to the impress of a source in their combination. More than once we have noted Marx's hesitation before "accessibility" (in this Marx could not be the "culture worker" Gellert explicitly favored) while also acknowledging the quality of a difficult idea is not necessarily resolved in simplification or by editing. Gellert reads accessibility as possibility; that is, the pictorial and re-figural offer a space for confronting crisis in a new analytic. The impetus is not new but the conjunction is evental. This might seem an obvious response to the Wall Street Crash of 1929 and the deep disruptions of its aftermath in the immiseration of millions in the United States, but Gellert's artistry and politics provide another dimension to the event of crisis, graphic Marxism if you will, that requires further comment.[2]

It is not just Gellert's sense of injustice that gives shape to the conditions of crisis but the ways in which he constellates *Capital* across different levels of abstraction and concreteness. Rather than either text or image being an unreflective précis of one another, their interaction produces at the very least a third term for their substance, that here I have been arguing for under the rubric of seriality. The graphic images of *Le Capital* are mostly in the form of decoration over illustration or comment. Their primary interaction is based on the conventions of contemporary serialization rather than through their interrogation. If there is a political unconscious in their array it is at odds with the text. The graphics take up space but do not occupy it with respect to thesis or critique. We have already suggested that for determinate reasons "serial Marx" is abrogated in its desire, a series that turns against its serial, the issues making up its number. What is in *Le Capital* an opportunity missed is for Gellert a condensation of his art, a series of lithographs that are an imaginative leap. It is as if in Marx's

2 The same impetus can be discerned in many other artists of the time of course, including Käthe Kollwitz, whose expressionism was often a theoretical exposition of beauty and critique by other means. A pertinent overview can be found in Hannelore Fischer (ed.), *Käthe Kollwitz* (Munich: Hirmer, 2022).

words Gellert finds an organic structure for his line that not only meets the road to science Marx draws but images the crisis of capitalism in the concreteness of its history. The effects are, at this level, quite extraordinary.

In his Foreword to the volume, Gellert only hints at the crisis in which it is enmeshed but draws on the extreme conditions that are lived experiences for the implied reader:

> In our America we live in a period of the greatest expropriation in history since we took the land from the Indian possessors. (Brave pioneers risked their lives for this land; now crafty bankers grab it, risking nothing.) Throughout our Southern states our black brothers have always known slavery. Under the NRA President Roosevelt makes slaves of all workers with the aid of strike proof 'labor unions,' after the pattern of Mussolini. Our last vestige of protection against the rapacious Trusts is being removed.[3]

The rhetorical conceits ("brave" pioneers, Roosevelt and Mussolini?) would need more context than Gellert provides but his art often points the way and underlines his flourish: "In this book only the most essential parts of the original are given. But with the aid of the drawings the necessary material for the understanding of the fundamentals of Marxism is included."[4]

If the aim is broadly educational the rabble rousing is very much part of the crisis response of the period. The Soviet Union has offered an example (the last image of the book is of Lenin) which is unique but in the imaging of Marx's texts the American masses will see the power in their own situation and the socio-economic relations in which such power is realized. Such of course is the theory of Gellert's artist activism even if the logic of the series both connects and divides. As noted, Gellert is a significant American artist of the twentieth century in his own right, so

---

3 Hugo Gellert, *Karl Marx: "Capital" in Lithographs* (New York: Ray Long and Richard R. Smith, 1934), p. 7. As noted below, original copies of this book, and indeed editions of the lithographs themselves, are collector items and feature on many art/bookseller sites. Facsimiles abound and I have cross-referenced one (from Delhi: Gyan Books, 2015) with the original.

4 Gellert, *Karl Marx: "Capital" in Lithographs*, p. *vii*.

the narrative of what makes *Capital in Lithographs* is reaccentuated and/or displaced by the status of his images. Indeed, the time/space that defines the crisis of the Thirties in the United States has become obscured or detached as the archive unhinges the syntax of Gellert's Marxism from a vision of more collectible proportions. This is not always the case: the Smithsonian Archives of American Art, for instance, provides a wide range of Gellert's materials that help to illuminate the rich complexity of Gellert's lifework. Still, one could point to MOMA's Gellert collection that permits one to consult his *Capital* images (the portfolio edition) without any reference to the accompanying text by Marx (the Whitney, by contrast, provides text and image side by side, yet labels the collection "Karl Marx in Pictures"—probably drawn from the trade book edition). This is an alienation effect of a different order yet is necessarily part of the possibility in revolutionary telling. Many of the lithographs from Gellert's *Capital* can be purchased individually or as portfolios (with signatures), not surprisingly, and reproductions of the work as a whole are relatively easy to source (offering two other versions of series in the life of the text—"original" copies are prized collector items). As early as 1930, Gellert was accepting pre-orders and pledges for the portfolio edition for $100 each (equivalent to around $1800 a set of 62 lithographs). Let us ponder the compositional effects of this *Capital*'s intervention and limits to the same.

An initial impression is made by the juxtaposition of images preceding Gellert's Foreword. The first is a reproduction of one of Gellert's somewhat notorious murals, the 1932 piece for the Museum of Modern Art titled, "Us Fellas Got to Stick Together," featuring at the top J. P. Morgan, Henry Ford, John D. Rockefeller, and President Hoover, all accompanied by a machine-gun firing Al Capone. Below them is a line of state enforcers (the police, the military), and below that what looks like an image of Thomas Mooney, the wrongly accused activist, behind bars. The reproduction of the image is sometimes subtitled with "the last defenses of capitalism." In the book version, the figures are facing a giant hammer and sickle and the slogan beneath them reads, "Workers of all Lands Unite!" Elements of this image will reappear later in the book as echoes of its guiding sentiment. While not subtle, it prepares the reader for the polemic, which subsequently will add nuance to its critique.

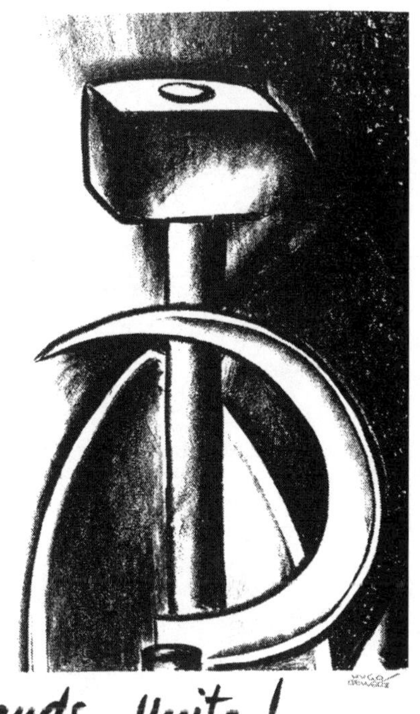

FIGURE 3. Hugo Gellert, "Workers of All Lands Unite" in *Karl Marx: "Capital" in Lithographs*, pp. *iii–iv*.

To the extent that *Capital in Lithographs* is abbreviated, historically situated, and illustrated this is not intended as *Das Kapital* according to Marx's project, or indeed the *Le Capital* serial. The challenge of Gellert's text is clearly stated: "The translation into graphic form of the revolutionary concepts of *Das Kapital* was a source of inspiration and stimulus." Can we both accept the difference of the text and the deployment of its repetition as a lesson not just for serializing Marx across forms, but for situating a radical politics of seriality in that array? The question is compounded by the phrase "translation into graphic form of [. . .] revolutionary concepts." I will link this formulation to a Benjaminian insistence on "heightened graphicness" (*Anschaulichkeit*—viewability and, among other meanings to be recalled, the vividness of the image), in my conclusion. Here one notes a kind of untranslatability immanent to Marx's critique that always fails its graphic representation (even in the socialist realism and American modernism of radical Left aesthetics of the Thirties) yet simultaneously nurtures its transformational demand. On the one hand, we have the commonplace of difference in repetition; on the other hand, repetition preserves the logic of rupture, and here the artist is neither cowed by the order of commodification in technological reproduction (everydayness is not simply consent) nor the limits of aesthetics in processes of social change. What is remarkable about *Capital in Lithographs* is not only that it seizes on a profound disaffection with the American institutional order in the Depression of the Thirties (in the state, in socio-economic structure) but it also imagines a series in the contingency of crisis that must disrupt, despite itself, the measure of Marxism for popular consciousness. The parts of Gellert's *Capital* are not released periodically but are published as a single volume in two forms 1933/34. Seriality can proceed in the absence of a serial (*Le Capital*) but here it is operative in several distinct modes: the relationship of the excerpts to their primary text, *Capital* (as intertext, as hypertext to hypotext);[5] the relationship of the excerpts to each other (as sequence and difference); the relationship of the images to a cultural

5 I am drawing here principally yet critically from Gérard Genette, *Palimpsests: Literature in the Second Degree* (Channa Newman and Claude Doubinsky trans) (Lincoln, NE: University of Nebraska Press, 1997). The basic idea is to think the stressed relationship of one text (or version) to another.

symbolic or system of referentiality (caricatures, political motifs); the relationship of the images to each other (as sequence, difference, afterimage, and consciousness); and also, most importantly, the relationship between the series of texts and images, where the dialogic exchange is uneven and contested, and very much part of the compositional compossibility of the combination in history. The last point does not suture or justify the relations preceding it; indeed, it is the dialectical constellation together that constitutes the challenge of seriality for social change and, of course, the reverse as inertia.

Following "Us Fellas" the book offers Gellert's sketch of Marx, whose stern demeanor suggests not only intellectual gravitas but a proximate rebuke to Messrs. Rockefeller and company (and even to the earlier Marx who looks away). The image signs the text although this by no means constitutes authorial consent or authentication, even as the hammer and sickle warrant a certain metonymy in the matter (these elements mark the ideological struggles in which this *Capital* performs). The text carries a dedication to Gellert's brother, Ernest, a "faithful soldier of the proletarian cause" whose conscientious objection to the Great War (First World War) ends in death in military custody, officially by suicide. We will not here examine every juxtaposition of Marx's text with Gellert's lithographs but certain patterns and stylistic elements are significant for the broader claims on serial engagement. Readers of *Capital* will know that it does not arrive without prefaces and notes on editions and translations (these framing devices resonate with what Derrida explores as *parerga*).[6] We have considered *Le Capital* within this array and it will continue to inform my final example below. Here, one notes Gellert's excerpt from Marx's preface to the first German edition, that includes the Latin phrase, "*De te fabula narratur*" (the story is told about you) and the comment about using individual capitalists as "personifications of economic categories" (which of course, Gellert himself has just done). The scene is set.

---

6 See Jacques Derrida, *The Truth in Painting* (Geoff Bennington and Ian McLeod trans) (Chicago, IL: University of Chicago Press, 1987). The *parergon*, or supplement, is also the space-off, or what is not seen, that permits the image to appear. The *parerga* of *Le Capital* are mostly ornamental but we have thought of the supplement in what the text does not represent, including the missing covers.

Let me briefly observe how Gellert determines to tell the story of *Capital* in its seriality for workers of all lands before moving to an analysis of its divisions. First of all, Gellert's invocation of abbreviation and accessibility gives us Marx's critique in a new and unique array (although he appears to use his own translations, he also uses and modifies the three-volume English translation—1906–1909—by another notable American socialist, Ernest Untermann, for the Marxist publishing house, Charles H. Kerr).[7] Gellert does not locate the excerpts, but doing this may prove useful for the critique that follows. Thus, schematically, he begins *Capital in Pictures* with almost the end of *Capital* (Volume One), Section 8, Chapter 26 on "primary" or "primitive" accumulation (Marx uses the term *ursprüngliche Akkumulation*, to signal original or initial—in general, in the age of technological reproduction, "original" is used ambivalently throughout the present study, especially around series as development).[8] The following two pages also feature selections from the same chapter, which is then tracked by four pages of excerpts from Chapter 27 on the

---

7 See Karl Marx, *Capital, A Critique of Political Economy: Volume One* (Ernest Untermann ed. and trans.) (Chicago, IL: Charles H. Kerr and Co., 1906–1909). Note: for Volume One, Untermann uses the Third German edition translated by Samuel Moore and Edward Aveling but then "revises" and "amplifies" using the Fourth German edition. His translation of Volume Two (from the Second German edition) appears in 1910. Volume Three (from the First German Edition) appears in 1909. Untermann provides a brief history of translations and editions of Marx's text in "an editor's note to the first American edition."

8 Although there is no space for this here, it would be interesting to analyze the extent to which Gellert translates or modifies the excerpts from *Capital* he uses (I see this in parallel with Marx and *Le Capital*, even if it is not as intensive). For instance, in the first excerpt on "primitive" accumulation, Marx offers a litany of violent procedures deployed for accumulation: "In der wirklichen Geschichte spielen bekanntlich Eroberung, Unterjochung, Raubmord, kurz Gewalt die große Rolle"; Marx, *Das Kapital*, p. 642. Both the first English translation and the first English translation in the United States (Untermann) render "Unterjochung" as" enslavement" or "Versklavung" (as does the later Ben Fowkes translation) but Gellert uses "subjugation" (a translation closer to the German and one used by Reitter/North in their new translation of Volume One). Obviously, Gellert does not offer a complete translation of *Das Kapital*, yet Marx in series should not abjure the ways in which a new version affects more than the form of presentation.

expropriation of the agricultural population from the land. We then have three pages with accompanying images drawn from Chapter 28 on "Bloody Legislation against the Expropriated," then one page that quotes both Chapter 29 and 30, followed by other excerpts from 30 ("Impact of the Agricultural Revolution on Industry"). After five pages of excerpts from Chapter 31 on the "Genesis of the Industrial Capitalist" Gellert moves to a few paragraphs from Chapter 32 on the "Historical tendency of Capitalist Accumulation." All of the pages of text to this point have been titled "primary accumulation." It is only after this long sequence of representations that Gellert moves to the beginning of *Capital* with the Commodity chapter and accompanying images. Skipping Chapter Two on the "Process of Exchange," Gellert moves to Chapter Three on "Money," then the "General Formula for Capital" (Chapter Four), and "The Sale and Purchase of Labor Power" (Chapter Six—excerpts from Chapter Five on "Contradictions in the General Formula" are omitted). Chapters 7 through 10 are represented over the following 9 pages, from the labor process to the working day. Chapter 11 on the "Rate and Mass of Surplus Value" is left out but then Gellert excerpts and illustrates Chapters 12 through 15, from "Relative Surplus Value" to "Machinery and Large-Scale Industry." Indeed, Chapter 15, with its many sub-headings, is the most quoted and illustrated chapter in Gellert's book (8 pages). We then jump forward to Chapter 19 on the "Transformation of the Value, or the Price, of Labor Power into the Wage," then back to 18 on "Different Formulae for the Rate of Surplus Value," followed by a shift to Chapter 23 on "Simple Reproduction." Skipping the chapter on "The Transformation of Surplus-Value into Capital," Gellert moves to Chapter 25 on the "General Law of Capitalist Accumulation (2 pages). If Gellert's first revision is by starting at the end with primary accumulation, his second is a dramatic shift to Volume Three of *Capital*, which features excerpts from Part Six, Chapter 37, introducing the "Transformation of Surplus Profit into Ground Rent" and Chapter 46 on the rent of buildings, etc. We then have four pages of excerpts from Chapter 47 on the "Genesis of Capitalist Ground Rent" before a final flourish featuring a juxtaposition of excerpts from Chapter 51 (Volume Three) on "Relations of Distribution and Relations of Production" and a reprise of Chapter 32 (Volume One). As we have noted, guides and introductions in and around *Capital* abound (Untermann published one himself in 1907), so what we are to make of this collage/montage against a background of socio-economic upheaval that was Gellert's primary concern?

Untermann adds his translations to a series of *Capital* editions and Gellert uses these as well as his own in producing *Capital in Lithographs*). Because the selections clearly offer a different vision of *Capital* (and not just literally) it is worth considering the contours of Gellert's intervention in relation to crisis, and also in connection to Marx's earlier appeal to worker accessibility. Some of the decisions are obvious (start with a history of accumulation rather than the opacity of the commodity) but Gellert's bold project is less about basic explanation (the illustrator does not always illustrate) and more to do with examining the text through inflections in experience among a projected working-class readership. When Marx sought a worker readership he believed division in seriality (with its periodical pricing) would largely do the work of dialogic address. As an activist and visual artist Gellert has a different relationship to the problem of *Capital's* readership. He is more confident that cultural engagement can speak to political economy as critique. The popular culture of the Bolshevik Revolution certainly feeds this belief but the various modes of American Marxist cultural work at the time were still more decisive. Everyday narratives of anti-capitalism (in fiction, documentary, reportage, poetry, theater, song, etc.) already had vibrant genealogies in Leftist populism and organizations like the IWW.[9] Nevertheless, Gellert is loathe to describe or summarize *Capital* for the masses. Gellert's daring is in offering a thought experiment that effectively rewrites *Capital* yet maintains Marx's text. It is a radical reduction, a difference and repetition, and necessarily impure (even as a stream of political unconscious) leaving us with neither the essential *Capital* nor the essence of Marxism (these are evident but necessarily in tension). In sixty pages of text with sixty accompanying lithographs plus opening material Gellert attempts his own version of *aplatir* as intervention. Like Marx, he does not smooth abstraction but

9 The importance of this period of radical expression cannot be overemphasized and takes its place with other key moments in the history of American radicalism. See, for instance, Bill Mullen and Sherry Linkon (eds), *Radical Revisions: Re-reading 1930s Culture* (Urbana/Champaign, IL: University of Illinois Press, 1996).

serializes its context. Although Gellert thinks of this as depth revelation (a trope favored by Marx in exploring the "hidden abode of production"),[10] its resonance is in community articulation against its absenting in capitalist socialization. Whether such a community can be produced by serial engagement is questioned rather than simply being answered by Gellert's conviction.

Foregrounding "primary accumulation" conjures a yesterday for the rapacity of the present. Marx writes of a theological compulsion (or delusion) in economics that says the wealthy worklessness of the few is based on their "chosen" status, and the masses should be happy with this "nursery tale" of the Fall, or "original" sin (hence, original accumulation). Marx continues, "In the real world, as every one knows, conquest, subjugation, robbery, murder—in a word, force—play leading roles."[11] Gellert accentuates this division of labor, the story of original division, by drawing hands, one holding a martini and a cigar; and above this, a pair of hands, sinewy and muscular, palms open, with nothing.

The image is basic but remains interrogative alongside the text: is your poverty based on original sin or is it socially and historically produced and reproduced? In an era of Prohibition and Depression the sense of divisions is fresh so one is invited to read on and examine how such disparity and immiseration structures the contemporary crisis. Indeed, the air of this section is not about the pastness of inequality as much as it highlights its persistence in the capitalism of the day (it remains "primary" and "original": the series of images exists both to confirm and confront this inertia, or seriality, dialectically). The issue of division in primary accumulation continues in the next juxtaposition of text and image—for Marx in the idea of a worker divided from their own means of production alongside Gellert's image of the result, a giant Henry Ford embracing a factory (and factory system) over a worker, who is forthright but alone and absent of productive means. Yet the United States was not just a Fordist

10 Marx, *Capital, Volume One* (Untermann trans.), p. 195; in the Reitter translation, "place of production"; Karl Marx, *Capital: Critique of Political Economy, Volume One* (Paul Reitter trans., Paul North and Paul Reitter eds) (Princeton: Princeton University Press, 2024), p. 148.

11 Gellert, *Karl Marx: "Capital" in Lithographs*, p. 2.

FIGURE 4. Hugo Gellert, "Primary Accumulation" in *Karl Marx: "Capital" in Lithographs*, p. 3.

dream of serial manufacture but a drama of dispossession Gellert reads from Marx's invocation of the enclosure of land, "the expropriation of the agricultural producers" and a "severance from the soil" Gellert sees in the many vacant and abandoned farms of the Thirties. It is true Marx's story of accumulation by dispossession is doggedly British and it is not clear references to the Highland Gaels on this page would reverberate. Yet Gellert appeals to local context and draws a farm family in the process of eviction (urban evictions were also rife at the time because millions could no longer afford rent or mortgages). In the background, the farmhouse is burning, but the farmer's extended (and again, muscular) arm with its clenched fist asserts this narrative is not over. The black and white (poster) realism of the image is not simply an illustration of Marx's critique but is a polemical personification. Indeed, this is a major difference with Marx's *Capital* because in addition to portraits and caricatures of capitalist powerbrokers Gellert foregrounds worker figuration, and not just through conventional masculinity. Where Marx may probe the nature of the production of working-class subjectivity Gellert is concerned to narrate its living forms, including the trauma of violence or unemployment lines (the Sartrean queue once more). The possibility of non-correspondence is where the dynamism of the text in its time begins. To be sure, both are positioned to assess the identity and difference of worker representation, yet Gellert's visualization challenges not just the laws of political economy but also the compositional limits of image approximation and verification. We might say, *Capital in Lithographs* both decodes the rich abstraction of Marx's writing while simultaneously encoding its visual impress for storytelling—a dialectics of seeing. Again, this does not solve the tension of the two (is the text *in* Gellert's rendering; is the image *in* Marx's *Capital*?). The power of explication is not equivalent to the force of consciousness in contradiction, and abridgement is not a foreshortening of imaginative engagement.

Not all Gellert's images are specific to the *Capital* project: the lithograph of Tom Mooney opposite an excerpt on "savage legislation," for instance, was used in the campaign to have Mooney released from prison.[12] Similarly,

12 The story of Tom Mooney's framing for the "San Francisco Preparedness Day Bombing" of 1916 has been told a number of times. Mooney's case became a cause

Gellert's depictions of Morgan, Ford, and Rockefeller are part of his radical vocabulary of anti-capitalism and offer a symbolic function for otherwise abstruse economic concepts across his work, especially during the Depression. Readers might be surprised Gellert uses passages on the value form where Marx draws on Aristotle by actually providing an image of Aristotle himself (in the bodily proportions of a Michelangelo sculpture no less—Michelangelo's representation of muscularity was influential on Gellert's art) yet Gellert, like Marx, is not averse to classicism (Perseus, for instance, appears earlier) and, as Sara Monoson has pointed out, the interest extends Gellert's "vernacular political theorizing."[13] Perhaps Gellert's most graphic representations, a kind of hermeneutics of Marxist contradiction, are elaborated around excerpts from Chapters 14 and 15 on labor, manufacture, and the transformation of the value of labor power. These pages are still a translation and fragmentary, but what holds them together is an argument about time and money. For Gellert, this is *Capital* in its sharpest potential.

Initially, Gellert illustrates a necessary structural division by simply picturing various implements for manufacturing and farming. The idea is to pinpoint the place in *Capital* where Marx articulates what the bearer of tools becomes when manufacture is subject to the demands of capital. Instruments turn into machines and labor is divided to rationalize what can be produced by them. Technological change (Gellert pictures a telephone and an airplane) signify transformations in scale and efficiency (the production of space in capitalism). The automaton that is the factory comes to envelop the worker as its extension, and it has to, because, as Marx argues in this section of *Capital*, machines may dominate the labor process but they are "fixed" in a way that the value-forming activities of labor are not. The dilemma is the value potential of embodied labor appears

---

célèbre for the American Left and he was eventually, after 22 years in prison, pardoned in 1939. See Estolv Ethan Ward, *The Gentle Dynamiter: A Biography of Tom Mooney* (Palo Alto, CA: Ramparts Press, 1983).

13 See S. Sara Monoson, "*Aesop Said So*: Ancient Wisdom and Radical Politics in 1930s New York," *Classical Receptions Journal* 8(1) (2016): 90–113. Monoson's essay on Gellert analyzes how he "illustrates" Aesop as a means to critique capitalism and fascism in the Thirties. This is a classicism of which Marx would have approved.

MACHINERY AND LARGE-SCALE INDUSTRY

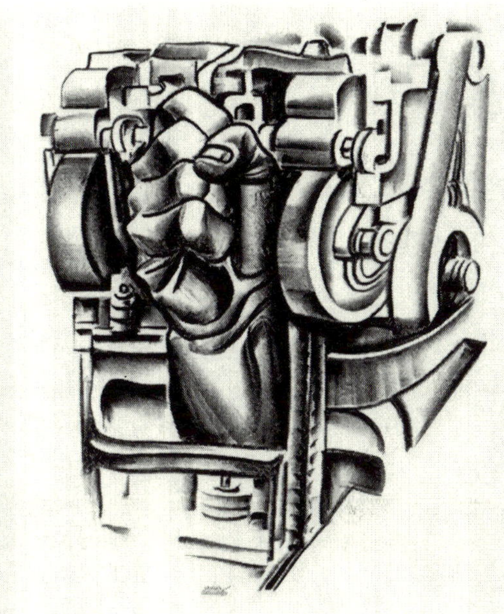

FIGURE 5. Hugo Gellert, "Machinery and Large-Scale Industry" in *Karl Marx*: *"Capital" in Lithographs*, p. 45.

trapped by the rationalization of the machine in large scale manufacture. The reader sees the machine with the worker's fist clasped within it. The task in Gellert's series of images is not to make *Capital* relatable as such; the real challenge is whether instances of identification (a dialectics of image I would adapt from Walter Benjamin as "awakening")[14] constitute a condition for social change. This is less a hermeneutics of healing but a leap of creation and imagination.

The limits to praxis appear compounded by capitalist rapacity. Capitalist revolution must deny alternatives to it. Thus, the "efficiency" of labor division divides not just laborers from each other but within families where such labor is seen to be socially reproduced. Gellert comments on this "primary effect" by picturing a woman about to breast feed. She is central to social reproduction and value-forming and is fully incorporated into surplus labor utilization (a logic that also awaits the child). A revolution in time is necessary for machinic incorporation of this kind, as Marx expounds, and that Gellert envisages initially with clichés: workers bound to cogs and a laborer strangled by a machine. But then Gellert refigures the notion of manufacturing machine man by first, imaging a worker held fast by a robot (the fear of "mechanical man" was very much part of the culture of the time, in cinema an arc discernible, say, from *Metropolis* [1927] to *Modern Times* [1936]), a symbolic mechanization answered by working-class revolts against specific inventions; and second, by a temporal transformation through which wages are paid for time but in lieu of a time that is unpaid, an "irrational expression" whereby surplus will be appropriated (accumulated). The abstraction (and extraction) of the process is complex but Gellert has already taken the idea of time incorporated to map labor temporality from *Capital* Chapters 7–10 in a series of clock images where labor is divided by time (initially, six hours for the average means of subsistence, then six hours for surplus value). In the quantification of quality, the clock face (with the clenched hand at its center) is a "precise

14 Walter Benjamin, *The Arcades Project* (Howard Eiland and Kevin McLaughlin trans) (Cambridge, MA: Harvard University Press, 1999), p. 462. This is Benjamin's way of salvaging the truth in dreams as a revolutionary consciousness, a truth that is itself a historical potential.

expression"[15] for the measure of exploitation. By Chapter 18, Marx opines that if the capitalist really paid labor at its value capital itself would be annulled, a realization Gellert signifies by emptying the clock of division. Time can begin again and it is this freedom Gellert draws for his reader, a measurelessness from measure latent in Marx's prose.

As noted, the jump to Volume Three is a way for Gellert to address the contemporary crisis of eviction and the ways that ground rent, rent, and debt manage and overdetermine worker experience of land and its powers of sustenance. On the one hand, Gellert reorganizes the text so that his pictorial can directly address current contingencies; on the other hand, however, it remains unclear whether his remix logically concludes a series of *Capital* in images or exists to refer the reader back to Marx's narrative of *Capital* in toto (or at least the totality extant). The tension of explication and articulation is the risk of Gellert's art: in making the images tell a story Gellert necessarily has to change what *Capital* means. How can this be "Capital in Pictures" if it is but 60 pages of the whole? Surely, an abbreviation or adaptation of the whole can indicate its totality? Or should a series match the labor of its origin? The distillation itself is the intimacy of crisis. Fidelity would seem to countermand the eventness or contingency of crisis (an absolute fidelity to *Capital* is, like Marx's, never to finish its representation). Yet the sequence of Gellert's images is more than convenience but represents an antinomy for working-class response. The compressed selections of the final page (from Chapters 32 of Volume One and 51 of Volume Three with the *Communist Manifesto* as a flourish) do not answer the "historical tendency of capitalist accumulation" with the historical predisposition of Lenin on the opposite page, yet the appeal (even as an imaginary resolution of a real contradiction) remains salutary. But is Gellert's intervention, for all of the urgency of crisis, any different from the plethora of *Capitals*, "illustrated," that conjure an image or two around some of Marx's more well-known ideas?

---

15 Karl Marx, *Capital: A Critique of Political Economy, Volume 1* (Ben Fowkes trans.) (London: Penguin, 1992), p. 326; "exact expression" (Untermann trans., p. 241); "accurately expresses" (Reitter trans., p. 190). "Der exakte Ausdruck" (Marx, *Das Kapital*, p. 196).

FIGURE 6. Hugo Gellert, "Transformation of the Value, or the Price, of Labor Power into Wages" in *Karl Marx: "Capital" in Lithographs*, p. 50.

Two elements are germane here: the first as a critique of a series of *Capitals*; the second as a radical reading practice where apprehension and comprehension are mutually interruptive. From Deleuze, we may think of series in a certain duality, here where Gellert's confabulation of text and lithographs repeat the text of Marx (via his and Untermann's translation) as a difference not just for understanding but as a dialectical breach mediated by the exigency of crisis and political practice (we have read Marx's *Le Capital* in this way as itself a concrete response to the civil war in France). To map editions in series and between series, a cartography of *Capital*, places peculiar demands on philology because Marxism cannot be anything other than an academic exercise without dissemination, where the *Manifesto* haunts the scientific exactitude of *Das Kapital* and the consummate professional precision of an archivist or translator. Marx, no doubt more than Engels, would see the solidarity and political pragmatism in Gellert's book, even if Chapter One is addressed a third of the way into the project (Marx himself once suggested beginning with Chapter Ten). The reshuffling is not primarily a response to difficulty (one thinks of the entreaties of Engels and Kugelmann to Marx over the latter's exegesis of the value form, which will eventually produce three versions, including a revised appendix to *Capital* inspired by Marx's attempt to explicate "as simply and even as schoolmasterly as possible."[16] Gellert seeks to interpellate a working-class reader (the masses) in a dialogic understanding of how capitalism works, how its processes inform labor's experience of the present. The result is demonstrably unscientific (just like Marx's supposition about French workers) and, in the spirit of measurelessness, there is little evidence of working-class readership of *Capital in Lithographs* beyond the comrades of the John Reed Club or *New Masses*. Nevertheless, Gellert's project is radically entangled with Leftist popular art of the Thirties and Forties, a graphic vernacular whose fidelity is first to revolutionary consciousness over and above scientificity as the truth in series.

---

16 See Michael Heinrich, *How to Read Marx's Capital: Commentary and Explanations of the Beginning Chapters* (Alexander Locascio trans.) (New York: Monthly Review Press, 2021), p. 93. Originally a two-volume set, Heinrich's erudition and textual scholarship sets a high bar but his basic question, "Why read *Capital* today?" is a major impetus for me in reading serial Marx. See also Michael Heinrich, *An Introduction to the Three Volumes of Marx's Capital* (Alexander Locascio trans.) (New York: Monthly Review Press, 2004).

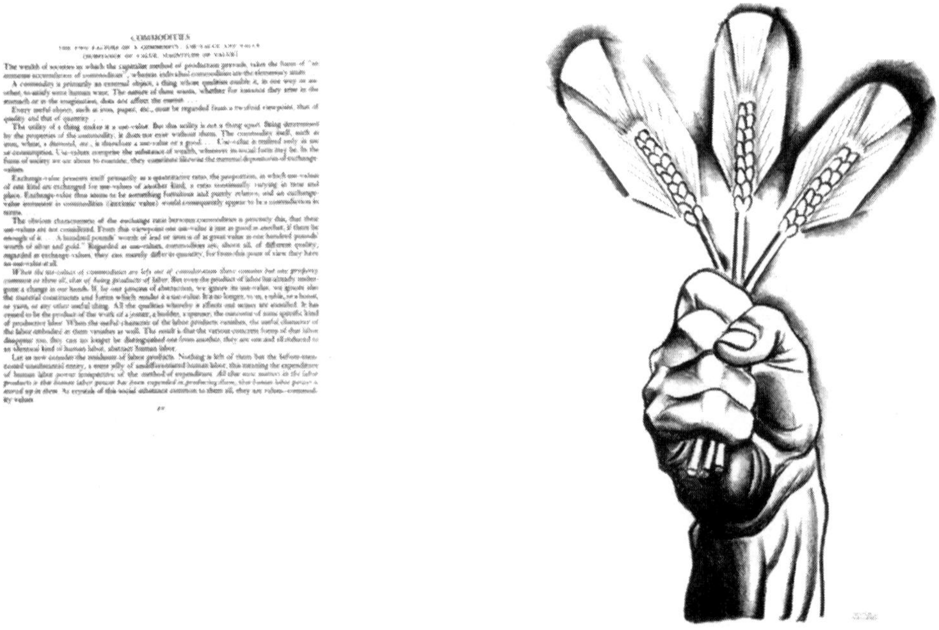

FIGURE 7. Hugo Gellert, "Commodities" in *Karl Marx: "Capital" in Lithographs*, p. 20.

When Gellert does focus on the commodity chapter, he provides a pertinent juxtaposition. In the first image, we see a hand clasping stalks of wheat (in the text, wheat is mentioned as a use value realized in consumption). The hand, labor, is what makes the wheat in the transformation of use value in exchange. Indeed, as Marx explains, remove this dimension of quality into quantity from the commodity and what one sees is "a mere jelly of undifferentiated human labor."[17] Not surprisingly, Gellert offers the hand of labor rather than its abstraction (instead of the jelly, therefore, labor power without specific laboring). This does not mean, however, Gellert abjures abstraction. The hand and wheat reappear in the next image, this time precisely in their congelation, which is to say they are inserted into a clock (the difference in the repetition of this motif [the clock is featured seven times] is a major part of the dynamism of the edition) which provides their measure. Commodity value is thus a calibration of labor power and labor time. True, this element of the commodity is subject to further qualification and calculation, yet the sequence of images and the text that grounds them lends credence to the idea illustration is not an innocent or easy complement to Marx's writing but constantly wrestles with the representational dilemma of making it true.

"*Capital* in series" is not just divided in itself, by period, by organization, but by generic difference, series that are themselves refigured by the form and time of their appearance. Gellert's work, for instance, is serially engaged not just with an "original" Marx, but with other graphic artists in and around *New Masses* at the time (including Gropper, Burck, Soglow, and Scigel) interested in the activism of art. Seriality is not simply about making connections (and divisions) by ordering reality but concerns the materialization of relation and the conditions of conjuncture, extension, and rupture. One cannot write this totality but one is always writing it, dialectically. In one series, versions of *Capital*, distinctions must be made

17 Gellert, *Karl Marx*: "*Capital*" *in Lithographs*, p. 20. Marx, *Capital, Volume One* (Untermann trans.), p. 45: "a mere congelation of homogeneous human labor"; *Capital* (Fowkes trans.), p. 128: "merely congealed quantities of homogeneous human labour"; Reitter translation, p. 16: "a bare gelatinous blob of undifferentiated human labor." Marx, *Das Kapital*, p. 21: "eine bloße Gallerte unterschiedsloser menschlicher Arbeit."

according to authors and authorization: definitive editions and translations are warranted (this labor is also the living on of specific revolutionary ideas). In another series, born of event as disjuncture, as concrete crisis, upheaval itself seems to be the editor/translator and it finds a text that meets its syntax, that strives in its form to articulate a grammar of change adequate to its moment. Seriality may attempt to norm the difference of series, yet it simultaneously names a space of contradiction and possibility. This indeed is the political and aesthetic substance between Marx's *Capital* and *Karl Marx's Capital in Lithographs*.

As we have noted, the reading practice of *Capital* pivots on its foundational existence as a complex critique of political economy with a prescience continually inviting further articulation. It is not outside the commodification processes it describes even if this is clearly not the sum of its participation in consciousness. Apprehension here is not necessarily fear, either in the intimidation of the text or in the nervousness around getting it wrong. It is that condition of comprehension introducing the salience of contradiction. To apprehend at this level is to experience the edge of exegesis, like dialectics at a standstill, to borrow from Benjamin once more. It is that part of understanding resisting the comprehensiveness of comprehension. It is the part of a guide that cannot describe its path. This is not a block on abstraction but a symptom where abstraction becomes generative, becomes alive to its new situation. Thus, on the one hand, one is always tempted to fill in or add to Gellert's project—given the pronounced and committed approach to race and class in many of the lithographs, why not end with *Capital Volume One*'s last chapter on colonization and complete the circle of primary accumulation? And, given the marked and repeated figuration of women workers, why not emphasize the patriarchal assumptions in division, including divisions of labor? On the other hand, why not take a problem of social representation, the representation of the laborer, and make this the substance of *Capital*? Marx himself notes this in relation to his celebrated text, that when it comes to personification, or even basic biography, his references are to capitalists and bourgeois thinkers, and his "figures" are mathematical calculation. If workers are a key agent in the dissolution of capitalism, *Capital* itself might usefully put flesh on the bones, which is also a "social substance [of] human labor."[18] Since absence feeds alienation Gellert draws workers as much as possible to fathom Marx's analysis (it could be argued the figuration chooses the excerpted passage although, as noted, he does draw from his established iconography, including the metonymic placement of the defiant fist). It is difficult to make a critique of political economy a people's story (which is why, once more, Marx's subtitle is omitted) but Gellert uses his experience, especially with his murals, posters, and, for example, the covers for *New Masses*, to project an intimacy and topicality that the fatiguing climb of Marx's steep paths to science might not otherwise provide. The difficulty remains—Gellert's excerpts do not edit out the brilliance or nuance of Marx's approach, and Gellert's art is much more than slogans of the hour. The serialization of politics in journals, pamphlets, posters, and murals is part of the language of mass movement of the period, a continuity in disjunction that attempts to foreground the possibility of a new political constituency and popular consciousness. It is not simply Gellert's articulation is latent in Marx's *Capital*, but that his art mediates crisis in such a way critique itself is serially connected. *Capital* exists in many editions and translations at the time but *Capital in Lithographs* abjures the definitive for the vital, for that which dialectically engages the conditions of crisis with a text alive to its contradictions.

Is Gellert's graphic Marxism an exception to the concept of seriality and social change advanced so far? Is it basically another example (one damn thing after another) rather than critical in its division? Gellert's bold aesthetics of the excerpt is much more than a casual serial array. Sometimes the sequence of images is determined by the tropological urgency of Gellert's commitment in the moment. Questions of race, gender, and class are suffused with comradely commitments bound to the socio-economic crisis of the time. The intervention reveals the extent to which seriality becomes dynamic in crisis by submitting the conventions of sequence to creative juxtaposition and a kind of frenetic disquiet with quotidian reproduction and representation. True, individual images may be deemed stock or staid: few would be surprised at the time by a caricature of Ford

18 Marx, *Capital* (Fowkes trans.), p. 138. Reitter translation, p. 25: "the same social denominator, human labor."

or Rockefeller. Nevertheless, Gellert reads *Capital* not to indulge in the mistakes of English translation (as if Marx has not already shown that an absolute, and German, truth does not root itself firmly in the peripeteia of his text—one can settle meaning without fossilizing it or aligning it with the ego of expertise), but to test its inspiration, to see how the graphic line both might draw on its promise and bring new insight to its analysis. One of the challenges of Gellert's *Capital* is its question for the terms of Deleuzean seriation. The relations of two series side by side contradicts the platitudes of correspondence as if their exposition, like Marx's explanation of method above, is contingent on the event of reading itself. Furthermore, we have suggested *that* event is mediated by projection and desire—the purported hermeneutical gaze of a working-class subject—which situates event in a dialectic of impossible series (the purloined series of revolutionary ardor) and concrete compossibility. *Capital in Lithographs* documents a certain irresolution in Marx's project that extends his interest in a series for the masses while offering a stark reminder crisis complicates the conditions of seriality itself. Gellert's work of art is not an unalloyed reflection on either the nature of social contradiction at the time nor on the talismanic transhistoricism of Marx's critique of political economy (again signaled by the absenting of the daunting subtitle). To say Gellert seeks relevance in Marx's text is to misconstrue the moment of intervention. If there is identification or a revelation of identity in the work it comes from an imaginative grasp of the conditions of crisis, not their proof. Perhaps this is one more alibi, one that rationalizes the continuing sales and collectability of Gellert's portfolio, or individual examples, over and above the serial challenge of *Capital* in pieces on the lefthand page. The meaning of social change exists in the constellation, one that *Capital* and capitalism necessarily reinscribe.

CAPITAL, THE MANGA

To deepen this sense of event still further while cleaving to the conditions of serial antinomy, I wish to consider how *Capital* comes to live in a Japanese manga published in 2008 (and subsequently translated and published globally, which will lead us back to *Le Capital*).[1] Obviously, given the intricate and specific history of Marx and Marxism in Japan these remarks remain prefatory but suggestive. It is noticeable, for instance, the first translated collected works of Marx appear in Japanese (in 1932) and there has been a robust attention to Marx in working out and complicating the meaning of modernity in Japan.[2] The tenor of the latter builds on Gellert's example in figuring worker subjectivity but only by returning to the ideas we have developed around Marx's serial engagement and the limits to the same (contradictions in desire, form, translation, and measure). No one is surprised there is a manga of *Capital*: of course there is, just as there is a musical of *Capital* in Chinese (directed by He Nian, 2010). In an era of media convergence, there is a certain inexorability in

---

1 Much of this section is devoted to a two volume manga based on *Capital* produced by Variety Artworks (a collective of illustrators and writers, more recently known as Team Banmikas) in 2008 and 2009. The books appeared as part of the series Manga de Dokuha (Japanese: まんがで読破, "Reading Through with Manga") and were originally published by East Press and sold primarily through convenience stores, most prominently 7-Eleven. The series as a whole was immensely popular (with sales approaching a million in 2008 alone) and the first volume of *Capital in manga* sold over six thousand copies in the first few days after publication, in part because of the success of another volume, *Kanikōsen* (蟹工船—*The Crab Cannery Ship*), based on the 1929 Japanese novel by Takiji Kobayashi. The novel was a central text of Japanese proletarian culture of the first decades of the twentieth century. Several official translations of *Capital in manga* have appeared (including Spanish, French, Arabic, plus, as noted, scanlations. A new Japanese edition of *Capital in manga*, *Volume One* appeared in 2020.

2 Gavin Walker's overview is very useful in this regard. See Gavin Walker, "Marxist Theory in Japan," *Historical Materialism*: rebrand.ly/8adbb0 (last accessed: August 26, 2025).

multi-platform Marxism. The appearance of a manga of *Capital* is not just specific, tied to a rediscovery of proletarian protest in light of the financial crisis of 2007–2008, but it recomposes a Japanese Marxist reading of *Capital* with a longer history in politics. As in the US in the 1920s and 1930s, there is a huge outpouring of popular and mass culture in Japan at that time, a space in which radicals reflected on both a Marxist tradition and the lessons of the 1917 Russian Revolution (the five-volume Japanese translation of *Capital* published in 1927–1928 was part of a wave of reflection and activism in response to the revolution), and also where a relatively mature industrialization and modernization permitted mass production and dissemination across culture (like Gellert, writers and artists in Japan could depend on high levels of cultural literacy). As several critics have pointed out, Japanese Marxism, unlike its counterparts both regionally and globally, was distinctly theoretical and university-based, even though many elements of anti-capitalism were debated by social activists and various oppositional parties, including the Communist Party of Japan. Introductions to Marxism in Japan intensified in the inter-war years, no doubt building on the example of Yamakawa Hitoshi, whose critique "Marx's *Capital*" was, of course, serialized (4 issues) in a newspaper he ran, the *Osaka heimin shinbun*, in 1908.[3] The flourish of proletarian literature and culture in Japan in the Twenties and Thirties certainly mediates a vernacular Marx and, while the concern here is considerably more narrow, several degrees of comparatism would help to elaborate the point (including Japanese relations to the US, the International, the specific nexus of capital and state, the contours of modernization, the place of imperialism in East Asia, and the longue durée of local and informal cultural traditions and innovations). Some of these concerns will emerge as symptoms in the following critique but the manga called *Capital* only begins to hint at the complex relations informing it.

3 Gavin Walker offers an in-depth critique of the history of Marxism in Japan. See Gavin Walker, *The Sublime Perversion of Capital* (Durham, NC: Duke University Press, 2016). See also Daniel Finn, "The Theory and Practice of Marxism in Japan: An Interview with Gavin Walker," *Jacobin* (July 3, 2021). Rather than a sublime perversion, I read the vernacular Marxism of *Capital in manga* as a political unconscious, in series.

Again, if the Paris Commune is the event that substantially grounds the project of *Le Capital*, *Capital in manga* finds its event in the global financial crisis of 2007–2008 and its aftermath.[4] There are several variations in debates about what produced the crisis but most analyses acknowledge the complex confluence of globalized and poorly-regulated speculative markets, particularly in derivatives and mortgage-backed securities, the sharp reduction of the US federal funds rate in the aftermath of 9/11, a housing boom that outstripped the market for mortgages (leading to predatory lending practices and the subprime loan), and a recession that sparked a liquidity crisis for banks attempting to cover defaults when interest rates began to turn. The role of the United States Federal Reserve in remedying this crisis is well known (via the Troubled Asset Relief Program [TARP] and the purchasing of trillions of dollars of mortgage-backed securities, for instance) but obviously the crisis was experienced very differently across global capital markets and national economies. Because of the sharp drop in US consumption of Japanese products (cars, electronics, etc.) in particular, Japan's GDP contracted far more and recovered more slowly than in the US. Thanks to Japan's Employment Adjustment Subsidy Program massive layoffs were avoided, but the sensitivity of Japan's economy to externalities, coming on the back of a "Lost Decade" (by this point, at least times two) in the winding down of asset bubbles intensified a sense that, along with a continuing contraction in real wages coupled with rising indebtedness, Japan's economic outlook was at best compromised and structurally suspect.[5] *Capital in manga* is

4 The crisis produced an outpouring of analysis, especially around the nexus of financialization and globalization. A pertinent history is Barry A. Wigmore, *The Financial Crisis of 2008: A History of US Financial Markets 2000–2012* (Cambridge: Cambridge University Press, 2022). For a critique of US quantitative easing through its Japanese counterpart, see Peter Hitchcock, "Kant at the Federal Reserve: On the Aesthetics of Quantitative Easing" in Jeffrey Di Leo, Peter Hitchcock and Sophia McClennen (eds), *The Debt Age* (New York: Routledge, 2018), pp. 27–41.

5 The crisis in Japan precedes its specific manifestation in 2008. See, for instance, Jennifer A. Amyx, *Japan's Financial Crisis: Institutional Rigidity and Reluctant Change* (Princeton, NJ: Princeton University Press, 2004). For more on the 2008 crisis itself, see Akira Kojima, "Japan's Economy and the Global Financial Crisis," *Asia-Pacific Review* 16(2) (2009): 15–25. See also Masahiro Kawai and Shinji Takagi, "Why Was

not responding explicitly to these conditions but the text reads the crisis as if it were writing it. Rather than argue the manga is paratextual, I am arguing its serialization is infrastructural, culturally and materially, in how capitalism is understood. Again, we might say that while seriality is not a direct cause of social change it is immanent to it as a condition of modernity as such. The narratological effects are neither casual references nor authorial intentions, a strain we have already discerned in the substantive limits of serial Marx. Instead, the living on of *Capital* is both overdetermined and internally logical, so that the manga can write the substance of *Capital* but as a serialization with its own materiality and translatability and/or transactional form.

Capital in manga appears in a series called Manga de Dokuha, basically "reading through [with] manga." There has been much debate in Japan and elsewhere about manga's effect on literacy (in Japan where literacy is about 100% this may appear overstated, but the relative influence of specific forms remains a subject of vigorous inquiry).[6] Certainly, this series intends to expand younger people's exposure to "classic" literature while using their visual and textual literacy in manga as form. What makes a classic is also a sign of cultural capital but one intention is to lead the reader from weekly manga magazines to bound manga series (*tankōbon*) and then books in general. The first five volumes in the Dokuha series were manga of vital Japanese literature (in forms not simply absorbed by manga itself), including Osamu Dazai's *Ningen Shikkaku* (*No Longer Human*), Natsume Soseki's *Kokoro*, first published as a serial, and Ryunosuke Akutagawa's short story, "Rashomon," from which Akira Kurosawa borrows the name

---

Japan Hit So Hard by the Global Financial Crisis?," *ADBI Working Paper Series* (Asia Development Bank Institute) 153 (October 2009): 1–15.

6 The question of writing and visual literacy in particular is the subject of much analysis. See, for instance, John E. Ingulsrud and Kate Allen, *Reading Japan Cool: Patterns of Manga Literacy and Discourse* (New York: Lexington, 2009). Several cultural histories of Japan have taken up this topic in relation to manga. See, for instance, Mark E. MacWilliams (ed.), *Explorations in the World of Manga and Anime* (London: M. E. Sharpe, 2008). See also Eike Exner, *Comics and the Origins of Manga* (New Brunswick, NJ: Rutgers University Press, 2022). The circulation of the visual in global commodity markets is not tangential to manga as a global literacy, as well as being a key integer of Japanese transnational trade.

for his film, although the movie is actually based on another Akutagawa story, "In a Grove." For the present discussion, the fifth volume is the most important, the manga of Takishi Kobayashi's *Kanikosen*, or *The Crab Cannery Ship*, Kobayashi's anti-capitalist novel of 1929. During the financial crisis of 2007–2008, both the novel and the manga received significant interest from young disaffected Japanese workers. Suddenly radical critiques of capitalism seemed not just relevant but intimately real. In 2008, *Kanikosen* the novel sold over half a million copies in Japan, and the four manga versions 200,000 copies. While the Dokuha series was not intended to foreground classic anti-capitalism (other titles include *Mein Kampf* and *King Lear*), the leftist texts have been its most successful volumes. And thus we come to *Capital in manga* (資本論–Shihon-ron).

As noted, the drawings and text are put together collectively by Variety Artworks, who produce the series in general. This process provides consistency and efficiency for Manga de Dokuha's publishing schedule, but not necessarily for a rendering of *Capital*. In this respect, the text feels closer to an explication, or an illustrated *Capital* (particularly in the second volume) rather than the sharp political and aesthetic articulation we have registered in Gellert's *Capital in Lithographs*. Neither the quality of the story nor the artwork are standouts even within this manga niche. We should note however that, like Gellert's project, *Capital in manga* provides a graphic story rather than the graphic ornamentation we noted in the cover and contents of Marx's *Le Capital*. Yet two narratives, at least, are in play: the first is around the exploits of Robin, a young cheesemaker lured by Daniel, an investor, into processes of mass production; and the second is as an initial primer on key elements of *Capital* (Volume One) in particular. The relation between the two can be crude and unproductive—here is what Robin is doing, here is what *Capital* says—as if the manga can only succeed by reducing abstraction and the possibility of contradiction (*aplatir* in the negative sense). We have remarked time and again that seriality's apparent desire for order and sequence is not secured by its representation, and particularly over decisions in division. The manga repeats elements of *Capital* but less in the content of Marx's text and more in the Deleuzean sense, an alignment/non-alignment of two series arrayed in difference. More than this, *Capital in manga* also stages the material

FIGURE 8. Variety Artworks, *Capital in Manga*!
(Tokyo: East Press/Team Banmikas, 2008).

contradictions of translation and translatability (we have remarked that Marx has long been available in Japanese but the Marx of Japan is not simply a translational strategy or technique). The context in which it is composed, a "great works" project of edumanga, is not necessarily the framework in which it is read, one based on a question about how capitalism works given the crisis of 2008. To some extent, this recalls the dilemma faced by Marx between the desire expressed in the famous letter to Lachâtre and the actual production of *Capital* as a serial in French. The differences are instructive since *Capital in manga* is in serial engagement with a Marxian project that in itself failed to serialize. The question of social change in my project is about whether it is incautious to view seriality as simply adjacent to its event. Here we should stress this negative dialectic reveals a provocative compulsion in seriality per se; namely, the possibility of specific and radical reinscription irrespective of authorial desire. The editors of the manga offer a much more modest agenda:

> This manga is a story based mainly on the first volume of the original book *Das Kapital*. The original *Das Kapital* is not only an elucidation of capitalism, but is also a major work that is imbued with revolutionary ideas and philosophy. We sincerely hope that this book will serve as a stepping stone and as a bridge between you and the original text.[7]

The sentiments change in translation (in the Spanish version, for instance, the editors hope the manga will enable readers to get closer [*acercarse*] to the original work, a sense both of intimacy and intimation). I will return to a logic of translation below, and especially in what returns to a French *Capital* in the form of a Japanese manga.

Rather than the English economy of the mid-nineteenth century (at the core of Marx's critique) the manga story is set close to the Alps at the

---

7 Each translation reframes the original manga, which is also part of its materiality. The English language version (which to date only reproduces the first volume of *Capital in manga* unlike, for instance, the French) is Variety Artworks, *Capital in manga*! (Guy Yasko trans.) (Ottawa: Red Quill Books, 2012). For a character analysis of this work and one that links it to visual representations of Marxism, see Magnus Nilsson, "Marxism across Media: Characterization and Montage in Variety Artwork's Capital in Manga," *International Journal of Comic Art* 21(1) (Spring–Summer 2019): 423–38

end of the nineteenth century, and it reveals a more intense industrialization and automation.[8] The vagaries of time and location underline that parables and principles are at stake more than historical verification—it is important to note, however, that de-locating the manga from its immediate context offers a provocative ambivalence about what makes it relevant in Japan. The point cannot be settled here but the dislocation of content and form suggest workers may find seeing a class in itself less abstract when elsewhere. Whatever the setting, we are much less naïve than the characters we meet in the opening pages of *Capital in manga*, which in part attempts to interpellate and project a young Japanese reader's understanding of political economy and/or a direct worker experience of capitalist order (including that of the so-called "Salaryman" (サラリーマン, sararīman).[9] Perhaps the thin characterizations result from a misapprehension of the primary audience, who are never simply dupes of capital/labor relations? Robin works with his father (Heinrich, a German ex-patriot) on a farm producing what one could call artisanal cheese which Robin sells at a local market. Enny (or Anna in some scanlations), a banker's daughter and the less than obscure object of Robin's desire, introduces him to a young entrepreneur, Daniel. Daniel is impressed by Robin's cheeses and gets him to industrialize his production. The tension in the story is partly about Robin's increasing guilt at what his workers must endure to realize value for the capitalist, but becomes more narrowly focused on whether or not the narrative conventions of manga are able to convey the complexities of Marx's critique of political economy as a narrative. In *Le Capital* we have a read a specificity that makes Marx's text persist very differently, formally and linguistically, a kind of concreteness that does not attempt to authenticate Marxian concepts or the expertise in claiming them but is sensitive to (but not as)

8 The actual locale is left fairly vague but is generally Western European, late nineteenth century (Engels will appear in Volume Two as a ghostly guide), although even then some of the signifiers are anachronistic (in one panel a portion of a twenty-pound note appears with the face of Queen Elizabeth II!). The presence of cheese with holes (eyes) might suggest Switzerland (perhaps Alps adjacent) or the Netherlands, but it is the degree of industrialization that is emphasized.

9 Again, the generalizability of the reader and experience is important to the marketing of the narrative and its organic presence for a Japanese popular culture audience.

a materialist methodology where Marx's critique lives in the possibility of social change. This becoming of *Capital* is seriality.

Gellert's *Capital in Lithographs* reveals a precise selection of Marx's text, in translation, that aesthetically and politically attempts both in images and text to galvanize its meaning for new readers for whom crises of capitalism are otherwise simultaneously redolent and mystified. The focus of *Capital in manga* necessarily changes the relationship of image and text. They are conjoint yet subject to the narratological exigencies of manga and the moment. Gellert may be the better artist and reader of *Capital* but that does not mean he is better at telling its story, which is the challenge between its explication and articulation. The manga begins from an entirely different premise. Even though the chapters of the manga refer to key elements of Marx's text ("The Process of Capitalist Production," "Exploitation," "The Buying and Selling of Labor," and "Value") these are indirect and uncited. The sense of reading by not reading we have invoked earlier is palpable and one could make the case what is Marx's text here is already someone else's summary or illustrated guide. We have also noted text in Marx (identified by the comments of Lachâtre) that French workers in the 1870s found basically unreadable. The level of abstraction is necessary—commodification as reification has to be understood as an abstraction of the social, or indeed the desire for its subsumption. Marx makes significant attempts at moving explication to articulation for instance, and the image of the congealed residue of labor-time in the commodity, irrespective of its form, helps to grasp the enigma of value across the text (a similar effect is achieved by the challenge of the dancing table in the opening chapter of *Das Kapital*). If the manga blunts the impact of Marx's modes of elaboration it yet conjures the spirit of articulation. It begins, for instance, in medias res: we are already living the processes of commodity desire the story will address. The first speech in the text is by a woman affirming the quality of Robin's cheese products and is an answer to dialogue that precedes the text. While Homer's *Iliad* might not be to mind, the economy of exposition works well and continually points to narrative silence in what the text can say. While this is a manga convention across many of its genres, it has a particular prescience in representing *Capital* Volume One which, as we have noted, is not beyond its own missing interlocutors and formal idiosyncrasies. A manga moves quickly and this volume takes less than an hour to read (an individual number of *Le Capital* the serial should have taken about forty minutes). With such a narrow window of serial engagement surely the form is a facile facility rather than a medium of critical consciousness, even as a "stepping stone" or "bridge" to Marx's celebrated work?

The comparative restlessness of the form neither denies critical abstraction nor radical apprehension. The epistemological grounds of social change, for instance, feature many levels of knowledge and understanding and thus, what composes political constituency is a problem of constellation rather than a formula for it. This does not obviate the need for primary texts or rigorous education in overcoming the social reproduction of inequality. Marx's *Capital* is, whatever else it is, a way to read capital as relation and as an economically dominant force, but neither in Volume One, nor in the notebooks known as the *Grundrisse*, do we look for more than a masterwork of methodology, a nuanced and highly-detailed diagnosis of political economy. To say the manga cannot provide the same critical depth as its inspiration is true regarding its formal methodology, but that is not the same as saying it cannot offer, in its apprehension of *Capital*, a working knowledge of the lived realities of capitalist hegemony. Marx both acknowledged and resisted such a possibility, and ultimately never reconciled himself to the alternative formal engagement seriality fostered, even as serial editions appeared in his lifetime. As a reflection chiefly on *Capital* Volume One, *Capital in manga* is reductionist and contrived, but as a serial (both with—eventually—a second volume within Manga de Dokuha, and with *Capital*'s longue durée) it is extensive, and what it extends, even as a contradiction, is a critical capacity for change, both in meaning and necessity. What is absent in the text (in what precedes it and in what is simply left out from Marx's work) remains a provocative non-said or unsaid in Pierre Macherey's sense,[10] sometimes as a conscious exigency (this is too detailed, this is too specific)

10 I am thinking here of Macherey's theory of literary production. See Pierre Macherey, *A Theory of Literary Production* (Geoffrey Wall trans.) (New York: Routledge, 2006). Macherey's work, which appeared in 1966, was itself embroiled in a rethinking of radical praxis and the role of the literary in such moments.

and sometimes as an unconscious struggle over what can be adequately narrated of socialization, especially through what appears always already reified.

Perhaps we can expand on the symptomatic here, the manga margins, through what we may term serial ellipses. The speed of consumption is a formal convention but does not exhaust the time/space of apprehension. Indeed, I would argue the elliptical logic of telling is closer to both how capital flow works and, perhaps more counter-intuitively, how it can be learned otherwise. It is in the demonstration and distance within its explication that capital is "in" manga, in the texture of its challenge as "mass" art or the popular. Certainly, much manga succeeds through melodrama and hyperbole but these are stylistic catalysts rather than grammatical screens. In *Capital in manga*, the ostensible love triangle of Robin, Enny, and Daniel drives part of the story (plucky artisan vies with dastardly factory owner for the attention of a banker's daughter, shades of amphisbetesis once more) but not all of the interest is in human interest. The missing text at the beginning of the manga is perhaps closer to the meaning of ellipsis for linguistics, especially in form/meaning articulation and in deletions that are essentially recovered in extant text. Some of this theorization is germane but there are other elements more focused on grammatical and formal conventions.

What is a serial ellipsis here? The economy of line in manga (which can also be read as the economy of the production line, materially as much as analogically) extends to speech and its absence. As a visual art, precision in compositional elements is vital, and especially if meaning is to be conveyed by subtraction, by a deliberate reduction in ornamentation in order to explain a kernel of meaning. Grammatically, of course, ellipses denote language that can be inferred rather than displayed, but it is also the plural of ellipse, the geometric term for falling short, and the latter can be used to describe an object so bound. While the plurals match, the singular forms do not and indeed represent a falling short in their own right, with a strong propensity for catachresis. This inappropriate mixing extends to the theoretical difference between grammatical and linguistic concerns for ellipsis, and both to its use in manga, where the economy of line and storyline is acute. To complicate the cultural concepts further, an ellipsis and ellipses also refer to the omission of a scene or scenes in narrative film that does not or do not advance the plot. Taken together, ellipses are a structural and thematic architectonic of manga, continually offering an apparent *vel* of non-meaning that yet composes story in its movement.[11] Serial here refers both to the literal representation of ellipses (dot, dot, dot—in Japanese, てんてんてん ten, ten, ten, or sometimes six dots, or more) and the sequencing of panels that permits the story to appear, in its absences (not every absence through ellipses is in itself significant as seriality per se). One part of the difficulty of manga beyond Japan and Japanese is the translation both of the serial and ellipses (which are culturally specific), as if falling short is in fact constitutive of its narrative mode and circulation. Manifest elision permits the manga to move as itself a visual language, yet this dynamic is contradictory because it both enhances the rapid scan of story but can pause interpretation (what is the character thinking, and how might this affect what happens or is said next?). Within manga seriality, ellipses are not so much a challenge as an invitation to imagine the character or object as a speaking subject. This is emphasized

---

11 The movement here is complex and in part borrows from Jacques Lacan, both from the work on the *vel* of alienation, an "or" in subjectivation where choosing implies the fading (*aphanisis*) of another subject, and to what this implies for the subject's relationship to language and signification. Ellipses in one sense describes a precise geometric intersection; and in another, the "or" of absence, of object, of missing text, of imaginary identification. Of course, the subject can be excentric to the ego but it does not seem to follow the ellipses of the Earth around the Sun. Both, however, are substantive. Lacan, for his part, invokes Kepler on orbital ellipsis because the law breaks with Copernicus, since it calculates an orbit from two foci in relation to the Sun rather than one. This "falling" as Lacan puts it, decenters the Sun and for me, elliptically, where the signifier cannot hold or center the subject. The image does not take up the shortfall signaled by grammatical ellipses to complete a subject, but extends them or breaks them up. See Jacques Lacan, *Encore: The Seminar of Jacques Lacan, Book XX, On Feminine Sexuality: The Limits of Love and Knowledge, 1972–1973* (Bruce Fink trans.) (New York: Norton, 1998), pp. 42–43. See also Jacques Lacan, "The Function and Field of Speech and Language in Psychoanalysis" in *Écrits: A Selection* (Alan Sheridan trans.) (London: Routledge, 1989), pp. 23–86. The question of the point and ellipses is also raised with regard to Lacan's work on the "Sinthome" or symptom, but not quite. See, for instance, Edward Dioguardi, "Lacan's Sinthome; or, the Point of Psychoanalysis," *The European Journal of Psychoanalysis* 7(2) (2021).

by a kinesis in panel to panel relations (a dialectics of elision is at stake between panels), further emphasized by using the sound effects of Japanese onomatopoeia (which are often retained in what is otherwise translated transnationally). Such aspect to aspect paneling within a scene is highly cinematic, although it is not necessarily filmic ellipses, even as this informs its possibility. Of course, this is only a small part of manga visual literacy and even less of its philosophy so why mention it here? Serial ellipses are apposite with a functional pause about the meaning of labor for capital. They have a literal and manifest meaning within the spatiality of capitalism highly evocative of capital's coding and circulation, what David Harvey refers to in *The Enigma of Capital*, as "flow" (this book, more so than the manga, is a direct response to the 2007–2008 financial crisis).[12]

In *Enigma* (not surprisingly available in Japanese translation), Harvey spends a good deal of time explaining how, once capital flow is understood, capital's enigma is illusory (a riposte to those who follow the opacity of capital's symbolic function as an end in itself, and ironically preserve the future of an illusion). While not consciously addressing its moment, *Capital in manga* is interlaced with the crisis Harvey explores. Both texts explicate Marx's *Capital* (although obviously the depth of Harvey's engagement across his career has had a massive impact on how *Capital* is understood, and not just in the anglophone world). Even with their second volume on *Capital*, about which more below, Variety Artworks is not presenting a comprehensive or critical reading of the text as an academic engagement much beyond the basic premises of edumanga. Again, Manga de Dokuha offers primers on great works in Japanese and world literature and on one level this is both consistent with manga's economic model, and the conflicted meanings attending world and literature in that endeavor. But on another level, the success of the publisher's Marxist texts in Japan, two volumes on *Capital* and another on the *Communist Manifesto*, is not altogether because the books ride the coat-tails of *Kanikosen* or the former Goldman Sachs executive Hideki Mitani's popular 強欲資本主義—ウォール街の自爆—*Gōyoku shihon shugi—u~ōru-gai no jibaku* (translated as "Greedy Capitalism: Wall Street's Self-Destruction"). It is because in their

12 David Harvey, *The Enigma of Capital and the Crises of Capitalism* (Oxford: Oxford University Press, 2010), especially the "Preamble."

formal engagement of Marxian critique Variety Artworks reveals an understanding of capitalist contradiction in producing them.

Capital circulation, labor exploitation, technical innovation, speed up, credit, realization (of profit), and labor resistance—all of these are themes shared by both the Harvey and Variety Artworks texts. Even Harvey's stirring "What is to be done? And who is going to do it?" has an albeit problematic answer by the workers at the end of the manga, "We are not slaves." Unlike *Le Capital*, the intended primary readers of *Capital in manga* are not factory laborers, and Harvey's outline of anti-capitalism similarly invokes constituencies beyond assumptions about industrial workers and traditional forms of organization (e.g. unions). Instead, Harvey invokes NGOs, anarchist, autonomist and grassroots organizations, and social and identity-based movements. How collectively these forces might seize the state (which Harvey sees as pivotal) constitutes not the enigma of capital but the contingent enigma about what might now compose the grounds of its sublation. Since neither Marx's *Capital* nor Harvey's critique of the crises of capitalism are prescriptive, one can hardly blame *Capital in manga* for being somewhat ambivalent in its polemic. Given the crisis at the time, for salarymen looking at the prospect of a company being downsized, and with a growing precariat of office and service workers, it is salutary that manga provides a refresher course about how capital might operate, at a few seconds per page on the morning commute. As Daisuke Asao, a senior officer in the National Confederation of Trades Unions in Japan notes:

> [T]he situation of those laborers in the book is very similar to modern temporary workers: the unpredictable contracts, the working under heavy supervision, violence from supervisors, the widespread sexual harassment and the pressure against unionization are all things that modern Japanese recognize every day.[13]

Such correlations may be relatively easy to find without engaging the formal elements that mediate the experience.

---

13 Quoted in Leo Lewis, "Karl Marx goes manga in a Kapital comic strip," *The Times* (November 18, 2008).

While serial ellipses are not an explanation of the logic within Harvey's reading of capital circulation, I am suggesting they point both to manga's affinity to capital in movement and to its conjunctural substance as a heuristic. At Daniel's recommendation, Robin scales up cheese production to standard capitalist factory foundations, where the series takes on its perfunctory guise of rationality: continuity, uniformity, regularity, order. The question of socially necessary labor time appears suspended; the calculus of a given product in a given time becomes "the technical law of the process of production itself." The idea here is it connects a whole process and is dynamic, the kind of living automaton Marx reads into the factory as an instance and as a system. Clearly, the organic concept of seriality would extend to manga as a publishing business and to its versions, its own series, its translations (including multiple translations of the same sequence), its *dojinshi* (fan and self-produced versions of manga), and scanlations, the serial bootlegging central to the digital industrial complex.

To sample ellipsis is also to appreciate how the manga challenges expectations around how capitalism "develops" or is lived. For instance, Figure 9 is drawn from the opening of *Capital in manga* and is a standard ellipsis.

Ostensibly, the mise en scene is premised on romance. Enni surprises Robin who is clearly smitten with Enni, but his view of her is complicated by the fact she is standing next to this young, dapper, businessman, Daniel. Robin is also embarrassed to be selling cheese in a market. The ellipses constitute a reaction shot where we are asked to read Robin's view of Enni and Daniel from within his understanding of the scene. Figure 10 shows the original Japanese version.

Note, obviously we are reading right to left so the standard English representation is a flipped version. The ellipses eschew grammar in this example of the Japanese text to accentuate Robin's thinking over the merely absent. Figure 11 is a scanlation that retains the panel order within the page, and the Japanese hyperbolic ellipses.

This is a form of abrogation since the anglophone reader is asked to follow language order in one direction with panel order in the other. The effect tends to disrupt narrative flow although clearly that in itself is not only a pause about the global circulation Harvey critiques, even if here it

FIGURE 9. Variety Artworks, *Capital in Manga*! (Guy Yasko trans.) (Ottawa: Red Quill Books, 2012), p. 7.

FIGURE 10. Variety Artworks, *Capital in Manga*! (2008), p. 7.

FIGURE 11. *Capital in Manga*!, Manga-Go.com, p. 7.

is an almost literal hesitation before capital, and the capitalist. Without over-emphasis on this sequence, it is notable both in the Japanese and in the occasional scanlation Daniel is given ellipses in the next panel as he ponders Robin, but he also contemplates Enni's comment that Robin is a rising star in the entrepreneurial world. This is not deemed central to the Red Quill English version but it does appear in the French (basically, it is a pause as a question: how do I present myself as a "rookie" investor to a producer I am attempting to persuade?). Although not all of these points hint at the problem of manga seriality, this example remains one of standard ellipsis. Minor differences that appear to smooth (*aplatir*) the text in fact produce new meaning, unsettling the tableau across translation and standing in sharp contrast to *Capital*, where the dialogics of such interaction as content are not at stake in the same way.

The next example is more complicated even as it appears to be an elementary technical or stylistic difference. Implicit ellipses describe where the mark of absent speech is itself absent or where extant speech is rendered elliptical. Figures 12 and 13 show the Japanese and MangaGo scanlation side by side.[14] Note also the Red Quill English version (Figure 14).

Here, Robin's awkward response (signaled by the bead of sweat and the conventional blush lines across the face) is accentuated by ellipses, and Enni's apology for Daniel's comment is given to Daniel (which is out of character for Daniel). Meanwhile, Daniel's ellipses, which concern his thoughts on the commerce of cheese are left out altogether, which alters the meaning of the exchange. Daniel might be teasing Robin, but he is simultaneously weighing an economic opportunity that is confirmed by the following panels. These are not just amateurish slips in the English version but are overdetermined by the conditions of translatability themselves, which have a specific logic within manga as a cultural form of exchange. This example is certainly not a key to manga translation and untranslatability but nevertheless it suggests such cultural phenomena are also enmeshed in reading practices within contemporary capitalist circulation.

---

14 Variety Artworks, *Capital in Manga*! (Tokyo: East Press/Team Banmikas, 2008), p. 16.

FIGURE 12. Variety Artworks, *Capital in Manga!* (2008), p. 15.

FIGURE 13. *Capital in Manga!*, Manga-Go.com, p. 12.

FIGURE 14. Variety Artworks, *Capital in Manga*! (Yasko trans.) (2012), p. 12.

The third example concerns the substance of serial ellipses. Rather than endorse standard readings of capitalist crisis, Harvey draws attention to the "perpetual repositioning."[15] of the limits to capital in its modes of circulation. One of the problems in reading capital as relation and indeed in opposing it, is that its moving contradictions occur at variable velocities: some, like its compound rate of accumulation, appear relatively fixed over centuries; others, like the niche marketing of commodified ephemera seem to approach the very edge of cognition (certainly faster than reading one page every few seconds). Here again, manga's significance is both its relationship to embedded structures of Japanese art, from woodcuts to classic brushwork, and to its visual materialization of capital circulation, particularly in its rise within the economic reconstruction after the Second World War (Harvey devotes several pages to post-war modernization, particularly as it shapes US relations with Japan). Such rapid industrialization is much more than the displaced commodification of cheese, of course, but the Japanese reader is being asked to measure the links and ellipses between this model of capitalist expansion and their own experience of the divisions of *Capital in manga*, commodities, exploitation, labor power, and value, in the present. In this scene the production process has reached breaking point. Robin wants to meet Daniel's demands for surplus value but this has brought the workers at the factory to exhaustion. Even the violence of Robin's foreman, the "enforcer," cannot promise further extraction.

Karl (yes, Karl) is a worker at the cheese factory whose life is collapsing under Daniel's desire for optimal exploitation. As he leaves work, Karl can see how the long hours and speed up are affecting worker well-being. "We have to work just to live" says one, and Karl thinks about the form of this necessity. He urges a fellow worker, who is sick, to stay home the next shift but the worker replies that he cannot take time off. Karl reminds him he is not a slave (奴隷—Dorei, the first time the word appears in the text) but the other worker insists he is like a slave. In the next panel Karl's thoughts on this possibility are represented by ellipses, which is both a standard invitation to the reader and one that shapes the intervention of the manga's engagement with *Capital*. What has work done to labor that could possibly sanction this identification?

15 Harvey, *Enigma*, p. 117.

FIGURE 15. Variety Artworks, *Capital in Manga*! (2008), p. 111.

FIGURE 16. Variety Artworks, *Capital in Manga*! (Yasko trans.) (2012), p. 111.

The use of "slave" to signify the immiseration and oppression of the workers in the narrative invokes a vexed topic in Japanese history, one that spans the prevalence of a slave system in Japan into the sixteenth century, the enslavement of Japanese by the Portuguese up to the end of the sixteenth century, the trafficking of Japanese women for sex work prior to the Second World War, to vast amounts of forced and enslaved labor by the Japanese before and during the Second World War itself. The ambivalence of the signifier extends both to acknowledgment of atrocities committed in the name of imperial Japan, and also to the humiliating conditions of defeat, all the way down to perceptions of the continuing "realignment" of US forces in contemporary Okinawa. If seriality comes to describe the inner workings of the factory, the automaton, and capital "flow," the figure of the slave and the racial differentiation at its heart make that modernization possible. In general, *Capital* is not expansive on the depth of this materiality, not because Marx does not recognize at once how value works between the plantation and the cotton mill, for instance, but because he was working through historical distinctions in the forms and distribution of labor exploitation the better to understand the nature of their equivalence. In fact, of course, Marx offers a great deal on slavery, particularly in his writings on the United States during and after the civil war. There are hundreds of references in *Capital* to slaves, slavery, and enslavement, and when Marx examines the "Genesis of the Industrial Capitalist" it is clear slavery substantially grounds this emergence. The metaphor employed in the "Genesis" chapter is open to conflicting interpretations: "the veiled slavery of the wage-laborers in Europe needed the unqualified slavery of the New World as its pedestal."[16] Slavery is quite literally the base but what sits on the pedestal is usually deemed more important. In Marx's defense, several critics have noted the metaphor probably derives from Marx's classicism and also that, while wage labor is

16 Marx, *Capital* (Fowkes trans.), p. 925. Marx, Das Kapital, p. 682: "Überhaupt bedurfte die verhüllte Sklaverei der Lohnarbeiter in Europa zum Piedestal die Sklaverei sans Phrase in der neuen Welt." Reitter translation, p. 688: "This, the slavery sans phrase of the New World, functioned as the pedestal that the veiled slavery of European wage laborers couldn't do without."

depicted as "veiled" or disguised slavery, it is not veiling slavery from the history of capitalism.

The manga refracts both the meaning of slavery in Japanese history and its key role in capitalist modernization. Indeed, more than this, and especially in the sections on exploitation and value, *Capital in manga* uses the idea of the slave as the seed of anti-capitalist consciousness. Spoken by several characters, the line "We are not slaves" is repeated again and again in the second half of Volume One of the manga in the face of factory exploitation, and it fills the last page of the book (as we have noted, repetition is also a mode or condition of refusal). Basically, if wage labor means this in cheese or any other commodity production then it must be resisted and emphatically so. Whereas *Capital* Volume One ends with a pointed critique of colonialism, the first volume of the manga concludes with a representation of capitalism as a specific colonization of social being. "We are not slaves" is true in terms of a specific economic history yet it is a revelation about the structural barbarism wage labor produces and reproduces. Wage labor does obscure or obfuscate the meanings of slavery but it also reveals a long history of exploitation in modernity as a totality. In Karl's response, as ellipses, to the worker's sense of slavery we also have a question for the silences of Marx's text on the concreteness of worker subjectivity, a notion the necessary abstraction of the critique (which is not a transhistoricism) can only be illustrated or elaborated by introducing an element of doubt in the convictions of political economy, which is a basic tension in the subject/object relations of labor. The working-class subject does not speak in *Capital* (it is not, after all, premised on sociological or anthropological fieldwork like Marx's subsequent "worker inquiry"), but the pauses in *Capital in manga* offer speechlessness as also a hesitation about the realization of its aims in extension. Even casual or radically contingent adaptations of *Capital* are active in reassessing the real foundations of its intervention and the answers it provides to questions it has not asked. Not all serial ellipses are actual ellipses in the text but the latter are often symptomatic a series is at stake, as if a capitalist crisis is in series dialectically with another crisis over the authentication of *Capital* as crisis critique. The "limits of capital" are not capital's alone.

After his exchange on the street, Karl returns home. It is late (a remark on the length of the working day Marx also discusses in Volume One) and his kids are already asleep. Karl thinks again about the nature of necessity—at least he has cheese for dinner! As he and his wife discuss the conditions of their existence, she reminds Karl that the reality is they need his work to get by. Again, the English version leaves out elements of their conversation. Angrily, Karl asks his wife why she does not call into question how they live. She replies—"I don't have time for that? I do what I can!" The exclamation marks do not do justice to this argument, and the question of reproductive labor in particular. While this is not a feminist manga, on more than one occasion the English version seems to minimize further such a possibility (especially in the exchanges between Robin and his childhood sweetheart Helena—who is working the fields as a day laborer and also the streets as a sex worker in order to subsist). It would be an exaggeration to say the text turns on such moments of consciousness but the ellipses in these sequences, both real and imagined, are intrinsic to the logic of seriality as concept, as a relation of measure. With his wife's final exhortation in mind, "We work to make a living," Karl returns to work the next day to assess the space between this promise and its material conditions. Once again, the English version simply drops the phrase ("to make a living") echoing in Karl's head as he faces Robin and the foreman, even though the image of his wife appears in the same panel. In the Japanese manga the phrase is rendered outside speech bubbles, and further accentuates its meaning.

The English version takes the ellipses of the foreman's reaction to be astonishment at worker resistance, but the Japanese text adds incredulity about the very idea of a decent working life for workers. Predictably, on the next page *Capital in manga* substitutes a question mark for Karl's thinking, but he is not thinking of a question, rather of the dominant declaration: "We are not slaves." The realization and subsequent exchanges elaborate a key meaning of "labor power" which is the subject of the chapter and a fulcrum for the last one on "value." I am not suggesting that ellipses (or their elision) are symbolic of capital consciousness (consciousness about capital) but within the manga they assume nevertheless an active trope, and sharpen the possibility of thinking through

FIGURE 17. Variety Artworks, *Capital in Manga*! (2008), p. 118.

FIGURE 18. Variety Artworks, *Capital in Manga*! (Yasko trans.) (2012), p. 118.

capital. The question mark is not on the page but in the mind of the reader. How far removed am I from Karl's predicament and what might constitute the ellipses in my own thinking, the conditions necessitating thought under and through capitalism?

This is a serial connection and not simply a teleological or causal one and is a longue durée of the meaning of *Das Kapital* across capitalism's dynamic. Certainly, such an understanding of capital flow does not necessitate ellipses to address its limits (here in the resistance of labor power). And, as I have noted, this does not fully acknowledge either the substantial formal components of manga, or the challenge of Marx's text, *Capital* (whose key ellipse, both in content and in mode of address, is the worker). While there is an ineluctability to ellipses within and between languages, the constitutive gap within seriality suggests other lines of inquiry. Much of the discussion about the emergence of *Capital in manga* in Japan circled around how the economic crisis was both expanding membership in the Japanese Communist Party and accentuating a new relevance for Marxist critique. Manga de dokuha's modest aims for the series were overdetermined and they subsequently seized on a demand opportunity to expand a line of their product (unsurprisingly, the very narrative their adaptation sought to tell). The phenomenon, like the credit crisis itself, quickly went global, initially via scanlation but subsequently in official multi-language versions. Yet it is not that a publishing event premised on the trials of capitalist crisis simply reproduces and exploits the conditions of globalization on which the crisis pivots. What manga seems to understand in *Capital* is in part that capitalist contradictions are, whatever else they are, problems of reading and that how its story gets told is a test of much more than relevancy, but of a kind of material embeddedness apposite with its real conditions, with the space between a decent life and the life produced.

Serial ellipsis constellates elements of the political unconscious of the manga so that what is selected as evidence of *Capital*'s analysis misses its exegesis while also engaging how misreading is mediated by more than what *Capital* can know in its serialization. On the one hand, manga, like the novel, like cinema, has the generic capacity to re-represent almost any text; on the other hand, its representational conventions do not automatically reproduce this desire, and the text becomes most interesting when its formal elisions are in dialogue with the silences of its hypertext. When Althusser suggests *Capital* answers a question it has not posed, "what is the value of labor?" he also identifies a logic in its serialization: not the eternal return of the same question, but the problem of extension and division in its very proposition. The banality of serialization, that includes its reproduction of the everyday, exists alongside a deconstruction of the quotidian itself, as if every function of seriality becomes a question about how to live the being it invokes.

The first volume of *Capital in manga* ends in crisis, with the echoed phrase "We are not slaves" signifying a proletarian refusal of Robin's embodiment of capitalist desire. The melodrama between language and line is unsurprising for the form yet creates something of a cliffhanger for the narrative presented: what is the endgame of the worker consciousness evoked? Marx concludes *Capital* with his own refusal, "we are not concerned here with the conditions of the colonies" and reminds his reader the focus is the fundamental condition of the capitalist mode of production and accumulation: "the expropriation of the worker." The dialectic of expropriation and its consciousness has a long history but finds expression in seriality as extension, which is both formal in the relationship of texts and individually constitutive in the Spinozist sense as a union of bodies, or in Marx's presupposition of socially determinate individuals. It is not simply that seriality constitutes the worker as subject but there are series nevertheless where such a subject wants to exist. The manga conjures *Capital* through this desire yet appears to need a guide to authorize the process. And thus we arrive at *Capital* in a disjunct continuation of the manga in the second volume (to be referred to as *Capital in manga II*).

The first volume of *Capital in manga* at once disabuses its reader that the bridge it hopes to build to Marx's text will be a short one or particularly sturdy and yet, as we have intimated, it symptomatically pursues the paths not taken in Marx's desire for a serialized *Le Capital*. Like capitalism, seriality depends on social connection but often in a reified moment where division is literally divisive. The queue is shared for instance, but each participant is divided in obligation, and convention flattens the contradictions in socialization. Serial form can do this too (it dis-connects) and mediates more than the logical split otherwise intends. The idea of an eight-page issue of *Le Capital* is an anodyne function of production, yet the tension in division is both divisive and decisive. "Manga Marx" both re-collects the massive contribution of his thought even as serialization necessarily challenges the capacity of its narration, not just because the manga is bound to illustrate, but because as a commodity it has already objectified the labor that is its possibility. On the one hand, *Capital* in its versions can enact the mystery of the commodity Marx describes in its first chapter; on the other hand, seriality seems determined to contradict such inexorability. How? Much of Marx's *Capital* is synchronic, in the sense that its critique of political economy hinges on a point of time where British industrialism provides the example. Marx's main concern, however, is capital and labor as a dynamic, so while the case studies might be a slice of economic history, Marx strongly resists essentializing from them. The complexity lies in the logic of relations and not in empirical description alone. Seriality may homogenize by abstracting from, for instance, individuality, but it also differentiates: its propensity to segment invites a question about the logic of division. Even if series do not state the question, the question dialectically constrains their apprehension. The material substantiation of a serial is coterminous with the question—how did this division come to be?

Capital in manga II does not begin with an insurrection based on the consciousness announced at the end of the first volume. Instead, a new character is introduced, Friedrich Engels, who will act as a guide and commentator on what passes for action in the book (personally, I love the idea Engels, who had derided the French version of *Capital*, is now explaining the book in Japanese, and in pictures). The conceit is loosely rationalized around the fact that Engels lived until 1895 and in theory could directly comment on the mise en scene of our cheese factory narrative. Engels edits and produces the second and third volumes of *Capital* after Marx's death based on Marx's work in progress and the extensive notes that accompanied it to that point. Engels' name now accompanies that of Marx on the title page of *Capital* included in *Capital in manga II*, while the list of characters in the manga contains Marx (about which more below), Engels, Gold (the president of a bank), and a nameless "businessman" who runs a factory supplying machinery for Robin's cheese manufacture. The contents page lists the chapter divisions: 1, Commodities, Money, Surplus Value; 2, The Pursuit of Profit; 3, The Contradictions of Capitalist Society; 4, Banks and Credit; and, most intriguingly, 5, Panic. There is a separate page filled with everyday goods bearing a caption that echoes the first line of *Capital* Volume One: "The wealth of societies in which the capitalist mode of production prevails appears as an 'immense collection of commodities.'" In effect, the first part of *Capital in manga II* returns us to *Capital* Volume One, particularly around the calculation of use and exchange values in the commodity form (just as for Gellert, a vernacular *Capital* required a different entry point than Marx's opening, even as the broader outlines of the critique are intimated) . The examples are also different—diamonds and bread, for instance—but there are ways in which this volume responds dialectically to the ellipses of the first manga with Engels in the role of teacher substituting for the appearance of Marx's ideas themselves as a narrative thread. There is an ambivalence about whether the story of the cheese factory can actually carry the weight of Marx's analysis. It is Engels, rather than Robin or the dastardly Daniel who thus offers explanatory notes on the central concepts of *Capital*. The project veers much closer to edumanga in this respect, and uses Japanese figures and/or caricatures to elaborate value in exchange. The tone is light, when money replaces gold, the currency note is called an "Engels" and, once the fetishism of money is introduced, we return, after 26 pages, to the story of *Capital in manga* offered in the first volume, but still continue with Engels as the narrator. For readers who might have been engaged by Robin's relationship with his father, or Robin's crush on Enni, or the tense reflections on his childhood sweetheart Helen, or even the psychological machinations of Daniel, Engels' storytelling prowess will come as a definitive letdown. The advantage of his participation is that he appears to move through Marx's text at ease (he is a consummate agent of "*aplatir*"). Engels handles basic questions like "what is capitalism?" without adornment and quotes more-or-less directly on complex ideas, like that of the worker being doubly-free, drawn from the chapter on "So-Called Primitive Accumulation" that we have discussed in terms of Gellert above.[17] When

17 And in Marx, *Capital* (Fowkes trans.), p. 874.

Robin and Daniel enter the text, it is usually to illustrate the concerns of a factory owner and an investor respectively or to remind the reader, albeit vaguely, that they also appeared in the earlier volume. We still get ellipses from Robin, of course, who retains a bad conscience about the stark formulae for economic exploitation. But Engels (and by extension, Variety Artworks) is less interested in character (an exigency of the publication process for this issue), and our protagonists are no sooner mentioned than we get down to *Capital* exegesis: "Key Concept—Depreciation: method through which the decline of the economic value of machinery and other assets because of their use and time passing is objectively quantified." It is not that character disappears (this will have importance for the conclusion of the manga) but it becomes an aspect of the explanation, and not the other way around, and thus it remains a problem for serial subjectivation and engagement, given the first volume.

Capital in manga II wants to re-establish its inner serial connection to Marx's text but does so in direct address while rendering its relationship to the first manga as relatively haphazard (despite declaring itself as a "continuation" and being published five months after the first volume). Given Marx's own difficulties over the prospects and publication process of a serialized *Capital* for the French working class, the difficulty of serial connection is appreciable, but clearly part of the rationale of *Capital in manga II* is to cash in on the success of the first volume as quickly as possible (which initially sold at a thousand copies a day) rather than figure out what might usefully follow the critical denouement of that book. Recall, *Capital in manga* says it wants to act as a bridge to Marx's original text but does not hint at a second volume nor claim to be part of such a series (a stark contrast to Marx's series in which the text pre-exists the project, although not in the form or language of its base). Analogically, we could simply remark that East Press looks at *Capital in manga* the way Daniel sees Robin's cheese manufacture, as an investment opportunity. Yet, whatever the cynicism regarding the manga's extension it nevertheless speaks to a necessary tension between *Capital* as critique and seriality as a narrative logic. From this perspective, the apparent randomness of *Capital in manga II* belies its mediatory function and the concreteness of its instance. It does more than reproduce the contradictions embedded in the economic crisis to which it opportunistically responds; it also reveals the living-on of Marx's critique in the limits of its representational attention.

As I have suggested, in *Capital in manga* the constitutive limits can be glimpsed in the non-said of the text, including the meanings of ellipsis for *Capital* in series. Because *Capital in manga II* is reacting more to the reception of the first volume over the place of Marx's *Capital* in the context of the economic crisis, its immediacy (a cultural logic I have described elsewhere as "immediation")[18] is a mode of realization, one that consumes *Capital* in series as an end in itself, rather than as a capacity of new narration. Having Engels explain the story of Robin's entrepreneurship in terms of key elements of *Capital* via comments, diagrams, and charts is very much in the edumanga mode and for some may have an advantage over Daniel's "how to do capitalist exploitation 101" pronouncements. It certainly increases the range of topics discussed (depreciation, variable versus constant capital, production cycles, etc.) but whether it draws readers closer to *Capital* itself is not a given, and especially in relation to the previous volume. Of course, one could argue the cheese factory narrative is no less contrived than adding Engels as an observer in the text. Two characters, however, complicate how *Capital in manga II* works in series, in parallel and as evidence of the manga's material conjuncture, and both are named Karl.

There is an intricate and braided relation between capitalism and seriality, between a mode of production and a logical form of socialization. One of the key lessons of *Capital*, that all of its serial iterations inflect and mediate, is that whatever represents the unity of capital in production, circulation, and consumption, it is a unity marked by systemic contradiction and disjunction. The scale of these disruptions is not predetermined because, as *Capital* meticulously details, the precise constellation of factors is necessarily dynamic. The conditions of seriality are always and never the material equivalence of economic contradiction; the question is about the nature of entanglement, one that is particularly instructive if the concrete life of Marx's central text is examined in this way. *Capital in*

---

18 See Peter Hitchcock, "Immediation" in Jeffrey Di Leo and Peter Hitchcock (eds), *The New Public Intellectual* (New York: Palgrave Macmillan, 2016), pp. 135–48. See also Anna Kornbluh, *Immediacy* (New York: Verso, 2023).

manga is in series with *Capital* but does not pose itself as a metonym for Marx's book, nor as a formal analog, even as manga as form is equally capable of producing both. *Capital* remains relevant for different reasons at different times, not out of some declarative transhistoricism but precisely out of the roiling specificity of its concepts. It could be that seriality maintains an understanding of living labor, but in *Capital* it relates a condition of living itself as a reading practice and as a critique of capitalist persistence. The moving contradictions of capitalism's differential unity are radically theorized in Marx's tome, and every part of that clause represents a question for the present, even as a political unconscious in popular imagination. It is the concreteness of Marx's theorization that compels serial engagement, not just in new editions, new translations, and rigorous scholarly debate, but as an understanding that the theory itself is constitutive in extension and division. What negates *Capital*'s serialization is not an inability to read its concrete abstraction but the dialectical terms of its historical supercession, at the very least a transformation of the mode of production which is its subject (the history of *Capital* can begin when the conditions of its critique are overreached).

Karl is not a misrepresentation of a laborer in *Capital in manga II*, but he does not embody what labor as relation has become, and therefore his story necessarily misses the nature of this provocation in Marx's critique of the labor/value nexus. If the first book of the manga on *Capital* shows increasing pressure (both from the experience of work and the extant conditions of Karl's family) to make Karl face reality, much of the exegesis of concepts from *Capital* in the second manga underline reality is a composite of complex socio-economic relations in the everyday that may not be discerned as such. Despite Engels' avuncular interjections, with his character directly facing the reader and raising his finger to make a point, Karl's understanding of his situation suggests an almost paratextual *Entfremdung*/alienation less assuaged by graphic representations of depreciation, variable capital, constant capital, or expanded reproduction (these subheadings, in the extreme margins of the Japanese manga, are often dropped from the translations, as if acknowledging the "alienating" effect of abstraction itself). The fact that much of *Capital in manga II* is dedicated to illustrating concepts via the exchanges of two capitalists,

Robin and Daniel (one an ambitious but increasingly ambivalent industrialist; the other, an investor for whom rapacity and accumulation are representationally as outsized as Gellert's depictions of Ford and Rockefeller) seems to echo Marx's predilections for capitalist caricature. Yet Karl's presence and disaffection offer a different form of readerly identification, like a punctum in Barthesian visuality, or the *objet petit a* in Lacanian critique.[19] The latter is a remnant in the Real, if not reality, the remains of the subject of the very desire for labor power as capital accumulation. On one level, the manga asks how can the worker be seen within this theorization of political economy?; on another level, the representation of Karl deepens the tension between visibility and verifiability, as if, like the subheadings, he floats at the edge of the narrative and voices what detailed calculation cannot possibly secure—a desire to live otherwise.

Karl is seen in only one panel in the first half of *Capital in manga II*, an "establishing shot" alongside Daniel, Robin, and the unnamed owner of a small factory. Significantly, the next time he appears is in the section on capitalist contradictions. First, he will not go for a drink with fellow workers on their way home (to which one worker basically responds, "Are you alive?" Karl's answer, of course, is ellipses). Then, at home, his wife notes his fatigue (he has two jobs) and she offers to work still more herself. The intimation of housework and social reproduction is salutary but if the understanding of gendered divisions of labor in the first manga was

---

19 See Roland Barthes, *Camera Lucida: Reflections on Photography* (Richard Howard trans.) (New York: Farrar, Straus and Giroux, 1981), pp. 42–62. For Barthes, the punctum is often a detail, a partial object, although it must be said his initial example, the photo of a Black family by James Van De Zee, at once calls the concept into question: what eye sanctions the acknowledgement of a girl's footwear? Mentioning the idea here also calls into question my vision of the text and the composition of its images. The point is that the detail does not escape its ideological mediation or somehow returns to artistic intent. Perhaps the second concept, the *objet petit a*, helps to elucidate the first. In a way, Barthes' sense of being pricked is just this Lacanian idea of the unattainable object of desire, although not quite a representational lack, as Lacan develops the concept. See Jacques Lacan, *The Four Fundamental Concepts of Psychoanalysis* (Alan Sheridan trans.), The Seminar of Jacques Lacan, Book XI (New York: Norton, 1978), pp. 67–122.

relatively superficial, in this volume it almost disappears. The wife, who is not named, is supported yet never rounded as a character. Women are seen working at the factory but do not speak. One could argue this is true to the male-centered predilections of *Capital*, but it does not engage the extensive genealogies of its interpretation. *Capital in manga* may be set elsewhere or beyond Japan, yet symptoms of patriarchy are not so far removed. In this scene, Karl thinks they will be ok and then, as if to remind us once more the event of this manga is the financial crisis of 2008, we see Karl at the bank checking on their savings and remarking it is not enough for the kids to go to college (not necessarily a late nineteenth century concern, one should note). The aura of savings, loans, and debt hangs over the narrative with different meanings for each participant. As Engels explains, when the machine factory owner expands production in order to maximize return, he also sells to Robin's rival, which produces price competition and puts further pressure on automation and the reduction of labor costs (more credit but potentially less demand) with every round of "uneven expansion" (a correlative of uneven development at other scales). As many commentators have noted, this is only one element of the global crisis of 2008, which is dominated by financialization (and addressed in the manga to some extent by the disquisition on fictive capital). For workers living under long-term wage stagnation, major outlays like mortgages, tuition, and automobiles are a difficult and receding horizon answered principally by the rapid expansion of credit instruments (from credit cards to long-term loans), all in the service of somehow maintaining effective demand and the belief in growth. The cheese industry might help Engels explain industrialization, but getting to grips with matters like money capital and real capital, some of the substance of *Capital* Volume Three, places great demands on Robin's business as a metonymic model, and on articulating the extent to which Marx's analysis remains to illuminate the present. At this level, the living on of both Marx and Karl pivots less on a simple relevancy test, but on the power of telling capital's story.

Engels attempts to globalize the tale ("The world is full of products," etc.), and Gold the banker, while obviously one-dimensional, conveys much of the uncertainty that comes to rest on the money form and trust.

It is interesting that, for the most part, Gold is drawn with eyes closed as if he sees the function of the bank but not necessarily its contradictions for socialization. Again, the hasty representations may be more to do with getting *Capital in manga II* into production (a process through which the speed of adaptation makes threading concepts with storyline a limit for an instant edumanga in series). The depiction of people in the manga is dramatically simplified when demonstrating economic processes (as are piles of money, numbers, and banks as smiling stick figures, etc.) and crisis is offered as a hardly innovative image of a storm at sea. Once more we see smoothing moved to simplification. Nevertheless, how the crisis unfolds leads us, as in the first volume, to the point of social conflagration. Karl joins a protest outside a bank and is told the bank has run out of money. "There is no money in the bank," he asks, "What does that mean?" The basic answer is a "bank run," in which customers demand their money deposits back, usually an amount far more than what the bank holds in cash or liquid assets. In 2008, the collapse of Washington Mutual in the United States was a bank run writ large.[20] After a credit downgrade of the bank (due to factors like exposure to failing mortgages) the next nine days saw customers collectively withdraw billions and the bank was closed by the Office of Thrift Supervision (like the name Gold, institutions do not shy from ironization). Eventually, the FDIC stripped out the bank assets and sold them to J. P. Morgan Chase, who of course was not liable for any of the claims of the bank's equity holders (many of the branches were quickly reopened as Chase Banks—crisis, what crisis?). For the most part, banks in Japan proved more resilient during the meltdown (quantitative easing was already in place and there was less volatile loan exposure) and the economic stress was located more in export industries but, as we have noted, both wage earners and "salarymen" were vulnerable to the knock-on effects of externalities.

What do the capitalists do in the manga? Daniel does not panic (after all, his mantra remains "You must exploit them [the workers]!"), he aims to downsize the business and reassign assets for accumulation elsewhere. Robin, who had previously exclaimed he wanted to be rich, is chastened

20 Kimberly Amadeo, "Washington Mutual (WaMu): How It Went Bankrupt," *The Balance* (August 23, 2021).

by the poverty and despair he witnesses (he is almost a conscious if not conscientious capitalist) and decides instead for a kind of "in-between" exploitation back at his father's small-scale facility, which could now be read as de-growth adjacent, even if hardly Kohei Saito's model for eco-economic transformation.[21] Meanwhile, Karl spots Mr. Gold doing his own version of a bank run by struggling down the street with a large suitcase of leaking cash.

As now, the reader in 2009 might wonder if only embezzlement was so easy to spot. Gold is confronted in an alleyway by the machine manufacturer whose business, bereft of the bank's lines of credit, has gone bankrupt. By the time Karl arrives the businessman has stabbed Mr. Gold to death. With an exchange of glances (and close-up panels that accentuate Karl's almost permanent bead of worry sweat, that we have also noted on Robin), Karl realizes he is not going to leave the alleyway without a deal and says his original bank deposit (100 Engels, no less) will be enough for his silence. The (ex) factory owner offers 200 for good measure. Does such melodramatic machination enhance or deplete the meaning of Marx for reading *Capital* today?

Part of the conceit of *Capital in manga*, in both volumes, is the idea Marx's understanding can be conveyed, like *Le Capital*, without a subtitle, as vernacular and as suggested, not just in explication, but in articulation. No one working on the Manga de Dokuha series believed individual classic titles could be rendered as manga without loss or misapprehension in the art of popularization (again, a different idea from Lachâtre's desire for *Le Capital*, serialized). On the other hand, the mangas of *Capital* still speak back to the genealogy from which they are drawn, and particularly since their emergence is galvanized by a material crisis of socio-economic relations for which *Capital* is no mere abstraction and manga is no passive

---

21 Saito has written extensively on degrowth as anti-capitalist in Japan and beyond. See Kohei Saito, *Marx in the Anthropocene*: *Towards the Idea of Degrowth Communism* (Cambridge: Cambridge University Press, 2022); and *Slow Down*: *The Degrowth Manifesto* (Brian Bergstrom trans.) (New York: Astra, 2024). While theoretically astute, Saito takes chances in his reading of Marx and this has helped spur a comparatively large readership in Japan where growth and the environment have garnered significant debate.

FIGURE 19. Variety Artworks, *Capital in Manga!* 2 (Tokyo: East Press/Team Banmikas, 2009), p. 171.

observer. The second character of interest is another Karl, Marx himself as a revenant both past and as a kind of future conditional (simultaneously a ghost of Japanese Marxism and an echo of Karl, the worker as a mode of becoming). If Engels appears as a living contemporary of our nineteenth century cheese factory narrative, and as a putative co-author of volumes two and three of *Capital* (the mini-bio in the manga describes him as an editor, but the title page of "the continuation of Capital" does not make this distinction), the arrival of Marx at the end of *Capital in manga II* is even more of a surprise. Marx, like communism, is a specter still haunting Europe at some level but it is amazing nevertheless to have his spirit alight upon this Japanese text. Engels, our teacher, has just stated recessions and crises are systemic to capitalism, to which Marx chimes in,

"Recession and Crisis are not necessarily bad things because they can reestablish equilibrium between supply and demand."[22] Engels, gobsmacked, asks how Marx is present, to which Marx replies "Even if I am dead, am I dead?" and, remarkably, has a halo over his head. Ostensibly, this is another lighthearted touch, by way of denouement (the patron saint of the working class with *Capital* as the worker's *Bible*, etc.), but it acts as a further defamiliarization of what *Capital* represents. It could be read as a shortcut to authentication—if you do not believe Engels' explanation so far you must be convinced by Marx himself. Both of course are fictional representations in a narrative that is hypertextually linked to several reciprocal series simultaneously (Volume Two to One, Manga de Dokuha, including the manga of the *Communist Manifesto*, to translations of this translation, and to translations and retranslations of Marx's original text, including his own, as well as subsequent editions). In effect, however, the appearance of Marx is not some tongue-in-cheek homage to the man from Trier but is a way for the manga to claim him and to ask in that representation what is operative in confronting capitalism today.

The appearance of Marx, the literal repetition and difference of Karl, is relatively conventional rather than resolutely Deleuzean in its implications yet, however playful, it opens up another line of inquiry regarding serial

22 Variety Artworks, *Capital in Manga*! *2* (Tokyo: East Press/Team Banmikas, 2009), p. 181.

FIGURE 20. Variety Artworks, *Capital in Manga! 2* (2009), p. 182.

FIGURE 21. Variety Artworks, *Capital in Manga! 2* (2009), p. 191.

FIGURE 22. Variety Artworks, *Le Capital 2* (Florent Georges trans.) (Paris: Soleil Manga, 2011), p. 191.

Marx in relation to social change. For the most part, the cameo simply repeats what Engels has already explained about constant and variable capital regarding the capacity to generate surplus value, and the related prospect of a falling rate of profit. The repetition is true to *Capital* but of course it does not engage the historical displacement of this theory in adjudicating the relevance or not of Marxist critique. Here we might say the manga could have spent more time on "The Rate and Mass of Surplus-Value," in *Capital*, or perhaps supplemented the idea with a consideration of Marx's other informing texts, as David Harvey has recently done (the idea being nuance rather than repeated declaration).[23] The reiteration of Marx at the end of *Capital in manga II* is a further sign the question of seriality in the serialization of *Capital* rests on hermeneutic exhaustibility. The text as a whole confirms the anxiety of the French reading public Marx noted in the letter to Lachâtre, a desire to press on when a new reading might be possible. It is not the page-turning logic of a manga that is at fault—wherever you look across the form one can find a richness of detail and aesthetic challenges of many kinds—but the missed opportunities for analysis that grates, when even ellipses themselves cannot do the work of reflection.

Yet still, there is division in extension, so that what is anachronistic in the template of industrialism drawn from the nineteenth century is often used to allegorize the present, the very reason for Marx's spectral return. The manga closes with the idea the version of *Capital*, the book that has been drawn, simultaneously intimates a process with shadows that are obviously but appreciably global. Then, with the admonishment to "Question common sense!" Marx (and Engels, who is also now represented with a halo!) takes flight.

This is not extraordinary for manga, and socialist comics are hardly beyond their superhero moments, but does this final panel merely confirm

---

23 It is a little unfair to pit *Capital in manga* against the lifetime research and elaboration of Marx and *Capital* in the works of David Harvey. Still, I do believe a dialogue is necessary, particularly because Harvey strongly believes in the pedagogical potential of Marx's central text (the dimension here referred to as "edumanga"). See, for instance, David Harvey, *The Anti-Capitalist Chronicles* (London: Pluto, 2020), where Harvey ends with discussion questions and references for further readings.

that *Capital* can only be banalized in serial extension unless it limits itself strictly to the missile Marx intended, and without the romantic figuration of a French working-class reader? To answer this, we finally return serial Marx to *Le Capital*, not to the single volume version in the BNF, but to the two-volume translation of *Capital in manga* that appeared in French as *Le Capital* in 2011 (and subsequently republished, just like Marx's serial, as a single volume "integrale" edition in 2016).[24] Within a dialectics of seriality *Le Capital* is shaped not just by a sanctioned adaptation and translation of the Variety Artworks/East Press project, but by serial connections to Marx's original project, both mediated and overdetermined by the concrete conditions of Marx and Marxism in France, and the political economy of its present. Consider, for instance, the French rendering of the panel above.

First, of course, we have a reprise of the epigraph from where we began—a reworking of Marx's borrowing from Dante, "Segui il tuo corso, e lascia dir le genti." Marx uses/adapts Dante to encourage you, the reader, to follow your own path and let people say what they will. The French here suggests there are people who are not able to face reality, whereas you should follow the path of justice. But how? The Japanese "question common sense" is deemed an insufficient flourish. Surely, given the nature of Marx's magnum opus, the charge "challenge capitalism!" is closer to its meaning? The Spanish version follows the Japanese, although a scanlation in English that uses the Herder Spanish edition as its source adds in red, "Translator's Note: the solution is socialism."[25] The differences are unsurprising, in part because translation is not a window but a lens. As with the many and multiple translations of Marx's work, the manga is repositioned by other languages in the material conditions of their moment. The French manga, however, seems intent on not only reproducing the Japanese version but also to maintain a conversation with the abstraction of *Capital* as a current contingency, which is another reason why Marx's critique of capitalism continues to be read. This contingency includes a French tradition of *bande*

24 Unlike the official English translation to date, the French version translates both volumes of *Capital in manga* (as does the Spanish translation): *Le Capital*, 2 VOLS (Florent Georges trans.) (Paris: Soleil Manga, 2011).

25 Karl Marx, *El Capital*: *Segunda Parte* (Maite Madinabeitia trans.) (Barcelona: Herder Editorial, SL, 2013), p. 199.

dessinées and a long engagement with Japanese manga as part of its own globalization. There is a dialectical stress in this version between respecting the efforts of Variety Artworks to bring *Capital* to the world as a Japanese manga, and offering an alternative argument that the whole "cheese factory in Europe in the late nineteenth century" narrative base is ultimately besides the point. In a strange way, this becomes the realization of Marx's serial he himself could not assure.

Unlike *Capital in manga*, *Le Capital* here is more directly linked to its contemporary political scene. For instance, the manga begins with a framing preface by the French politician, Olivier Besancenot. In 2002 he ran for the French Presidency as a revolutionary socialist (at 28, the youngest candidate in French history) and he garnered over a million votes. In 2007 he ran again, this time for the *Ligue communiste revolutionnaire* (Fourth International). He then helped found the New Anti-capitalist Party, which he led until 2011, the year of the manga *Le Capital*'s publication. Besancenot's career illustrates divisions in the French Left over the place of anti-capitalism in national politics (his book with Michael Löwy on *Revolutionary Affinities* is also an example of rethinking the relationship of Marxism and anarchism, a topic with its own longue durée).[26] Besancenot's preface to *Le Capital* is populist by design, while simultaneously offering lessons why the form and content of *Capital* matters. Besancenot invokes the filmmaker Ken Loach (who Besancenot admires and who had previously endorsed his candidacy) and remarks on Loach's image of capitalism as a wheel with a mouse caught and continually running within it. The problem is not the mouse but it is the wheel that must be dismantled. Besancenot dialogically positions the French translation of the manga as an appeal to the reader's understanding of lived injustice rather than only extensively calculated surplus extraction. The formulae of Marx's *Capital* are not changed but the form is alive to the manner of their inscription. More than this, the framing accentuates the

---

26 Michael Löwy and Olivier Besancenot, *Revolutionary Affinities: Toward a Marxist-Anarchist Solidarity* (David Campbell trans.) (Binghamton, NY: PM Press, 2023). Originally published as Michael Löwy and Olivier Besancenot, *Affinités révolutionnaires: Nos étoiles rouges et noires: Pour une solidarité entre marxistes et libertaires* (Paris: Éditions Mille et Une Nuits, 2014).

specificity of both the translation and the line, or the line in translation. True, even Besancenot has his Engels moments of explication, but his idea in redescribing value extraction is to puncture the "liberal fantasy" of equality as a discourse that, by reform or by ideological obfuscation, seeks to maintain the core of capitalist exploitation. The very fact of *Le Capital*'s extension in seriality, not just to the bound volume of 1875, but to the return of *Le Capital* as a manga, reveals the contradictory logic of two serials that in their relation generate politics and culture. Both serials appear unbounded, the apeiron of appearance, one in the inertial persistence of capital accumulation; the other, in the repetition and difference of its critique of political economy. Yet both are resolutely historical and, while Besancenot remarks that the world of capitalism Marx analyzes has not fundamentally changed, there is enough dynamism to warrant thinking and reading through its story as a movement in history itself.

We have noted the point in *Capital in manga* where exploitation fosters resistance and the repeated cry to deny enslavement. The French version takes up Karl's plea to other workers to ask questions and to oppose capitalism's domination of everyday life but adds sentiment to sharpen the distinctions in play. Thus, whereas the Japanese manga asks what are we working for, *Le Capital* also questions why workers are compelled to labor under any conditions, like fatigue and immiseration, as if to concretize the necessity to question in this instance. The issue is not a better text but one that dialogically engages a reader familiar with the question and the political discourse in which it lives. Much of the exegesis of Marx's definitions and calculations remains the same and, although a cheese factory narrative might seem more contrived or clichéd in a French context, *Le Capital* appears intent on bearing witness to a different genealogy in Marx's text, "une libre adaptation en manga" as it puts it, that simultaneously speaks back to Marx's translation/serialization. Obviously, this is not simply the project Marx had in mind for his translation and editing in *Le Capital*, nor does it provide the conceptual and critical nous of Michael Heinrich's "*Le Capital* après la MEGA," which seeks to assess some of the impact of the original MEGA project (an effort truncated by Stalinism) and its refiguration/extension in MEGA^{2}, the massive and ongoing attempt to gather and publish a more complete archive (at least 140 volumes in four parts) of Marx and Engels' writings.[27] *Le Capital*, the manga, is also "after" the MEGA but it does not seek to "complete" Marx's *Le Capital* in any explicit manner. The manga is undoubtedly a "minor" or "small" literature in Deleuze and Guattari's sense, in its framing of collective experience, political expression, and most pointedly in its deterritorialization of language and form.[28] In seriality, the line of flight is at least doubled in the sense that *Le Capital* the manga claims a new space of understanding from *Le Capital* while simultaneously representing a scission with capitalist command. The substance of value Marx explicates is necessarily irreducible to its serialization, or to a sampling in manga form, yet the point is that how this Soleil Manga comes to be is not only after Marx's *Le Capital*, or indeed after MEGA, but within the substance of its value for a class critique of political economy. In this way, to understand the living-on of Marx's desire to reach a working-class readership, the manga is not a microscopic reproduction of *Capital* in pictures (in lithographs, or as a bande dessinée) but is an abstraction of its immanent present (as I suggested earlier, the impossibility of serial authenticity is precisely a present conjunction) This is another way "Le mort saisit le vif" as Marx puts it in his preface to *Le Capital*, a preface to his own appearance as a "serial figure" in the sense of

---

27 See Michael Heinrich, "*Le Capital* après la MEGA" in Alix Bouffard, Alexandre Feron, Guillaume Fondu and Michael Heinrich, *Ce qu'est Le Capital de Marx* (Paris: Les éditions sociales, 2017), pp. 7–90. In the essay that follows, "Les éditions françaises du Capital" (pp. 91–145), the authors, Bouffard, Feron and Fondu, provide a detailed chronology of *Le Capital* across its editions in French. Two dimensions are notable: first, although "livraisons successive" are mentioned regarding Roy's translation, nothing is said about the innovation of this form for the French version nor indeed what is extant of it; second, the book asks what is Marx's *Capital*, but there is no consideration of a French version that, in its translation of a Japanese manga, asks the same question for a contemporary French readership. Obviously, *Le Capital* is not Marx's *Le Capital*, but part of the argument here is that Marx's *Le Capital* is not *Capital* either, and productively so.

28 See Gilles Deleuze and Félix Guattari, *Kafka: Toward a Minor Literature* (Dana Polan trans.) (Minneapolis, MN: University of Minnesota Press, 1986). The minor emerges as a much larger topic—politics—and is essential to the reading practice.

Denson and Mayer,[29] a spirit of resistance in *Capital in manga* ("Even if I am dead am I dead?") or in the French version, where Engels' question is about living and Marx answers, "et plus que jamais, sacrebleu."

The repositioning of the Japanese manga in French is not interested in correcting it or in normalizing its representation of *Capital*, but in meeting the challenge of a French reader at the time. *Capital in manga*, for instance, may represent the 2008 crisis as potentially a tornadic turmoil but this is experienced differently across the manga's serial production.

On the one hand, *Capital in manga* attempts to draw the consequences of a classic contradiction examined in Marx's critique of capitalism. Thus, the expansion of capital disrupts the balance between supply and demand and, if a financial crisis follows this, "a great storm called the depression" is heading our way. It is a crude analysis and adds a little alarmism for good measure (accentuated by sound effect words) since no one was quite sure how the globality of the 2007–2008 crisis would specifically impact the Japanese economy (one could argue the real "storm" for Japan was unleashed a little later by the quake, tsunami, and Fukushima disaster of 2011). By contrast, the French understanding of the crisis has the benefit not just of two or more years of hindsight, but also its mediation of French exception to capitalist trauma, even within the EU. The narrative (in figure 24 below) suggests the increase in capital needs to produce more and more goods which creates an imbalance between supply and demand, and can lead to a panic in the markets, which in turn results, "undeniably," in a financial crisis. There is a difference here between what is surmised and what is experienced and, while the French interpretation reproduces the gist of the Japanese text (the section on "panic," and adds its own sound effect, "broooh") it draws simultaneously on the concrete conjunction of the crisis for the French economy. Even if *Capital in manga* does not begin as a direct reflection of capitalist crisis, its own globality in mediation and translation permits precisely this entanglement, one that cannot sit still with its status as edumanga because of the socio-economic relations it confronts.

29 See Shane Denson and Ruth Meyer, "Spectral Seriality: The Sights and Sounds of Count Dracula" in Frank Kelleter (ed.), *The Media of Serial Narrative* (Columbus, OH: Ohio State University Press, 2017), pp. 108–24.

FIGURE 23. Variety Artworks, *Capital in Manga*! *2* (2009), p. 159.

FIGURE 24. Variety Artworks, *Le Capital 2*, p. 159.

After the final declaration of the first volume of the manga *Le Capital*, "Nous ne sommes . . . Les esclaves de personne!", with Karl arrested for protesting and Robin remaining the ever-anxious capitalist, Soleil Manga makes sure to add a hook to maintain its series and publishing project. It explains the manga is drawn primarily from Marx's *Capital* Volume One, a critique that reveals not just capitalist processes but also provides a "materialist philosophical method" to trace its emergence and overthrow ("renversement") capitalism. If the Japanese manga promotes itself as a bridge to Marx's magnum opus, the French translation offers an "entryway," then approximately quotes the Eleventh Thesis on Feuerbach, "Les philosophes ont diversement interprété le monde. Il s'agit maintenant de le transformer" (a variation on "Les philosophes n'ont fait qu'interpréter diversement le monde, il s'agit maintenant de le transformer"). The note is salutary, and emphasizes, however modestly, the role serial engagement plays in world changing or, in the case of *Le Capital*, the difference between reprinting and imprinting. Recall the moment of Marx's *Le Capital* was significantly linked to the crisis represented by the violent suppression of the Paris Commune a few months before (although Marx had considered a French translation of *Capital* earlier). In their "résumé du volume 2" Soleil Manga further situate the "storm" figured above by referring to "les crises générales du marché mondial comme celle qui a démarré en 2007 aux Etats-Unis et s'est etendue à tous les pays développés." Rather than assume the relevance of the text the reader is invited to imagine the depth of its connections. There is a further challenge, however, which we will address by way of conclusion: if seriality finds new readers, in different languages and forms, does its division and extension remain at the level of interpretation and how is its logic in itself a mode of active participation in social change and transformation?

CONCLUSION: TELLING CAPITAL

Revolution implies a transformation in storytelling, of socialization, perhaps of socio-economic organization, and even of the means of production. The claim may be justified for most of these dimensions, but storytelling? Stories are not so much revolutionized by social change but attempt to inscribe and participate in how such a process takes place, even if storytelling is never limited to that compulsion. We speak of storytelling as a human reflex and its modes are capacious and historical. Walter Benjamin, of course, argued that whatever the stories, the storyteller themselves was a reduced figure, and ponders Nikolai Leskov in this regard. He then notes, "The art of storytelling is reaching its end because the epic side of truth, wisdom, is dying out. This, however, is a process that has been going on for a long time. And nothing would be more fatuous than to want to see in it merely a "symptom of decay," let alone a "modern" symptom. It is, rather, only a concomitant symptom of the secular productive forces of history, a concomitant that has quite gradually removed narrative from the realm of living speech and at the same time is making it possible to see a new beauty in what is vanishing."[1] The theoretical implications of what Benjamin suggests are profound even as I remain more sanguine about the living speech of the storyteller (not because of technology like audible books which no doubt are succumbing to AI avatars, but because the raconteur in general continues to help array the everyday). It may well be that serialization is a counter valence of storytelling's "gradual removal" but that its logic necessarily reconfigures how stories are composed, disseminated, and by all means survive. We have noted this push and pull of narrative desire in the examples above, and especially in the context of a book project that critiques how economic oppression occurs and how reading this critique might reach those whose

1 See Walter Benjamin, "The Storyteller: Observations on the Works of Nikolai Leskov" in *Selected Writings*, 3: *1935–1938* (Howard Eiland and Michael W. Jennings eds) (Cambridge, MA: Harvard University Press, 2006), pp. 143–62; here, p. 146.

agency is not outside the conditions of capitalism's demise. Yet one might also say in response to Benjamin that, even with the serial survivre of *Capital*, whatever the working-class agency of its readers, to storytell *Capital* is only to realize once more its diminished capacity and anachronistic impress in praxis across a range of social contestation. Conversely, if there is no archetype of such storytelling or storyteller it is because of the link to the process of transformation itself, the uniqueness immanent to change: a story contingent precisely on the event of revolution, an expressivity born in the degree zero of a world turned upside down. Narrative contradictions abound. Trotsky, of course, tells the story of the Russian Revolution as a history, and to the extent that a revolution is pinned to the syntax of history, it is documented first within such a grammar. The event of revolution without history is still an event, but more one of ideology and fantastic projection, perhaps even of false consciousness, even as a world still to win is a challenge, a world before us. Trotsky, however, suggests a specific kind of history is at stake:

> The history of a revolution, like every other history, ought first of all to tell what happened and how. That, however, is little enough. From the very telling it ought to become clear why it happened thus and not otherwise. Events can neither be regarded as a series of adventures, nor strung on the thread of a preconceived moral. They must obey their own laws. The discovery of these laws is the author's task.[2]

In "serial Marx" we do not see necessarily the laws specific to an event of revolution that may not live beyond the moment, and yet it is still possible to discern a logic of structure in the telling, *Capital* as story, one that allows a spirit of revolution itself to live on—a series then not of adventures but of a concept that grounds their possibility (while avoiding, of course, all trace of what Trotsky refers to as "pedantic schematism"!). The challenge from the outset here has been the series is at once out of step with the event as irruption, and to storytell in series would seem to undo the notion a transformation is taking or has taken place. In this we conjecture that

---

2 Leon Trotsky, *History of the Russian Revolution* (Chicago, IL: Haymarket Books, 2008), p. *xv*.

the time of revolution in series is posed as a future conditional, like the frightful hobgoblin haunting Europe in the *Communist Manifesto*. History congeals in the moment the future meets its series, as if the series realizes its history in coming to an end. One is reminded the proletariat does not seek to extend its being but finish it, a moment that is the beginning of its history if not history as such. Seriality, like revolution itself, is replete with such dialectical antinomies, which must necessarily evince a discrepant and distinct relation to narrating social change.

But anything can happen in series: it is, to borrow from Bakhtin, an adventure time of storytelling and its chronotope (not a list of adventures in Trotsky's sense), that might usefully be made episodic in extension.[3] But what if serial division, for instance, was itself a mediation of historic process? This would not negate other factors (an axiology of accumulation or a convenience of allotted time), and indeed these are by far the most evident, quotidian almost, in social practice. Clearly, we have only begun to address the political, theoretical, and formal problems of serializing *Capital*, and by taking only one thread in reading *Capital* and representing it, via *Le Capital*, *Capital in lithographs*, *Capital in manga*, and *Le Capital* (encore), one cannot purport to have solved its enigma, or capital's in general. This is not to say, however, that the heuristic of *Capital* in series is not a provocation, especially if one takes seriously the idea seriality (again, somewhat contra Sartre) enables a story of capital, modernity in a specific key, where an ending is dialectically concretized. Culture is alive to capital's unfinished series, one that is paradoxically bound to historical sublation even as culture simultaneously nourishes its extension. The conundrum can be stated thus: the extension of *Capital* in series is necessarily imbricated, directly or symptomatically, to capital's persistence, yet simultaneously marks a division across its logic or hegemonic pretensions. By itself, the revelation of content in reading *Capital*—"Yes, this is what capital does or capitalism is doing"—is not decisive (somebody else reading in the queue, waiting perhaps for work at Ford or Toyota, may simply recoil at *Capital*'s abstractions or recalcitrant Germanisms); but neither is

3 See Mikhail Bakhtin, "Forms of Time and of the Chronotope in The Novel" in *The Dialogic Imagination* (Michael Holquist ed., Caryl Emerson and Michael Holquist trans) (Austin, TX: University of Texas Press, 1981).

formal innovation alone, particularly in manga (which predates *Capital*) a guarantee that consciousness will find in critique an insurrectionary idea. What the logic, or law in Trotsky's reckoning, suggests is that without prescribing form a form is always at stake (just as for Benjamin, in a living voice the storyteller's fate is in play), one that dares to suggest what might seem like an individual or monadic experience can become, in a moment of crisis and critique, a time of collective reciprocity, a serial engagement in the social. Capitalist hegemony does not abjure bad reading and anti-capitalism demonstrably has no monopoly on a good reading. All seriality says in this context is that what exhausts a story is not a lack of imagination but the historical conditions for its extension. The critique of *Capital* is in its title not its subtitle and seriality, whatever else it is, is its death sentence (*l'arrêt de mort* as both a sign of execution and its stay). The limits of the example, however, weigh heavily on the capacity to theorize from it.

Perhaps, to draw further from Benjamin's comments, to storytell capital (as relation) is to reflect upon the tension between seriality as a harbinger of a certain entropy in its story (not necessarily of a falling rate of profit, but of constitutive limits in expansion and maintenance) and the potential for new beauty, the liveliness of manga aesthetics for instance, or the stark presencing of the lithographic line. Benjamin argues a story is not about its information or that which is pinned to its present and, in a time of live feeds and meme virality, one should add the time of information itself has been radically foreshortened. Instead, "A story is different. It does not expend itself. It preserves and concentrates its strength and is capable of releasing it even after a long time."[4] This is something of the *potenza* and *potentia* where I began, where seriality confounds the dogma of containment, or the attempt to individuate in isolation all who participate in it. The dialectics of seriality, however, do not in themselves provide an exit from the contradictions of storytelling capital, which extend well beyond how inventively one might sample Marx's *Capital*.

To engage the series that is *Capital* is never simply to add to it but is to confront the grounds for its extension—as a new edition, as a new translation, as another volume in MEGA², as an inspiration for various

4 Benjamin, "Storyteller," p. 148.

kinds of creative rearticulation. These efforts may find a newness in Marx's vast and intensive project and indeed realize their own "new beauty" by addressing what lives beyond its moment. Gellert's graphic reinscription and juxtaposition of text and image, for example, is an amazing way to experience concrete elements of Marx's critique, but as a direct engagement with the class, race, and gender relations of the United States at that time. The drawings and order of Gellert's understanding of *Capital* are mediated by the upheavals of the Thirties and by Gellert's commitment to identify key areas of social contradiction and struggle. The serialization of *Le Capital* is the beginning of an idea in this direction, yet whose own process is thwarted by the overdeterminations of crisis in post-Commune France, and by seriality chasing Marx's text all over the map. If not initially, then eventually, *Capital in manga* is also mediated by crisis, yet we have noted a certain detachment in its formal engagement that on the one hand finds in manga a storytelling that is much more than illustration; but, on the other hand, is not necessarily driven by a political commitment to remedy the economic conditions explored. The mise en scene of late nineteenth century White European capitalism as a conceit in situating the history of Marx's text works as a historical phenomenon, and sanctions to an extent Engels' appearance in the second volume of the manga. Does the popularity of the Japanese manga prove the organic relation of its representations to the experience of crisis in Japan 2007–2008? This is certainly not a manga project that resonates strongly with concepts of racial capitalism, the anticolonialism of the Global South, or with contemporary discourses of gender and sexuality, all of which engage the meanings of *Capital* by struggling forcefully with and against the spirit of its critical mode. There are symptoms of reaccentuation, some of which I have invoked, but it is noticeable subsequent translations of *Capital in manga* have attempted to reframe its intervention as something that is globalist by *Capital*'s design, even if this is hardly incidental to manga's global circulation as a cultural symbolic. Clearly, *Le Capital* the manga is inspired by manga as formal innovation (as Besancenot underlines) not by its specific representation of capitalism's story, the cheese factory correlative, etc. In provocative fashion, these limits demonstrate the material force of seriality for social change. How?

Marx probes serial logic for its capacity for commitment. How does one come to *Capital*, or to the Marxism of which it is a pivotal part? Marx knows he cannot adjudicate response directly but he is confident serialization can encourage a deeper worker and working knowledge of the conditions of existence. The cultural logic of the serial embraces, albeit contingently, a habit of engagement. What Marx, and Lachâtre for that matter, sees in *Le Capital* as serial is an opening to reflection which, by division and extension, intimates a commonplace of anti-capitalism adequate to the challenge of everyday capitalist command in post-Commune France. By reflecting on the philosophical elements of seriality we have traced several limits not just in the social imprint of series, but in its immanent design, where the relay of radical thinking meets the challenge of storytelling in general (what can be articulated, by whom, with story itself as a metonym of concretization, the real, the living). These limits remain constitutive, even if the desire to reach a broader audience, to have *Capital* read by any means necessary, is not in itself an idealistic whim or a project shorn of practicality. The question of seriality does not mediate the form of crisis or its response in any mechanical fashion, but we have suggested the return or extension of Marx's critique is greater than a nostalgic tic and is linked to the dynamic persistence of capitalism and the concreteness of specific socio-economic contradictions. In series there is an appropriateness of form and not just an opportunism in one. To reframe Benjamin once more, the series permits a storytelling process that, in light of the present, accentuates a past is at stake (in contradistinction to the idea this potential has been irredeemably lost). Social change in this respect is not caused by seriality but is an opening onto what is contingent in it taking place. Marx's writing finds life in series yet this does not mean that it can only persist in serialization. The abruption of capitalist crisis draws on Marx's critique of political economy because of a desire to tell not just its correspondence but also its difference in persistence. Storytelling perhaps resists the history and positivism of *Capital*'s critique even if, in edumanga and endless guides, it is easily reducible to information and graphic replication. It is not enough to say manga is another way of telling capital, even if, in the reach of its commodification and consumption, it is one more example of serial manufacture. The reason I have stressed the lacunae or ellipses of *Capital in manga* is because they are symptomatic of more than Marx's *Capital* can possibly say. They are an index of silences in *Capital*, about capital, and the marks of seriality. Marx himself realized the possible shortfall in attempting a serialized *Le Capital*, but tried anyway, in large part because of the inkling of periodicity and readership learned from years of professional journalism (which similarly offered engagement via dissemination). Yet consciousness of vernacular is not consciousness through vernacularization, and it is important to stress again that assuming a reader does not mean finding one. We might say the working-class reader is no less absent for *Capital in manga* than it was for Marx's serial project in French. The series only motivates a desire, a singularity without affiliation, as Deleuze puts it, but in its process it finds a logic of story integral to how singularity takes place, or the evental in revolutionary change. *Capital* is not a story of capital but, because so many people have a lifelong experience of the dynamic conditions of capitalism, seriality extends familiarity with its meanings, which is also the capacity to change them. In John Berger's *Once in Europa* (the second volume of the trilogy, *Into Their Labors*) the narrator notes, "If every event which occurred could be given a name, there would be no need for stories. As things are here, life outstrips our vocabulary. A word is missing and so the story has to be told."[5] Clearly, to storytell capital does not end capitalism but in seriality maintains a vigilance to the missing word or event in its attenuation. Vigilance here is a creative form of unsettling. Even if Marx's vocabulary may have outstripped his desired reader, serial engagement can find his text and crisis will discover its story necessary to tell. One can engage *Capital* and capitalism outside series, but in seriality one may yet grasp both the necessary conditions of their persistence but also, for determinate and concrete reasons, the ways in which their stories are overreached.

5 John Berger, *Once in Europa* (New York: Pantheon, 1987), p. 77.

PART TWO

"Other" Serializations

Serialization as Other

"What effect does the life we lead have on you?"
"Well, I say, the effect is like seeing a riverbank before us which one must reach."
"Me," he went on, "it feels like reading a book with images."
—Louise Michel, *La commune*, 1898

There is some confusion about the identity of Michel's interlocutor here. She is accompanied by an old "zouave pontifical" who, several passages earlier had been characterized as "jet black," although, because of vagaries in the punctuation, he has also been interpreted as two separate comrades. If anything, the text favors the former, yet the various histories of the zouaves pontifical (or the smaller "Volontaires de l'Ouest," as the French contingent fighting the Prussians was called) mention only one to three soldiers of African descent, out of at least five thousand at the time. Further, while the French "volontaires" disbanded when Prussians troops entered Paris at the end of the siege, almost all of the remaining zouaves pontifical, the international force, went to Poitiers, then on to Rennes, and subsequently fought with Thiers' forces. Members of the zouaves pontifical are known to have participated in the massacre of Communards in May 1871. This zouave force (rather than the "volontaires") was eventually dissolved in August of 1871. It is certain that zouaves joined the uprising, but these were much more likely to be long-standing regulars from light infantry regiments of the French army, originally drawn from Zwawa Berbers of Algeria from the 1830s on, rather than the Papal Zouaves, despite the obvious similarities in uniform.

TOWARDS THE SERIAL AS HISTORY AND IMAGE

Radical change exists in seriality when serialization confronts its prescriptions. Repetition without difference sharply constrains the alternative possibilities of the social dynamic it presents and represents. Some inertia is to be expected, but order for its own sake masks the propensities of division in extension. In the case of *Capital*, lots of versions of Marx's text maintain its serial impress not simply by reasserting a hermeneutical fidelity, but also by taking its critique as a representational challenge of reading the present. The issue here is not the status of *Capital* as a historical document; the emphasis is rather on its next issue, the extent to which its serial conditions, both within and between its representations, animate the presence of its challenge to the ways in which political economy is lived today. This is much more than a question of relevance: seriality examines living-on as a capacity for living differently. The bulk of serials and series, of course, maintain seriality's primary function to mediate the social as a recognizable continuum. There are other serializations that question this logic as a social compact, as a narrative mode, and as an understanding of sequence in its material abstractions. Similarly, the other in serialization is not limited to a variation on subject apprehension (another subject in series) but it can confront the recuperation of difference in series as a means to make such difference count differently. Othering of this kind is both narratological (a kind of compositional difference) and necessarily ontological, since it thinks through what makes up being. Part Two, then, will not only provide other examples of seriality's claims to "tell" differently but will also examine how elements of othering inflect the ways social change is conceived in series. To begin, let us pick up on where we found Marx in 1871.

As Marx reflected on the civil war in France and the violent denouement of the Paris Commune, he not only pondered the political consequences of a massive conflagration as class war but also the problem between representing the revolution in time and the idea of revolutionary time. The radical leftist in the face of defeat is often caricatured through stoic resignation—words to the effect that the collapse of the Commune in 1871 just means the time was not right, the conditions were not ripe, all that makes the moment did not conjoin. The ascriptions are justified to the extent that the facts of defeat appear largely uncontestable and that the plethora of information (it was an event plump with documentation and archival élan, some of which will be referenced below) accentuates not a caesura of history but its inveterate inertia, especially prized by those who benefit from the latter. The Commune failed because this is the truth of history that dares exception and any attendant narrative disconnection. Conversely, the Commune is a revolutionary inspiration and its defeat is a success waiting to happen; or rather, social change does not wait on historical judgment but continues to fight every historical inevitability deemed to contain it. What makes history at this level also means confronting an event in its pre-history, that the conjunction is never simply a line of flight from the material substance of possibility. The triumph of the Haitian Revolution, for instance, is neither accident nor incident but a long-formed constellation of anti-colonial and anti-racist desire.[1] A rendezvous of victory is a moment for celebration and is also a turning point where history might begin or begin again.

In Part One we addressed the troubled conceptualization of seriality in dialectical tension with Marx's attempt to serialize *Le Capital* (a project that emerged between a publisher notably exiled as a Communard and an exile from both Germany and France living in London). *Le Capital* was read as a provocation to investigate how one might "tell" capital, not just as Marx's text, but as a story of a socio-economic relation. The contemporary pertinence of capital as relation does not automatically grant unalloyed applicability to Marx's *Capital*, yet the exploration of its renewed manifestations has provided lessons about the exigent role of seriality in the living on of anti-capitalist critique and culture. Is this a genre of radical cultural history? Serialization in culture might seem to offer a typology of forms and genres: from the novel, journal, and magazine

---

1 The importance of this event cannot be overemphasized. See, for instance, C. L. R. James, *The Black Jacobins: Toussaint L'Ouverture and the San Domingo Revolution* (New York: Vintage, 1989).

to manga, the blog, the podcast, TikTok videos, Instagram and various social feeds, the phenomenon of the franchise, and prestige tv. Each mode promises extension and division, and none are simply outside the capacity or will to commodification under capitalism, crosscut by powerful contradictions in modernity, technological change, and crucially, in time. Is an adaptation of Marx's text more successful than the effort spurred by Marx's original idea for a French serial of *Capital*? Are workers more likely to read *Capital in manga* cover to cover than any expert translation of Marx's disquisition on the value form? Such questions of likelihood and success are somewhat empty gestures and a misrecognition of what is at stake in taking seriality seriously. David Harvey's online courses in reading *Capital* provide brilliant exegesis and commentary on the complex ideas and processes in Marx's work, but at no point does Harvey offer these as a substitute for reading *Capital* itself.[2] Perhaps the "bridge" to *Capital* is sturdier in Harvey's pedagogy than that of Variety Artworks, but in general it is seriality's demand that is at issue, and specifically in relation to what grounds social understanding of the contradictory conditions of existence. Such a demand is not in itself a return to *Capital* qua capital as some form of narrow orthodoxy (the MEGA^2 is not in the service of future-proofing the critique of *Capital* as a critique of capital). Instead, seriality attends to what is manifest in extension and division as a kind of unfinished business in socioeconomic contradiction. The end of a series is only one dimension of historical closure.

A history of seriality has been invoked earlier, and it is clearly in an uneven relationship to how history is composed. Rather than a reattachment to linearity as a normative series of events, seriality suggests something more volatile, disjunctive, and oblique where even the apparent conformity of the queue lines up exception. While this is not the place to discuss variant theorizations of the compositional elements of history, these too do not simply inform how social change is conceived and arrayed. Indeed, the anodyne phrase "subject to history" is particularly resonant for the subjectivation of seriality (as the historical distinction of the subject

2 Harvey's lifelong dedication to understanding and teaching Marx and Marxism is exemplary. For more on his projects and publications, see davidharvey.org (last accessed: August 26, 2025).

in series, which I have used to connect characterization in storytelling capital). Such a view, however, is inexorably tested both by concrete histories of subjection, and by history interrupted, when what is subject to history calls history itself to a historical reckoning. Seriality is hardly a metonym of this rupture, yet it interrogates the logic in which it may be understood. From this perspective, seriality is not a functional explanation of the forces and relations of production but an entry point into the time and space of their contradictions. Crisis intensifies serial engagement. Whenever history is announced as secure in its endgame, crisis appears to trouble its teleology. Marx himself responds to the historical crisis of the Paris Commune not just by directly addressing comrades who seek an understanding of its promise and paroxysm, but by throwing his energy into an intellectual project that might forcefully connect with those living the uprising in immediate proximity.

The crisis and immediacy of history is very much to the fore in Marx's Third Address to the General Worker's Council of May 1871.[3] If the earlier addresses outline a basic litany of causes, of macropolitical machinations and economic dysfunction, the Third Address (split into four sections) crystallizes not just a sense of crisis but of a crisis in the concept of history that attends to it. The enormity of the historical question, for class war and social struggle, for an otherwise obtuse rendering of event and change, is not settled by Marx's address, not least because of the Paris Commune's historical immediacy; yet the framing of Marx's analysis will help us move from the telling of capital to the telling of history as a conditional crux of seriality. Seriality enables a sense of event, which is an important part of its shaping as history. I do not mean this in terms of the series of addresses Marx makes themselves, but in terms of the historical challenge and the challenge to history the Paris Commune represents to Marx and Marxism. Twenty years after the Paris Commune, in his preface to the collected addresses on the civil war in France, Engels offers a textbook example of Marxist history.[4] It is not just a detailed description of the events precipitating the Commune but it offers an approach replete with a narrative

3 Marx's work on the civil war in France has been collated on marxists.org: rebrand.ly/3cedd6 (last accessed: August 26, 2025).

4 See Engels's 1891 Postscript here: rebrand.ly/1c3250 (last accessed: August 26, 2025).

of class war. Eschewing both a tale of "great men" and a story limited to the difference of belligerent states, Engels instead focuses on determinate schisms of class and the challenge of overcoming them. Initially, the method seems bound to the declarative ("the position of Paris has been such that no revolutions could break out there without assuming a proletarian character") but then Engels quickly settles in to a discussion of the class characteristics of the key factions before and during the civil war. True, specific circumstances, the rise of Louis Bonaparte, the war with Prussia, did not in themselves make for proletarian uprising, yet Engels braids these processes with those of longstanding political constituency, economic conditions, and elements of chance (that the National Guard effectively armed the workers in the face of Prussian advances on Paris would prove crucial in mounting an insurrection). Engels records how the Commune built rapidly on its advantage and consciousness of its moment by reorganizing social divisions towards a common good but, as we will shortly examine in more detail, the proximity of the Prussian army and the collusions of the Versailles government of Adolphe Thiers would not permit these infrastructural transformations to take root.

It is not a long piece, but Engels' postscript as preface is packed with pertinent dimensions for a historical understanding of the Paris Commune. Its role, formally, is to set the scene for the distinctiveness of Marx's rousing presentations, which is to say generically, and symptomatically, Marx's approach to the Paris Commune is history in another key. There are several ways to think of this, not least in the contrast between class antagonism as the history of event and the temporality of immediate interpretation. Marx's addresses, like his journalism and critique, lean more towards a hermeneutics of history rather than history as such (hence the contrast and perhaps necessity of Engels' preface). His predilection was, like Brecht many years later, to start with the "bad new things"[5] then work these into a longue durée (labor in its pre-history) so that history emerges in the situational poised on the recollection. *Le Capital* and "The Civil War in France" are both responses to the Paris Commune and are bound by a serial desire to articulate/translate the meaning of anti-capitalism for labor.

5 See Walter Benjamin, "Conversations with Brecht" in Ernst Bloch et al. *Aesthetics and Politics* (Anna Bostock trans.) (London: Verso, 1980), p. 69.

In a sense, such writing interpellates labor as an absent/presence, not as an actual reader/listener, but as the form of subject that would "make" the history the texts do not otherwise contain.

Engels' concern for the happening of history and Marx's inkling for its emergence are central to a Marxist dialectic of history but do not exhaust the potential in its expressive forms, which below will be explored in terms of the Commune's "graphic ideas." Symptoms of this promise can certainly be discerned in the *Jeztzeit* or now time of Marx's third address,[6] although the logic of such time hardly assures victory (one thinks, for instance, of Robyn C. Spencer's evocative history of the Black Panthers where the reversals of Black Power are pointedly referred to as "changing same").[7] Marx grasps the "turmoil of surprise" as a quickly shifting scene of betrayal and opportunity. Arming the citizens in the cause of national defense could be propitious but for the fact Parisian workers might not smile on a republic forged (as in forgery, as Marx makes clear) with class hegemony over worker alternatives in mind. As always, Marx is unflinching in his ridicule of the government's maneuvers before the Prussian aggressors (he terms them the "capitulards," and Thiers is a "monstrous gnome"), yet the tone cannot avoid grim resolution given the magnitude of defeat. Indeed, despite the pillorying of those who would deny the people's desire for radical change, Marx's address channels the aura of a requiem of revolution, a teachable series for radical opposition. If the substance of revolutionary fervor is to be understood, the address wants to hold at bay for as long as possible the finality of defeat in favor of appreciating the internal logic that structures the contingency of its moment.

True, Marx does not offer his account as impassive or studiously neutral. His representation of the Commune's non-violence is notable, although it is fair to say the cannons at Montmartre had a little more than symbolic value. Similarly, the summary execution on March 18, 1871, of

6 *Jetztzeit* is redolent in Benjamin's notion that "The dialectical image is an image that emerges suddenly, in a flash." See Benjamin, *Arcades Project*, p. 473 [N9,7].

7 See Robyn C. Spencer, *The Revolution Has Come: Black Power, Gender, and the Black Panther Party in Oakland* (Durham, NC: Duke University Press, 2016), p. 1. The contingent tension rests between a change that is the same and a same that is irrevocably changed. A different order of time is at stake in revolution.

both General Claude Lecomte and General Jacques Léon Clément-Thomas in the aftermath of the failed attempt by the National Assembly to capture the Montmartre cannons is read as either "they had it coming" or as regrettable collateral damage. Marx also intimates that not being more proactive militarily, as in immediately marching to Versailles to depose Thiers, fatally compromised the uprising, an initial reaction that would take on the substance of tactical, if not historical truth (conditional elements would have to include the relative strength of the military of the Third Republic, and again, the looming position of the Prussian army). On the whole, Marx eschews the subjunctive and the speculative for lessons from a history that is, in pondering revolution (post-1848 in particular), largely understood: "After every revolution marking a progressive phase in the class struggle, the purely repressive character of the state power stands out in bolder and bolder relief." If history has a discernible yet variable shape, its path for Marx, according to a science of productive modes (forces and relations of production), leads to communism. His reflections on the Paris Commune explicitly acknowledge the event as a demonstrable symptom of such transformation, but it is just as clear the countervailing forces, including "state power," heavily mitigate the prospect of worker victory and any future of classlessness. Statements like "the working class had not yet acquired the faculty of ruling the nation" are not history but they abound with provocation. Is this a consciousness derived from social being or is this faculty in fact a false consciousness since the eclipse of proletarianization could also lead to the sublation of its national form? Then there is the scale of transformation. A revolution in one country from Marx to now has continually been questioned for the limited scope and generalization of its aims, particularly since it can be isolated or otherwise ostracized. Here, Marx wants to emphasize the work of change itself as a powerful resource which, if not history in the way Engels writes it, is a radically materialist disposition.

Marx asserts the Commune is the antithesis of Empire, and is the positive form of the "social republic" outlined earlier in 1871 as the French people tried to extricate themselves from the forces represented by both Thiers and Bismarck. He outlines some of its rapid achievements and modes of organization regarding policing, property, and the free provision of education. The ambition of the Commune cannot be overstated—for a few weeks in Paris in 1871 the world witnessed a striking representation of people power; neither a model nor a blueprint, the Commune has yet inspired any number of attempts to wrest control of the means of production in the name of a thoroughgoing equitable redistribution of public good. But how does this bear on history, and seriality which is our main concern? Because Marx is elaborating the Paris Commune from the position of its proximate defeat a few days earlier, he accentuates not just its extraordinary achievements but also the outline of its desire. Again, in his address Marx is less concerned with the "what ifs" or permutations of revolutionary possibility but the real foundations of social change, the base on which a political and economic vision is constructed. Marx notes the Commune's very presence "presupposed the non-existence of monarchy" and, much to the alarm of those who favored a bourgeois status quo and monarchical gesture, "the Commune intended to abolish that class property which makes the labor of the many the wealth of the few." The force of change was driven by desire not expectation—this is the possibility in the otherwise impossible conditions of the Commune's brief existence, and this, for Marx, is a moment for history without meeting the conditions, at least in his Third Address, of a history made. These are not rhetorical gestures alone on Marx's part, although he well understands the dialogical necessity of engaging the crisis without resignation. We might say that while Marx was often brief on historical method (the concision of the concept of materialist history in the 1859 Preface to *A Contribution to the Critique of Political Economy* is an invitation to theorization rather than a procedure in itself)[8] he is continually broaching the terms of its apprehension. Eric Hobsbawm clarifies this approach:

> [T]he mode of production is the base of our understanding of the variety of human societies and their interactions, as well as of their historical dynamics. The mode of production is not identical with a society: "society" is a system of human relations, or, to be more precise, of relations between human groups. The "mode of

8 See, for instance, Marx's Preface to *A Contribution to the Critique of Political Economy*, in which he writes of the movement from the concise to the general: rebrand.ly/747feb (last accessed: August 26, 2025).

> production" (MOP) concept serves to identify the forces guiding the alignment of these groups—which can be done variously in different societies, within a certain range. Do the MOPs form a series of evolutionary stages, ordered chronologically or otherwise? There seems to be little doubt that Marx himself saw them as forming a series in which man's growing emancipation from, and control over, nature affected both the forces and the relations of production.[9]

The modes of production form a series in the ways they are enmeshed in uneven processes of division and extension in human socialization. It is important, however, to emphasize this a determinate rather than determinist instance of seriality's logic because the exact terms of socio-economic organization do not line up in a formulaic manner. The base of understanding does not account for the modes of its apprehension (although this is not a rationalization for missteps in Marx's conceptualizations, like the Asiatic mode of production). Again, seriality is not the cause of change but it is operative in what change can become. Interestingly, Hobsbawm ends his essay on Marx and history by suggesting there may come a time when no one asks whether a history is Marxist or not and this could be a sign that history has been so transformed by Marxist ideas its separate identity is no longer discernible. That the transformation precedes the one indicated in the mode of production critique itself underlines one series is not coterminous with the other and may indeed be in contradiction. Could the same be said of forms of representation of history?

Engels' preface to the *Civil War in France* offers a timeline of the Paris Commune in a history of class struggle. As we have noted, for his part, Marx wants to assure his listeners that what has not been defeated in the crushing of the Commune is its demonstrable desire, both in its brilliant activism and in the bravery of its social demand. Whereas Engels' statement predominantly follows the Paris Commune as event, allowing a form of history to, as it were, congeal, Marx's response lives the moment for a

9 Eric Hobsbawm, "Marx and History," *New Left Review* 143 (January–February 1984): 46.

history that history itself has not settled, the commune to come. Thus, "Within sight of that Prussian army, that had annexed to Germany two French provinces, the Commune annexed to France the working people all over the world." Rhetorically, the Commune achieved this in the name of the workers of the world and that is its lesson *for* history not *as* history. There is a form of time in revolution that permits such distinction, what Marx in the *Grundrisse* calls the living, form-giving fire of labor.[10] Obviously, labor time in capitalism is not identical with its form in social change and the difference itself may be thought of as historical contradiction. The time of labor in one can be posed as that of preservation through cycles of production and exchange; the time of the other is pinned to sublation and/or subsumption, in which the measure of the working day for instance is thoroughly reconstituted (not just in hours but in its experiential coordinates). The time of labor is also distinguished in its modes, a theoretical and practical challenge in so-called advanced or mature capitalist economies where classic factory practices of production have been either superseded or relocated by labor costs in globalization and by technological change. The differentiation of labor time coordinates contrasting forms of the labor subject and subjection. The immateriality of labor in one place is necessarily in dialectical tension with the material production of proletarianization elsewhere, a totality marked by forms of time (it is the inability to "see" time that erases or mystifies the constitution of labor elsewhere). The chronotope of the commune is not a simple allegorization of labor time, but I would suggest it challenges the logic of historical apprehension. Whereas Engels sees the history of the Paris Commune as a series of events, its now-time for Marx is part of a series yet to be, a time for labor unencumbered by capitalist command.

Seriality presupposes a problem of measure which here I am reading as a challenge of historical representation, one that could account both for the facts of the Paris Commune as event but also for its contested logic, "the form-giving fire." Marx, for instance, notes "The great social measure of the Commune was its own working existence. Its special measures could but betoken the tendency of a government of the people by the people." The measure here is to some extent spontaneous and improvised yet it

10 Marx, *Grundrisse* (Martin Nicolaus trans.), p. 286.

builds on political practices and forms of organization that precede and prepare March 18, 1871. Marx celebrates the creativity and the liberatory acts of the Commune but again, in the knowledge these have already been vanquished by *le semaine sanglante*. The experience of time itself is fractured and out of joint, seen for instance in the contrast between the bourgeois of the Versailles government quickly repopulating the restaurants of the Paris "freed" by Thiers' army (a motley yet heavily armed crew supplemented by prisoners of war released via negotiations with Bismarck), and the scenes of intense fighting and wholesale slaughter occurring just kilometers away. Marx notes how the Versailles government complains that the Communards are burning buildings as they retreat and that the bourgeois is revolted not by the mass killing but rather "is convulsed by horror at the desecration of brick and mortar!" There is indeed a convulsion at work in the destruction of property, yet also in the seeming irreconcilability of a roasted bird pulled apart at the dinner table in one space and women and children blown to pieces by cannon fire not far away. But then, as Marx also attempts to explain, when the Communards are prevented from using hostages for a truce, those prisoners, including most famously the Archbishop Darboy, are executed. Not surprisingly, these deaths are used to sanction not just further massacres by the Versaillais but all of the killing of the innocent up to that point. Marx is not trying to excuse Communard violence but he sees already how this history of conflagration will be written.

Given the coordination of France and Prussia in the defeat of the Commune, Marx asserts the international character of class war, and this too mediates what the chronotope the Paris Commune represents. Dialogically and polemically, of course, Marx reveals this time/space as in part the necessity for forming the International Working Men's Association and the General Council of the International, who he is addressing. The rhetorical and interpretive challenge is clear, but again serial engagement with the immediacy of the event does not produce history, or at least the kind of history represented by, for instance, Prosper Olivier Lissagaray's later *History of the Commune of 1871*.[11] In the introduction to her

11 Prosper-Olivier Lissagaray, *History of the Paris Commune of 1871* (Eleanor Marx trans.) (London: Verso, 2012).

translation of this work, Eleanor Marx notes it is "the only authentic and reliable history as yet written" about the Commune, in part because Lissagaray was directly involved in its moment (Marx maintains it is impartial because the account does not excuse the many missteps of the Commune in its constituency and activities). Lissagaray's history is closer to Engels' assessment although, like her father, Eleanor Marx takes the Commune as event to be a symptom and lesson of socialism's future. Again, like Karl, Eleanor does not seek to capture the moment that was the Paris Commune, but release it, to take its intervention as a political imaginary. On the one hand, we have the narrative of the Commune in its basic repetition: this is its recounting. On the other hand, Karl Marx's Third Address in May 1871 in particular, seeks a form for the Commune's revolutionary idea, what counts in his accounting. We have considered this living on, this logic of sense, in the story of *Capital*, but how does the chronotope of the Paris Commune come to live in this way?

When we imagine the Commune we do not simply reproduce its history but necessarily engage its presence, which is not its unalloyed truth, even in Alain Badiou's rendering of the Commune, but its desire, its call to articulation.[12] In their wonderfully inventive historical fiction, *Marx in Paris*, Michael Löwy and Olivier Besancenot (we have discussed Besancenot above in relation to *Le Capital*, the manga) offer a tantalizing conceit: what if Marx and his daughter Jenny went to Paris during the Commune and bore witness to the spirit Marx conjures in his address up close? Jenny tells Marx not to pack *Capital* (whose distribution in Paris, of course, is another story), so instead he takes Balzac's *Illusions Perdues*, itself a serial novel that on one level allegorizes how telling is being changed by paper manufacture and commercialization. The unspoken of *Marx in Paris* is that some illusions are lost for good historical reasons yet the articulation of revolutionary desire seeks new accounts. In a fictional diary by Jenny, Löwy/Besancenot insert formal markers into *Marx in Paris* to situate/authenticate the narrative. It is a playful yet reflective story that wonders aloud what a direct experience of the Commune would do to Marx's sense of political possibility. There are unsurprising moments of

12 See Alain Badiou, "The Paris Commune: A Political Declaration on Politics" in *Polemics* (Bruno Bosteels et al. trans) (London: Verso, 2006), pp. 257–90.

tendentiousness and potted dialogue (Marx, "shouldn't we also propose initiatives that call into question the private ownership of the means of production?" and "The infinite accumulation of fictitious capital is only one of the symptoms of economic crisis")[13] and the text borrows phrasing directly from Marx's addresses, but in general the narrative attempts to place Marx not just within the history "The Civil War in France" invokes but to intensify the "form-giving fire" of living the insurrection itself that Marx wants to carry forward and bring to any crisis of contradiction class war produces.

The meetings in *Marx in Paris* are "commune ex machina," allowing for some fairly basic explications of the Commune's work (the meeting with Lisa on the Union des Femmes, the chance encounter with a "revolutionary artist" who offers a brochure on the Federation of Artists and who emphasizes "we aim to put our motto, 'communal luxury,' within everyone's reach," etc.). Nevertheless, Löwy/Besancenot inscribe a more intimate people's history with a humanized Marx as part of its defamiliarization. Their reading of Marx's Third Address includes the idea that Marx wants to live the event of the uprising, so they have him "walk through insurgent Paris." How would Marx react to seeing the revolution and talking to prominent participants, like Eugène Varlin and Louise Michel? Because such figures are relatively well-known, they help to place the event for the contemporary reader, although the significance of the Commune lies in other parts of Karl and Jenny's walk, including the visit to a factory making wooden crates, where the workers have assumed complete control over the means of production. Louise Michel herself is presented as a firebrand but also as self-deprecating ("I am nothing, the Commune is everything").[14] Despite the meetings, overall, one gets very little sense that Karl or Jenny (or the reader) have reason to change their impressions of the Commune's historical meaning. The point seems to be to dramatize literally, to place Marx in the middle of the revolutionary action he so fervently contemplated and theorized. Marx, Löwy/Besancenot imply, had a special relationship to Paris, having lived there and written

13 Michael Löwy and Olivier Besancenot, *Marx in Paris* (Todd Cretien trans.) (Chicago, IL: Haymarket Books, 2022), pp. 19 and 59.

14 Löwy and Besancenot, *Marx in Paris*, p. 86.

about its historical role in social change. In their Postface, the authors describe their work as political fiction or imaginary history, one in which they hoped to reveal how Marx "learned from the event." In a vibrant flourish Löwy/Besancenot aver "the motivation for this attempt is entirely subjective" and "we tried to give shape to our dream through an imaginary story."[15] Readers with some familiarity about the Commune will not miss the history nor the fiction the authors offer. One could still say, however, that even if we do not witness what Marx learns from the event beyond the evidence of "The Civil War in France," the invocation of the imagination still conjures how the text of the event might continue to live in a political imaginary. *Marx in Paris* maintains the Left populism we noted in Besancenot's preface to the manga of *Le Capital*, yet steps back from the idea of "lived injustice" the earlier text conveyed. This is ironic, given much of Marx's Third Address channels the lived as an expression of crisis, and conveys a history that is living but has not been lived (the congelation of revolutionary event that arrives from the future). In a way, *Marx in Paris* notes the living history without being able to show it. The problem is not a lack of imagination, but rests to an important degree in the relationship of the imaginary to image.

So far, we have approached Marx's reading of the Paris Commune as in large part a dialectical and dialogical understanding of the time of contradiction, one caught between history's demand (indicated in my comments on Engels) and "the living, form-giving fire of labor" that inspires Marx's response. Fictionalizing this moment, as *Marx in Paris* does, provides a significant and not just supplementary dimension to the telling of uprising (much as we have attempted to do in the telling of *Capital*). In Part One, we have taken the challenge of reading *Capital* as one of seriality and sequential art (telling capital in both its articulation and in its illustration). To image capital raises a whole set of problems around the representation and explanation of what is properly a relation and not just a thing of human socialization and economic interaction. Although there are certainly images of revolution, the epistemological grounds of a revolutionary image are also much disputed. In the following case study, therefore, the "othering" of serialization is in part the problem of imaging

15 Löwy and Besancenot, *Marx in Paris*, p. 108.

relation and social transformation in both their distinction and imbrication. This is particularly important in how to read the Paris Commune, whose event and understanding as reported was cast against a backdrop of a complex and shifting terrain in the relationship of illustrated news and the graphic (via woodcuts, the daguerreotype, and the advent of glass plate photography). The "othering" of perception, linked to what Marx once referred to as the history of the five senses, is here taken to mean that imaging has among its developments, specific class components. Serialization in the nineteenth century, of course, was intensified by technological changes in production and distribution, with illustration enabling, among other factors, a much broader readership. As we have seen with *Le Capital*, low-priced serialization was seen to potentially engage a working-class readership. That edition, however, did not use illustration or images which, in a period of relatively low literacy levels, was often presented as a complementary path to rendering narrative, whether fiction or daily news—a kind of "literarization" in Benjamin's sense galvanized by technological reproducibility. On the one hand, the democratization of imaging was seen to bolster the impress of the visual artist: "The great end of the whole art of engraving is to render the spirit and genius of a great artist accessible to the thousands, or the millions, by embodying them in cheap and portable forms";[16] on the other hand, critics constantly bemoaned the role and impact of such imaging, noting a "partial return to baby literature—to a second childhood of learning—the eye is often appealed to instead of the understanding [. . .] a low utilitarian wish to give and receive the greatest possible amount of knowledge at the least possible expense of time, trouble, money, and we may add, of intellect."[17] These are not absolute positions or some codified binary but the relationship of class and illustration continues to play a key role in how the need for social change is articulated and distributed. What John Berger refers to as "the enigma of appearance"[18] inflects both the ideology of image for class

16 Henry Cole, "Modern Wood Engraving," *London and Westminster Review* 28 (1838): 268–69.

17 John Holmes, "Illustrated Books," *Quarterly Review* 74 (June 1844): 170–71.

18 John Berger, *Understanding a Photograph* (Geoff Dyer ed.) (London: Penguin, 2013), p. 86.

composition and significant contestation in the art of "profane illumination" (Walter Benjamin).[19] We have been thinking about seriality as an active logic in the critique of capital and capitalism across a variety of narrative forms. Here we will apply elements of that analysis, serial heuristics, to the graphic representation of history, where sequential art wrestles with serialization as an opening to the idea of radical social change. This will mean reconfiguring the temporal problematic of the Paris Commune outlined above as a historical graphic and grapheme. Later, we will offer the Paris Commune as a serial demand without closure that unpicks the sutures that otherwise hold its event. On one level, this extends the lessons of serial Marx so far; on another level, it necessarily connects the antinomies of seriality to paradigms of radical representation themselves.

19 See Walter Benjamin, "Surrealism: the Last Snapshot of the European Intelligentsia," *New Left Review* 108 (March–April 1978): 47–56.

With the greatest care and understanding Karl Marx had followed the fortunes of the Commune. Immediately after its fall, he spoke to the workers of the world on the lessons of its rise and fall.

"Workingmen's Paris," he said, "with its Commune, will forever be celebrated as the glorious harbinger of a new society."

28

FIGURE 25. William Siegel, *The Paris Commune: A Story in Pictures* (New York: International Pamphlets, 1932), p. 28.

After the collapse of "actually existing socialism" in the early Nineteen Nineties, history did not end in Francis Fukuyama's fatalistic fashion but began anew in several strains of radical thought and practice. Around socialism and communism, critique quickly diverged around matters of process, authentication, failure, and rearticulation. Attempts to wrest such radicalism away from state or party interpretations were and are relatively easy, since state or party versions of communism had been all but vanquished. Socialism and communism, however, continue to have a significant "actual" material presence, if not always global living correlatives under such names. There is no space here to detail the range of difference this represents but the dialectical dynamics are instructive, not least because they signal what is living and dead in the "idea of communism." The latter, while insistently and symptomatically spectral or phantomatic, took on a new reality in light of the deep economic crisis of 2007–2008 to which we have earlier referred, when globalization had cause to doubt the nature of its capitalist expertise, a symptom read above in the emergence of *Capital in manga*. Well-attended conferences on the communist idea, and a corresponding outpouring of books (including those by Badiou, Zizek, and Ali),[1] provided fresh insights on a body of theory tuned both to explain and counter the globalization of capital as relation, while also acknowledging the limits of previous specific interpretive modes (something further highlighted by the improvisations and innovations of the so-called "Arab Spring" and the "Occupy Wall Street" movements in 2011, and the impact of Black Lives Matter from 2013 on).

1 See, for instance, Alain Badiou, *The Communist Hypothesis* (David Macey and Steve Corcoran trans) (London: Verso, 2015); Costas Douzinas and Slavoj Žižek (eds), *The Idea of Communism* (London: Verso, 2010); and Tariq Ali, *The Idea of Communism* (London: Seagull Books, 2009). I will not here be principally considering the event of the idea in terms of the idea of the event which is a complementary approach to the dialectically enmeshed.

Lineaments of a "communist idea" live serially in a number of ways, and here we will focus on an elaboration of an expressive form in which the concept creatively maintains a concrete if contradictory persistence and challenge. I am concerned with a cultural relay between memory as nostalgia and as the ground of political imperatives (within "moments of danger," as Walter Benjamin puts it).[2] Specifically, if the Paris Commune articulates a living communism, a possible communism, as Marx suggests,[3] how does it continue to live expressively? We have remarked upon *Marx in Paris* in this regard, but are images, or let us say, graphic reinscription, or what Benjamin once termed "heightened graphicness" (*Anschaulichkeit*—viewability and, among other interpretations, the vividness of the image),[4] decisive or critical to that living on as a form of citational communality? Instead of limiting the notion to written reflection, what if we thought of the Commune as also a graphic instantiation of the communist idea? Would this throw any light on the texture of the Paris Commune's intervention, a veritable theater of all of our struggles and all of our ideas (to invoke Benjamin once more)? Conversely and concomitantly, is not the graphicness of the Commune nevertheless problematized by the very idea of the graphic, specifically, graphic representation, the graphic as a sign in technological reproducibility? This speculative leap from a long drawn-out process of history to processes of

2 Drawn from Benjamin's "Theses on the Philosophy of History." See Walter Benjamin, *Illuminations* (Hannah Arendt ed., Harry Zohn trans.) (New York: Schocken, 1969).

3 See Karl Marx, *The Civil War in France* (Beijing: Foreign Languages Press, 1970), p. 68.

4 Although the direction in the following critique does not comport directly with Benjamin's provocation in *Das Passagen-Werk*, the argument below will build on the conceptual challenge it represents. Benjamin notes: "A central problem of historical materialism that ought to be seen in the end: Must the Marxist understanding of history necessarily be acquired at the expense of the perceptibility of history? Or: in what way is it possible to conjoin a heightened graphicness (*Anschaulichkeit*) to the realization of the Marxist method? The first stage in this undertaking will be to carry over the principle of montage into history. That is, to assemble large-scale constructions out of the smallest and most precisely cut components. Indeed, to discover in the analysis of the small individual moment the crystal of the total event." What follows is a graphic montage. See Benjamin, *Arcades Project*, p. 461 [N2,6].

drawing history (seen in Part One, but also below in graphic novels) might be deemed to compromise the serious political implications of social transformation the Paris Commune poignantly represents. Again, I wish to press the notion that the living on, or sur-vivre as Derrida puts it,[5] of the communist idea is intimately braided with the vexed history of cultural forms as constitutive rather than destituent. To recall, just as Marx, in 1872, praised the idea that the French edition of *Capital* was to be serialized, so we might think further on the complementary appropriateness of narrating struggle itself as a form of serialization, even as a serialized graphic. Accepting that the epigraph to Part Two is not an endorsement, can the Commune live on like "a book with images," and why would this matter?

Much depends on the components of historical movement and how they might be lived, communicated. The tension between the abstract and the real (and within real abstraction) as a mainstay of materialist critique here takes the form of a schism between communism and the commune, between the seemingly always represented and the unrepresentable, or between what Alain Badiou calls the fact and the singularity.[6] In Engels' précis, the notion of the Paris Commune of 1871 as a verifiable event is not in question, but how that moment might be realizable or cognized today is a continuing narrative provocation. Badiou, for instance, notes that not long ago in France the subject of the Paris Commune was removed from school history syllabi, and that formal fidelity to the idea and moment is observed only by a fraction of the organized Left. For him the issue is not one of memory or lessons derived from it, but one of truth. The problem for Badiou is not just of fidelity to the event, but of the truth procedures in its putative representation. Extrapolating from such positions, one might say the question is not about the right way to meet the prescience

---

5 See Jacques Derrida, "Survivre: journal de bord" in *Parages* (Paris: Éditions Galilée, 1986), pp. 117–218. Translated as "Living On / Borderlines" (James Hulbert trans.) in Harold Bloom, Paul de Man, Jacques Derrida, Geoffrey H. Hartman and J. Hillis Miller, *Deconstruction and Criticism* (London & New York: Continuum, 2004), pp. 62–142.

6 Badiou, *Communist Hypothesis*, p. 215. Badiou makes this distinction to mark the Paris Commune as an event: "We will call a site whose intensity of existence is not maximal a fact. We will call a site whose intensity of existence is maximal a singularity."

of the worker uprising in Paris of 1871, but the manner in which its cognitive challenge can be addressed. Thus, as with *Capital*, how is revolution told?

John Merriman's *Massacre* is in many ways an exemplary study in this regard, and it draws on an extensive historical archive to reconstruct the emergence and defeat of the Paris Commune.[7] Primary sources consulted include national archives, police records, Archives de la Défense (Vincennes), and other individual library collections. Merriman also uses some of the hundreds of available memoirs and "contemporary accounts" (those of the 1870s) of the event, including journalism, public inquiries, annals, military records, letters, diaries, and personal histories. Some three hundred "official accounts" about what happened appeared by 1873 alone, and that is just the beginning of an explosion of research and disputation. A state desire to "fix" the history of rebellion in short order is a narratological prerogative in its own right and is demonstrable around the explication of the Commune. If the primary sources are voluminous, the secondary material is gargantuan and, while the Paris Commune may be off the syllabus, it is definitely and massively discernible in bibliographies of French history, socialist and anarchist revolution, and capital critique. One could argue that the sheer volume of evidence and criticism works to inhibit expertise if not novel approaches. Knowledge of the Commune is summarily niched, allowing for perspective against a largely settled panorama.

Badiou, for example, in order to advance his analysis of the Paris Commune as a "singularity," as a "site" and as an "event" (concepts that are ultimately arrayed as a logic), must quickly characterize the facts and established views (beginning with Marx's addresses to the General Council of the International discussed above). Yet the recycling of such facts (with their dates and drama) is not necessarily out of step with the main thrust of subsequent classical, Leninist, or Maoist interpretations to which Badiou also refers, that assume such determinations in shaping political, ideological, and philosophical *différance*. Meanwhile, historians of the period continue

7 See John Merriman, *Massacre: The Life and Death of The Paris Commune of 1871* (New Haven, CT: Yale University Press, 2014).

to hotly contest the evidentiary substance of the Commune's brief existence, not to dismiss it, but to ward off what they feel to be deleterious mythification or selective ideological redeployments. True, no historian is outside the conditions of ideology or myth (as Hobsbawm above would agree), but there is sufficient historical argument about the facts of the Paris Commune to render even Badiou's somber summary something of a false positive. For instance, buried in a footnote in Merriman's *Massacre* is a nod to Robert Tombs' research on the number of Communards murdered during the "*La semaine sanglante*" (the massacres in Paris of May 21 to 28, 1871). Referenced everywhere else in the book with some reverence, Tombs is questioned by Merriman on his findings that corroboration of the uppermost limit on executions/murders of Communards reveals a number of between 5,700 and 7,400.[8] No one denies that brutal, systematic, and extensive massacres occurred, but a figure that places it below the 1790s in terms of bloody carnage (during the days of "*la terreur*") changes the dimensions of the historical impress as "a constructed understanding of the past."[9] Merriman correctly points out that a number of Communards were buried after May 30, 1871 (something that Tombs acknowledges but are figures about which he will not speculate), yet basically accepts the "official" tally of 17,000, adding that some estimates have reached as high as 35,000 dead (although this is uncorroborated—Merriman's focus on "massacre" inevitably necessitates numerical punch or, as Robert St. Clair puts it, "a mathematical sublime").[10] For his part, Marx does not count the dead except to say that "the men [sic] who fell were really dead" (to which we might add Louise Michel's resignation: "Paris is truly dead").[11] Badiou,

8 See Robert Tombs, "How Bloody was 'La Semaine Sanglante' of 1871? A Revision," *The Historical Journal* 55 (September 3, 2012): 679–704.

9 Tombs, "How Bloody was 'La Semaine Sanglante' of 1871?": 703.

10 St. Clair notes: "By many accounts, the violence that explodes in the capital in the final days of the Commune in some sense defies visual representation. it strays into the domain of the mathematical sublime." I like the idea here that number fights (other) modes of visualization, particularly given St. Clair's focus on Tardi. See Robert St. Clair, "Reframing the Commune: Violence, intertextuality, and event in Tardi's Cri du people," *Romance Notes* 55(1) (2015): 147–59.

11 Marx, *Civil War*, p. 83. See also Edith Thomas, *Louise Michel* (Penelope Williams trans.) (Montreal: Black Rose, 1980), p. 129.

FIGURE 26. Jacques Tardi, *Le Cri du peuple*, VOL. 3: *Les Heures sanglantes* (Paris: Casterman, 2003), p. 73.

who philosophizes on the truth of number and ontology as mathematics, simply states "at least twenty thousand are shot dead." The numbers are important, since they too, for several reasons, provide a graphic idea of the commune, the nature of its rupture as event and (to borrow from Badiou once more) its generic procedure.

If the numbers are graphic in themselves, can we yet provide an alternative perspective on revolutionary substance and substantiation that broaches the representational fix of articulating the event of uprising as a living provocation? One of the important representational distinctions between the French Revolution and the Paris Commune is not just the conditions of class antagonism in France (and/or variations in the murdered and terrorized), but that the Commune was extensively imaged; indeed, like the US Civil War before it, its iconography is critically marked by the photographic and the pictorial. Much of the visual representation occurs in commercial woodcuts used to embellish stories in the illustrated dailies and weeklies of the time—including *Le Monde Illustré* and *L'Illustration* (both the London paper, *The Graphic*, and t*he Illustrated London News* had several artists in Paris during the Spring of 1871, and the American press, like *Everyday Saturday* and *Harper's Weekly*, reproduced much of this work). For the most part, such news coverage was not sympathetic to the Commune's cause (this includes many representations by caricaturists), but some expressed significant consternation concerning the massacres of its final week. Although the photographic apparatus was still relatively young, production was already commercialized and industrialized (or technologically reproducible) by the 1870s and basic equipment was more widely available. The photographers of the American Civil War had proved the power of the image as a documentary medium of social conflagration, one that could affect how events were cognized and disseminated; indeed, how the time/space of change could be articulated otherwise in its immediacy. This does not mean, however, that the understanding of the Paris Commune is technologically determined, but that its conditions of possibility are dialectically mediated by the status of the image itself. Even if one accepts, as Benjamin notes, photography is "the first truly revolutionary means of reproduction,"[12] no one would argue that it can

12 Benjamin, *Illuminations*, p. 224.

simply reproduce the means of true revolution (some kind of purity beyond "possible communism"). The written account, the first-hand memoir, remains a primary source within the constitution of the Commune's archive and it is generally considered in relation to "official" accounts mentioned and the normative metrics of record. The truth procedures of the visual, like those of fiction, do not necessarily contradict in advance the eventness of the event, but neither are their logical processes simply an extension of revolutionary measure (the production of series, seriality, and serialization are not just teleological chains in the understanding and production of social change). In the case of the Paris Commune, the initial conditions of imaging appear to reify the "must be seen" of worker uprising.

Most of the photographs taken during the Commune are of barricades. These are photogenic and "photo-generic" regarding the Commune's interruption of history and its primary mode of defense. What is being defended is generally not documented in this way—it is enough that it is being defended (the "it" here remains an abstraction before the viewer—if there are captions to the photos of the time they refer to location, the concrete spatiality of the revolution, not its process). As commentators have pointed out, the exposure time required for each photo means that static poses at the barricades are more easily captured and display the visible presence of the Commune's control.

Some of the most famous photographs are of Communards standing among the debris of the felled Vendôme Column with its broken statue of Napoleon. Gustave Courbet, the most prominent artist among the Communard leadership, was particularly vocal in wanting the column destroyed and replaced by an appropriate symbol of the March 18 takeover (this is noted with gusto in *Marx in Paris*). Initially the Commune had voted against the column's destruction, but by the May 16 the symbolic weight of its toppling overcame all manner of political strategy. In the midst of revolution, the demolition was presented as a ticketed event, although most who attended did not pay the fee. One American, however, did allegedly hand over $80 in order to be the last to climb the column before it was torn down. As to the photos of the Vendôme Column that day, many were taken by Bruno Braquehais (in a series published as "Paris under the Commune"), and they reveal the extent to which it was an event

FIGURE 27. Jacques Tardi, *Le Cri du peuple*, VOL. 3, p. 39.

FIGURE 28. Anonymous, *Barricade de la Chaussée Ménilmontant, 18 mars 1871, Musée Carnavalet.*

while hinting that its substance may lie elsewhere.[13] Many of the photos express a sense of achievement and joy at the destruction of a resented testament to imperial power and state repression. Others convey a formal solemnity befitting the enormity of the historical act. One, taken just before the column is toppled, seems to combine intimations of both, with elements of determination and spontaneous whimsy, although whether this was Braquehais' intent or the carnivalesque overcoming formality the viewer is left to ponder. Felling statues always culminates political desire, yet this is barely even a preface of its social syntax if the photographs are indeed considered evidentiary.

Braquehais' photos come closest to conveying the stakes involved in the Commune's project, particularly since they show the workers of Paris reclaiming the space of their city (something that is largely absent from the paintings, drawings, and engravings of established artists of the time, even those directly associated with the Commune), and occupying the space of photography itself (from which workers to that point had been resolutely excluded). While the Commune had no official photographer, Braquehais (and another photographer of note, Auguste-Hyppolyte Collard) made up for this undersight. Even the posing at barricades (and by the fallen statue of Napoleon) accentuate resistance and taking a stand in the face of inevitable and devastating counter-insurgency. Posing, of course, is not unproblematic, but in this instance could be dangerous (as a mark of unintended consequences, the quality of such photos was later used by the opposing Versaillais to help identify Communards for prosecution, execution, or deportation—an early and definitive sign of photography's place in the discourse of "*surveiller et punir*"). Lapostolle suggests that when Braquehais describes his work as that of "*un témoin fidèle*" (a faithful witness) he tends to understate the nature of consent (and solidarity) required in the situation.[14] For those with limited

13 Auguste Bruno Braquehais was a professional photographer who took stock portraits and also images of nude women. Largely unknown before the Commune, Braquehais' photos of its existence are vital to its archive. Many of these images can now be accessed on the web and they have been featured in several exhibitions. After the Commune, Braquehais returned to obscurity and within three years declared bankruptcy.

14 See Christine Lapostolle, "Plus vrai que le vrai: Stratégie photographique et Commune de Paris," *Actes de la recherche en sciences sociales* 73 (1988): 67–76.

FIGURE 29. Bruno Braquehais, *Place Vendôme*, May 1871.

FIGURE 30. Bruno Braquehais, *Battery at Porte Maillot, 1871*, in "La Commune photographiée," Musée d'Orsay, Paris, exhibition March 14 – June 11, 2000.

experience of viewing photographs, what criteria are foremost in measuring their fidelity to the event? Indeed, the photography of the Paris Commune and its aftermath still asks pertinent questions of representationality and the nature of its chronotope. What or who is the subject of change? The photos reveal the defense of the Commune but what of its promise? Is this also collectible?

The ambiguity in such representation is unsurprising, even alongside Marx's "instant" assessment of the Commune. Yet there are other edges to the photographs' invitation to history that cast doubt on the image as a "faithful witness" of change. Infamously, we have the work of Ernest Eugène Appert who, in order to bolster the triumph (and brutality) of the Versaillais, put together a series, "Crimes of the Commune," to counter Braquehais' efforts.[15] Using actors to "recreate" scenes from the Commune, Appert then cut and pasted head shots of Communards into the frame (both found images and those he had gleaned from photographing prisoners for the Versaillais as a record for possible prosecution) then re-photographed the subsequent tableaux. The photos purported to show wanton assassination and executions by the Commune and helped to stir righteous narratives of justice. As noted, the Communards had executed prisoners, but Appert's method, while crude, was extremely effective and affective in justifying the rectitude of the Third Republic's "revenge" (Appert's work on the image demonstrated photomontage included deception in its aesthetic innovations, a propensity that has hardly receded even as the technology of reproducibility has changed demonstrably).

In the catalog accompanying the exhibition in 2000, "La Commune photographiée," at the Musée D'Orsay, Quentin Bajac considers how the meaning of the Commune is constructed photographically.[16] He includes discussions of both Braquehais and Appert, while further bolstering the claim that photographs of the Commune could be partial and easily

---

15 Like Braquehais, Appert is much discussed regarding the representation of the Commune. Interestingly, during the trials of the Communards he photographed several leading figures, including Louise Michel, in exchange for a few photos that they could keep. Given his role in discrediting the Commune, such consent is extraordinary.

16 See Quentin Bajac (ed.), *La Commune photographiée* (Paris: Éditions de la Réunion des Musées Nationaux, 2000).

misinterpreted. In addition to Appert's efforts, one famous photograph by Disdéri, for instance, purported to represent a line of coffins of dead Communards killed by the Versaillais, but the image is most likely the product of an earlier Commune project to record the French killed in the Franco-Prussian War (specifically during the siege of Paris). The life of the photograph does not necessarily suture the image conveyed. The ontology of the archive is dynamic even as the Commune's imaging appears static for long periods. The largest number of photographs related to the Commune, larger than those of Communards defined by their barricades, are those dedicated to depicting the aftermath of its defeat, principally in the imaging of Parisian ruins.

It is not always clear who or what started the fires that destroyed so many buildings during the conflict. The Hôtel de Ville, the Tuileries Palace, and the Palais de Justice were certainly targets of the Communards, but the work of so-called "petroleuses," bands of pro-Commune working-class women arsonists, was just as assuredly overstated or simply invented, a sexist demonization of feminist praxis common in much conservative coverage of the Commune, and further enhanced by the extraordinary clay figure dramas photographed in "*vue stéréoscopique*" by Jules Raudnitz.[17] Nevertheless, the interest in recording the subsequent ruins was phenomenal, as if the burned out and blasted buildings were the most lasting signifiers of communal remnants—"*les vestiges communaux*" beyond the oft-noted "*luxe communal*"; or rather, *luxus* (excess) as that which remains rather than that which was desired.[18] Viewers seemed drawn to the city's devastation much more than the implications in the conflagration.

---

17 Raudnitz's "Le Sabbat rouge" is a symptomatic visualization of the fear of worker uprising at the time. See Jules Raudnitz, "Le Sabbat rouge," Série stéréoscopique (Paris: BNF, 1871).

18 "Luxe communal" or "communal luxury" is, of course, a key term of the manifesto of the Federation of Artists that appeared in the April 15 edition of the *Journal Officiel* (1871) and is the title of Kristin Ross's vital book on the aesthetic legacies of the Commune in, for instance, the works of William Morris, Elisée Reclus, and Peter Kropotkin. Ross also explores the seedbed for commune thinking among French workers after the revolutionary activities of 1848. As a political imaginary, "communal luxury" is a powerful and radical resource of hope. Here, I mark the tension between luxe and luxus in the imaging of the Commune at the time. See Kristin Ross, *Communal Luxury: The Political Imaginary of the Paris Commune* (New York: Verso, 2015).

FIGURE 31. *Ruins of the Hôtel de Ville de Paris*, 1871, Bibliothèque nationale de France, Paris.

The *luxus*, and not simply the *luxe*, is something of a utopian persistence and here measures in part the difference between artisanal and proletarian visions of worker insurrection. Copies of the photographs themselves proved quite popular, whatever the political affiliation, and survived the ban on Commune photographs instituted by the Third Republic at the end of 1871 (Appert's influence, for instance, had proved disturbing even to those it benefited). Indeed, by that time tourism of the ruins had become quite the business, with Thomas Cook among other companies facilitating sightseeing excursions to notable addresses in the city (a correlative to the production of memorabilia in postcards, posters and the like). Exhibitions of the photographed ruins, rather than of the revolution, were staged in several countries, and thus we might say the imaging of the Paris Commune contributes to its own disappearance in figuring alternatives to state and trade at the time. If photography can replicate, then the dissemination of images of ruin directly undermines the otherwise positive elements of revolutionary desire (this would be the relative triumph of salability over recognition). The ruins are the spectral remains of a subject that had not been but whose possibility was to be grasped, if not graphed, in the interpretations of Marx and after.

There has been much interest in this remainder as the historical potential in the photograph—the idea that, whatever the confused or downright manipulated the surfaces of the photograph might be, it yet may narrate a different story at the level of the optical unconscious, that which exists outside or beyond the authorial intent "exposed." Benjamin thought of the history captured by the photograph as coterminous with the history of the photograph itself.[19] The dialectical image is never only that relation but it is the first principle of the photograph's meaning ("revolution at a standstill," as Jeannene Przyblyski pithily puts it).[20] The limits of the photograph in depicting the Paris Commune are obviously mediated by the conditions of technological reproducibility, but do these

---

19 See Walter Benjamin, *On Photography* (Esther Leslie trans.) (London: Reaktion Books, 2015)—especially "Small History of Photography" and, in light of my other comments, "Nothing Wrong with the Illustrated Press."

20 See Jeannene Przyblyski, "Revolution at a Standstill: Photography and the Paris Commune of 1871," *Yale French Studies* 101 (2001): 54–78. Przyblyski's essay looks again at the complex repertoires of barricade photography.

in any way refract the confines in which the Commune is lived as history, as event? Does the memory of such images affect the "now of recognizability" in the Paris Commune's provocation? And what if the force of the image for articulating the Commune's disruption lies outside the graphing of the photograph, but in the imaging of art itself, in the aesthetic fidelity also active in the Commune's field of representationality?

That the Commune was deeply invested in its aesthetic self-representation is made clear in the Federation of Artists Manifesto and the number of artists who committed to the Commune's cause. When the Federation's committee of 47 members was constituted in this regard on April 7, 1871, Courbet and fifteen other painters formed its core (with 10 sculptors, 5 architects, 6 engravers and lithographers, and 10 industrial or decorative artists). Not surprisingly, the artistic merits of photography were not considered important (and would not be for decades), which is particularly notable given that photographs, not art by any members of the Federation, formed by far the most Commune-produced visual record of its existence—if not its event as such (and even then, the relative number of photographs is small, since many professional photographers, like many painters, fled the city when the fighting erupted). Perhaps it is not the Federation's exclusion of photographers that is crucial, but that the artistic output of Communard photographers justifies their absence. Yet the discussion itself is not internal to the claims for art made by the Commune, or indeed by most critics since. We should also note that, although the life of the Commune was extensively illustrated by outsiders, its main declarations and activities (including the artists' manifesto) were published in the *Journal Officiel*, a serial produced without the luxury of pictures (striking, given the popular appetite for illustrated news among the urban working class—we have discussed this elision in the original serialization of *Le Capital*). For their part, the artists explicitly allied with the Commune generally did not produce work during the Spring of 1871. Édouard Manet's famous lithograph, "Civil War" (originally sketched just after "*La Semaine sanglante*" and marked 1871, was probably made in 1872–1873, then published in 1874)[21] is a prominent example—although Manet was listed in the Federation, he was not in Paris during the Commune. Courbet did

21 Manet returned to Paris a few days after the collapse of the Commune and "Civil War" is a testimony to the affect/effect of that moment.

make a few sketches, but the project announced by the manifesto needed the luxury of *time* in the moment of revolution more than the "luxe communal" promised by the Federation's declaration. The announcement of the Federation is more significantly about the place of art in the society envisaged than about any of the directives regarding modes of expression (including, for instance, how to organize and make available the treasures of the French state). As the declaration put it, art should develop freely and independently of government and privilege; there should be equal rights among artists of the federation; and the independence and dignity of each artist should be safeguarded by the universal suffrage of artists (concomitant, clearly, with the suffrage practiced by the Commune as a whole). Art history has focused on the degree to which this level of social engagement fostered or denatured the impressionism, post-impressionism, and neo-impressionism of the following decades, yet the art itself, if it did reflect on the Paris Commune, did so in ways very similar to original Paris Commune photography, at least in measuring the violence, death, and ruin of the event. Such later representation, of course, also explored the nature of mourning and its role in confronting the tension between the judgments of history and the unresolved promise in the uprising itself. Again, this is not to assign a function to the image, the luxury of mourning, perhaps (mourning is more than that, and could be linked back to the question of immediacy in Marx's Third Address); rather, the attention is to the problem of imaging itself in the specific revolutionary desire of the women and men of the French working class.

In general, painting of the Commune does not simply copy its photography (a reproduction of reproducibility), but comments on the shortfall of both in grasping the Commune's meaning. Death in its instant or in its aftermath is a prevailing theme but, not surprisingly, the art is also thinking about whether the limits of instaneity provoke other ways to narrate the visuality of the Commune. In later paintings, this is linked to art as its own historical visualization. Maximilien Luce's painting, "A Paris Street in 1871" (1905), for instance, renders what might be deemed typological elements of Commune representation, bits of a barricade and dead Communards in an otherwise discrepant configuration.

FIGURE 32. Maximilien Luce, *A Paris Street in 1871* (1905), Musée d'Orsay, Paris.

As Alastair Wright has pointed out, Luce is simultaneously negotiating the conditions of painting's possibilities in his own present with the promise of change violently deracinated in the moment depicted.[22] The arrangement of the dead, therefore, is as much an address to art history (Wright notes its citations—perhaps Delacroix, certainly Manet, Meissonier, and Gerome) as it is to that flash of memory in revolution's prospect. While one could take issue with Wright's assignation of "crudely illustrational" technique meant to appeal, apparently, to less discerning working-class viewers (a problem I have already noted in what images get prioritized), whose eye is overdetermined by industrialism, Luce's painting buckles under the strain of its position in commitment: could not the image in memory be more than memorial?

Often when radical theory thinks of specters, it is both to conjure the haunting from the future that opens the *Communist Manifesto*, but it is also to wonder again about the ghostly vestiges scattered across history of the communist idea. Images can make of that narrative tension something new and strange, yet not by simply re-describing it, nor by filling in its putative absence around current constellations. The dilemma of representing the living idea of the commune as a worker uprising contains within it a graphic injunction, the drawing out of elements (literally and figuratively) that conjure fictions of fact and singularity as nevertheless historically composed. Such an interpretation is not simply that imaging is a generic extension of narrating the Paris Commune—an equivalent to photo-graphing once more the still life of stolen lives. Instead, the emphasis is on its serial relationship, in this case whether the conditions of technological reproducibility are active in a material resonance of the Commune's transformational demand, the narrative as it could be today (and where "graphicness" is heightened in its telling). I want to provide a few brief examples of this dialectics of reconfiguration as a fulcrum of serial extension.

One could start with a key character in the Commune's meaning, the aforementioned Louise Michel, whose symbolic presence is itself a catalyst of the communist idea.

---

22 Alastair Wright, "Mourning, Painting, and the Commune: Maximilien Luce's A Paris Street in 1871," *Oxford Art Journal* 32(2) (2009): 223–42.

FIGURE 33. Mary M. Talbot and Bryan Talbot, *The Red Virgin and the Vision of Utopia* (Milwaukie, OR: Dark Horse Books, 2016), p. 41.

Among the leading revolutionaries of the Commune (that included Blanqui—albeit like Manet an absent presence—Vallès, Ferre, and Rigault), Michel is represented as a historical embodiment of the claims for social and economic justice. Eventually dubbed the "Red Virgin," itself an assignation of radical essence (and therefore at once politically contradictory as Gayle Gullickson has shown),[23] Michel's story has been told many times, beginning with those around her in the Spring of 1871 and in her subsequent memoirs of her life and of the Commune itself. A feminist, anti-colonialist, soldier, teacher, anarchist, anarchist teacher, poet, novelist—Michel in her life and politics is at once greater and less than the Paris Commune as idea and event. Her anarchism alone is a subreption of all that binds unproblematically the Commune to communism, just as her feminism significantly challenges socio-political norms (including those of her "radical" comrades). Accepting that the heroification or hagiography of the individual revolutionary risks eliding the communist for the commodity (Che being an obvious reference point), how might imaging Michel graphically instantiate the revolutionary force of the Commune?

Michel has an active visual presence that greatly expands upon the few photographs and portraits produced during her lifetime. The French TV film *Louise Michel, La Rebelle* (2009) is typical in this light, as is Paul Mason's play about Michel's life as a deportee in New Caledonia, "Divine Chaos of Starry Things."[24] The visual exploration of the Paris Commune in recent years (again, particularly after the collapse of actually existing socialism and the later financial crisis of 2007–2008) is generally undertheorized in contrast to its written conceptualization/narration (like the question of the photograph alongside the historical accounts in the

23 See Gayle L. Gullickson, *Unruly Women of Paris: Images of the Commune* (Ithaca, NY: Cornell University Press, 1996), pp. 154–56. Gullickson's extensive research reveals a number of ways that femininity and woman as subject get figured, visually and otherwise, in the historical discourse of the Commune. The effulgence of the "Red Virgin" moniker for Louise Michel is typical, and now denotes Michel during the Commune, even though the term was invented some years later.

24 Mason's play was first performed in the Spring of 2017 in London, UK. *Louise Michel, La Rebelle* (2009) was directed by Sólveig Anspach, produced by Jem Productions, and was exhibited primarily as a telefilm.

immediate aftermath of the Commune itself—there are exceptions—the work of James A. Leith in particular).[25] Michel's extraordinary life and unflagging desire for social change, however (she certainly was not the "false revolutionary legend" that Lissagaray warned of in others),[26] offers a complex provocation for imaging the Commune's idea when the triumph of collectivity is measured against its historical symbolic: the hydra-headed contradictions signifying both inspiring individual heroism and the conditions of defeat. Pertinently, the question of the role of imaging is brought up by Michel herself in her suggestions about pedagogy for the Commune. Acknowledging the low levels of literacy among the poor and the dispossessed of Paris, Michel believed a relatively small number of words could be taught initially and that teaching should be primarily imaged based, including giant tableaux representing major historical events (a storytelling seen in the muralism invoked via Gellert in Part One, and a contrast, obviously, with Marx's project in *Le Capital*).[27] The communist idea is, whatever else it is, a way of seeing.

Mary and Bryan Talbot's graphic novel on Louise Michel, *The Red Virgin and the Vision of Utopia*, captures in its very title the difficulties of the task, if not the possibilities of the form in addressing them.[28] The book

---

25 See James A. Leith, "The War of Images Surrounding the Commune" in *Images of the Commune/Images de la Commune* (James A. Leith ed.) (Montreal: McGill–Queen's University Press, 1978), pp. 102–50. Image, for Leith, is a scene of formal struggle over the representability of the Commune, especially as an event whose real implications were otherwise too transformative to fathom.

26 See Prosper-Olivier Lissagaray, *History of the Commune of 1871* (Eleanor Marx Aveling trans.) (London: T. Fisher Unwin, 1902). While obviously sympathetic to the Commune, Lissagaray understood the degree to which heroification might act as an ideological displacement.

27 The visual economy of revolution is diverse but Michel here is sensitive to the material realities of "reading" images. The success or not of narrating transformation in images hinges on visual literacy, so that the process of learning is itself a realization of revolution's meaning. In this way, murals, posters, photographs and the like are not simply a salve for limited reading and writing but create a language of change itself. I read "graphic" as an injunction in this regard.

28 Mary M. Talbot and Bryan Talbot, *The Red Virgin and the Vision of Utopia* (Milwaukie, OR: Dark Horse Books, 2016). The Talbots provide a number of significant insights into Michel's worldview without necessarily using this to address the question

begins with panels depicting an early airplane flight and an inventor (the reference is to Franz Reichelt) stumbling onto the idea of a parachute (surely a remark more on scientific progress than a salve for communism! Reichelt is shown with his parachute leaping from the Eiffel Tower in 1912 at the end of the novel—unfortunately to his death, as history records). A few years after the timeframe for *Capital in manga*, we are in 1905 when Michel's body (she has recently passed away in Marseille) is brought to Paris for a large funeral march and burial. At the same railway station, Charlotte Perkins Gilman is being met while on a break between speaking engagements. The tale is drawn in black and white, save for pertinent if slightly more obvious splashes of red (and a patina to indicate flashbacks). Using Gilman as a framing device is intriguing, since it acts as bridge to American correlatives for Michel's feminism and utopian instincts (the Talbots also build in a critique of Gilman's racism because it is so clearly out of step with many of Michel's "visions" for social transformation). Gilman, who in the story has previously met Michel in London (she claims Michel is full of "fantastical ideas"), asks to learn more about the revolutionary figure, and Monique, her French companion and daughter of a Communard close to Michel, duly obliges. While the backstory, beginning with the Siege of Paris, is familiar, Badiou's "facts" once more, the novel gets much more interesting around visualizing the nature of Michel's participation in history and the formation of her worldview. This is predominantly an education in history, edumanga, and one can imagine using the narrative pedagogically as a complementary commentary (and

---

of utopian thinking, visually. An earlier "picture book" that takes up this challenge in relation to the Paris Commune is the work of William Siegel, a frequent contributor to the *New Masses*. See William Siegel, *The Paris Commune: A Story in Pictures* (New York: International Pamphlets, 1932). In his introduction Alexander Trachtenberg notes the heuristic (and ideological) impact: "In the following pages the reader will find the story of the Paris Commune told in pictures. This is a medium in which little working-class literature has previously been done. It is graphic, dramatic and simple and should give to the reader the story of the Commune" (p. 12). Despite the whiff of condescension Trachtenberg's comment is echoing Michel's point about visual literacy. While there is no space here, it would be interesting to compare the Talbot's visual representation of Michel's ideas with that of Kate Evans biography of Rosa Luxemburg, in which the latter's thoughts are both explained and radically illustrated. See Kate Evans, *Red Rosa* (London: Verso, 2015).

a restoration of the missing event in contemporary French teaching to which Badiou refers) on the articulation of a revolutionary life. This function is enhanced when Michel's beliefs are delivered in panels where her face directly addresses the reader). Part of the dialogue is used so that Michel can channel or repeat the main demands of the National Guard, whose initiative was crucial in establishing the necessity for the Commune. The Talbots dramatize a key moment we have mentioned, the army's mission to recapture the cannons stored in Montmartre (basic questions have been raised about whether such a military maneuver could have been attempted without horses to pull them away). Michel is "bloodied" in this moment when she tends to a comrade (Turpin) shot by the advancing troops, and in the following panels her hands remain red. The tension is palpable, as lines of uniformed soldiers are ordered to fire upon the civilians blocking their path to the cannons. Eventually, the soldiers refuse and the officer in charge is summarily dispatched (Michel is depicted arguing for due process. The officer in question is most likely General Claude Lecomte. As we have noted, General Jacques Léon Clément-Thomas, who had been reconnoitering in disguise the barricades of Montmartre was discovered and executed shortly afterwards). We quickly move to the Hôtel de Ville, where debates ensue about what to do in order to consolidate the uprising. Michel famously advocates striking back at the seat of government in Versailles (something supported by Blanquists like Émile Duval) and also suggests assassinating its leader, Thiers, but the panels here emphasize solidarity and process, with voting a central committee becoming a first priority (the novel is not the first account, however, to downplay the factionalism that considerably weakened the Commune's day to day organization and, crucially, its defense).[29] By the March 28, 1871, the

29 Most of the histories mentioned so far discuss the issue of mounting an attack on Thiers' Versailles base. Militarily this would have been daunting but it would have had the advantage of surprise (Marx too believed this would have been strategically vital). Michel's advocacy for assassination was not taken seriously yet she showed, by going to Versailles and returning unchallenged, that such an idea was not necessarily outlandish. Once the opposing forces had time to reassemble (and had negotiated corresponding agreements with the Prussians in place) any opportunity to consolidate the gains of the uprising all but disappeared. If the Commune began in the spectral language of the *Communist Manifesto*, historically it returned to spectrality by the beginning of April 1871.

Commune was declared, but by this time a surprise attack on Versailles was foreclosed and Thiers, in notable consultation with the Prussians, was able to consolidate a massive counter-revolutionary force.

What is fascinating is not this basic retelling of the fateful weeks after, but the flashes of revolutionary promise the Talbots have Michel dramatize (again, mostly from the historical record, but as an activity with composition, framing, shading, and focal distance all used to punctuate and create a personal story as living history). "And now we build a perfect world," says Michel, and she and her companion, Elianne, set about the tasks at hand, in education, in childcare, in food distribution, in property redistribution, and in unleashing the social power of women. The list seems less abstract over the pages because of the spatial coordinates in which its text is arrayed; indeed, this is one way the process beyond the freeze frames of barricades is communicated. Critically, the graphic presses a dynamic instantiation that, while not assuming a crude equivalence, conjures an elemental praxis and serial connection to the moment. All of the familiar graphic techniques to indicate movement are employed (minus for the most part motion lines and the grammar of sound we have touched on earlier, for which alternating panels with changed positions in bodies are usually substituted), but the activities of the political movement are expressed by the intimacy of the vignettes with one another. How does the imaging negotiate the history depicted with that of the medium used? Does the *Red Virgin* ever challenge the conventions given to the graphic in its history, or is it enough that Michel's drama is drawn at all? Can the graphic envision the utopia invoked? Is this its *Anschaulichkeit*?

On a basic level, one could say drawing utopia simply negates the principle of utopia in play; on another, if, as the Talbots suggest, Michel does not embody the Commune outright she might yet signify the persistence of utopia and the idea of the Commune in her figuration and dreams. Whatever is transcendent in the idea is only discernible in the constellation of her life as situated, as materially resonant. This quality is then used to place Michel in the verifiable processes of the Commune. One panel, for instance, has Michel in the foreground of the scene where the Commune is declared (see above—the background is clearly taken from a woodcut of the moment that appeared in the aforementioned illustrated press). We know that Michel often voiced the slogan "Vive la Commune!" so why not here? This does not validate Appert's pernicious intent in photomontage but nevertheless affirms the graphic is not innocent in its apprehension. In general, the graphic allows the Talbots to make connections around the idea of utopia in its perseverance that are not there to echo just the facts of the Paris Commune, or indeed the veracity of Michel's self-representation, but rather they point to an imaginary itself with drawing as an expressive narrative desire of the dreamworld dreamed from catastrophe. Thus, while most of the novel cleaves to life representation as conventionally realist, the imaginary asks one to figure what is not being drawn as true to life. The technical solution is to frame Michel's story with Gilman's thoughts on utopian fiction (that includes commentary on Bellamy, Wells, and Gilman's own contributions). Gilman reads to Michel from H. G. Wells' novel, *When the Sleeper Wakes*, serialized of course in the English illustrated newspaper, *The Graphic*. For her part, we have Michel dreaming through Jules Verne's science fiction and imagining, on her voyage of deportation, New Caledonia as a utopian paradise. While Michel's "ethnographic" work with the Kanaks on the islands has been appropriately questioned, it is represented here as an extension of her social responsibility and genuine solidarity. She does not find her utopia, of course, but continues to hold to the truth of its possibility, steeled by the Kanak revolt of 1878.[30] It is this sense, rather than illustrating the facts of Michel's existence, that the graphic dares to convey.

Is the Talbots' *Red Virgin* merely a supplement to the extant archive, an entertaining history with less words than Michel's memoirs of 1886, or her book on the Commune from 1898?[31] This reminds us of *Capital, the*

30 The Kanak rebellion against French colonialism is well known and the struggle for independence in New Caledonia continues to the present day. Overviews include, Jean-Marie Colombani, *Double Calédonie: d'une utopie à l'autre* (Paris: Denoël, 1999); Jacqueline Sénès, *La Vie quotidienne en Nouvelle-Calédonie de 1850 à nos jours* (Mesnil-sur-l'Estrée: Société Nouvelle Firmin-Didot, 1987); and Martyn Lyons, *The Totem and the Tricolour: A Short History of New Caledonia since 1774* (Randwick: New South Wales University Press, 1986).

31 In addition to *La commune*, already noted, see *The Red Virgin: Memoirs of Louise Michel* (Bullitt Lowry and Elizabeth Ellington Gunther eds and trans) (Tuscaloosa, AL: University of Alabama Press, 1981). This is a translation of *Memoires de Louise*

manga once more and the constitutive tension between adaptation and transformation (in the history of forms as a social demand). Clearly, the graphic novel is not intended to stand in for Michel's life, yet it is important to assess whether its "graphicness" accentuates the unrepresentativeness of representation itself in the meaning of a revolutionary's self-understanding. Recall that Michel's memoirs were written while she was imprisoned in solitary confinement for three years (an extraordinary circumstance—her science fiction novel, *Les Microbes humain*, was written contemporaneously and is a symptomatic measure of Michel's extreme situation).[32] In her biography *Louise Michel*, Edith Thomas gently chides Michel for the distance between what can be corroborated and her somewhat effervescent self-representation (Michel, ever the revolutionary, yet also the author of Catholic, royalist, and Bonapartist poetry!).[33] Hagiography? No. Thomas says bluntly, "we must discount her testimony." That Thomas views Michel's life as a "*roman picaresque*" is not a rejection of its truth, but is an indication of the fraught nature of the material content of the idea of the commune she is held to speak, which composes its truth in representation. For Thomas, the core of Michel's revolutionary feminism and anarchism does not lie in the purification of their spirit but in the force, not the content, of Michel's expression (a contrast with those studies

Michel, ecrits par elle-meme (Paris: F. Roy, 1886). Nowhere in her memoir does Michel remember herself as the "red virgin." By referencing a number of versions of Michel's story I do not offer a composite as such. I am more interested in whether narrative finds an adequate expressive form through or within revolutionary ardor.

32 See Louise Michel, *Trois romans: Les Microbes humains, Le Monde nouveau, Le Claque-dents* (Lyon: PUL, 2013). Despite the hardships of prison Michel planned a classic feuilleton serial of six parts that would move from establishing a utopia on Earth to producing one in space.

33 Thomas continually wrestles with the angel of Michel's characterizations but it is not just to challenge revolutionary romanticization. What sometimes comes across as cynicism is a deep engagement with how Michel, an agent of history, comes to make history in her telling. This marks Thomas's work as refreshing even if its style is every bit as effervescent as Michel's self-representation, which carries through both a spirit of radical feminism and anarchism. See Édith Thomas, *Louise Michel ou la Velleda de l'anarchie* (Paris: Gallimard, 1971). Translated as, *Louis Michel* (Penelope Williams trans.) (Montreal: Black Rose Books, 1980).

that persistently use Michel's memoir as definitive historical corroboration). Thomas accepts, therefore, that Michel was apt to "play" her life as much as live it, but such a comment in itself is no reason to discount the power that animates revolutionary performance (posing, therefore, not just as pretense but as provocation, something we have already noted in the photography of the Commune). This may also warrant the Talbot's graphic exuberance while also underlining how the graphic novel can extend and visualize Michel's affective embrace of meaningful solidarity. Again, the facts are not irrelevant, but it is the truth in Michel's fidelity that is striking rather than any status, like that of Braquehais, as "un témoin fidèle." Measuring Michel's politics across her life is always about correlations not declarations or definitions. In this regard, as Bullitt Lowry and Elizabeth Ellington Gunter put it, "Michel's anarchism was emotional, not theoretical." Not every fiction of memory is a necessary truth, but the image can negotiate the difference in poignant if sometimes literal ways.

One of the most noted events of Michel's life was her trial in December 1871, for which there is a great deal of official documentation. At this point, there seemed little doubt in Michel's mind that she would be executed like other central Commune figures, and so she greets her impending martyrdom with eloquent gusto. The Talbots devote several panels to the trial and include verbatim excerpts from Michel's well-known final speech, including the flourish, "I have finished. If you are not cowards, kill me." It is a brilliant text of defiance that needs no embellishment. Michel will include an unexpurgated official account of her trial, with her speech taken from the *Gazette de Tribunaux*, as an appendix to her memoirs. In her statement to the Council of War at the trial Michel takes responsibility for all of the accusations made, even those for which no evidentiary corroboration by the prosecution was actually supplied: "As for the burning of Paris, yes, I participated in it . . . I had no accomplices in that. I acted on my own." Michel then claims to have attended all the meetings at the Hôtel de Ville about Commune decisions, a statement, Thomas notes, contradicted by her reported simultaneous activities elsewhere in the city as an ambulance nurse, soldier, and teacher. As Thomas goes through the charges, she can find very little that sticks, that is consistent either with the extant testimony Michel provided over several months of interrogations, or with the substantial testimony recorded by others on her behalf. In the end, it was the pre-trial documentation that prevailed over Michel's court day challenge. The prosecutor withdrew all of the charges except the one about carrying a weapon during an insurrection. Michel would be deported to New Caledonia with thousands of other Communards and their sympathizers.

Gullickson points out that Michel presented the Council with a bourgeois dilemma: ostensibly, a comparatively well-educated and professional woman of their own, but who dared to express solidarity and actively support an uprising of working-class women and men. This is also a representational dilemma for imaging the Commune (in fine art fashion) that the Talbots attempt to address and refigure in their graphic novel. To individuate and heroify is perhaps the easiest route, to mark the exception in what is already an exceptional revolutionary life. The narrative framing, the kinetic tension between centering Michel in some panels (particularly her pulpit-delivered speeches to the women's club at the church of Saint-Germain l'Auxerrois), and casting her among the crowds in others, asks the reader and viewer for another way to see commitment and praxis, even when figured against massacre and defeat. The novelization in images of Louise Michel does not attempt to reclaim a revolutionary essence from the vagaries of her memory (again, in Michel's case, either recalled in solitary confinement, or 27 years after the Paris Commune in her book on the event), nor the concrete hypostatization of her life as the real of transformation—of gender, of class, of the very idea of communism. The graphic re-records and is replicated but, like serialization, it is not replication for its own sake. Here, it does not contain the lost or the absent of the photograph, or the death in the image as countlessly recalled by critics (usually via Kracauer and Benjamin, plus plentiful critical metonyms drawn from Blanchot), but "graphicness" does share something with the graphing of the photo, which is its capacity to ghost or spectralize the time of its presence. Just as Badiou teases out Marx's ambiguity about the Commune between its anti-statist stance and certain quasi-state imperatives (including an organized military defense—what we might call in this situation a strategy of the sensible) so the graphic hovers between impression and expression of a communist idea, where the *Red Virgin* in particular becomes a kind of spectral mode of verisimilitude—fiction as constitutively more than a refraction on the real. For all of its conventional artwork, then, the *Red Virgin* yet holds true to its central thesis about representational history: imagine otherwise.

This does not settle important questions of Michel's fidelity or not to truths in feminism or in anarchism, both of which offer a graphic line that does not simply trace the "political visibility of the Paris Commune today," as Badiou puts it in his assessment of the event. There are, however, others ways to read its spirit or specter as graphic representation, as a realization if not reality of utopia, as an image of singularity rather than fact. Jacques Tardi's extraordinary tetralogy of comics, *Le Cri du peuple* (2001, adapted from a novel of the same name by Jean Vautrin that originally appeared in 1998) also draws on Michel's revolutionary ardor, and the repertoire of central tropes to which we have already alluded, yet Tardi's work is much more insistent about seeing the event of the Commune as resolutely *à propos* graphic narrative, or as Eric Fournier puts it, "an element as present."[34] *Le Cri du peuple* was a prominent newspaper (again, without graphics) of the Commune edited by Jules Vallès, himself the author of a trilogy on revolutionary life, *Jacques Vingtras* (*L'Enfant*, *Le Bachelier*, *L'Insurgé*).[35] Neither the word of the people, nor its image, are necessarily

34 See Jacques Tardi, *Le Cri du people*, VOLS 1–4 (Paris: Castermann, 2001–2004). Like the Talbots' adaptation of Michel's life, Tardi's visual reworking of Vautrin's novel of the same name would require more extensive formal critique than here, where the focus is chiefly on the mediation of the graphic. Rather than argue that graphic novels do the work of history, or that of photography during the Commune, the visual genealogy here is symptomatic and traces a "heightened" inclusivity active in the maintenance of a popular base. Political antinomies remain: it is not clear, for instance, that a graphic novel is any less niche-bound than a salon painting or a limited-edition wallpaper. We are thinking here, principally, of visual disturbances in what constitutes a living archive. See also Jean Vautrin, *Le Cri du peuple* (Paris: Éditions Grasset et Fasquelle, 1999), translated into English as *The Voice of the People* (John Howe trans.) (London: Phoenix House, 2002). The conversations between Tardi and Vautrin on *Le Cri* would be an alternative research trajectory, not least because Vautrin worked extensively in visual culture as a film director, screenwriter, and actor.

35 See Jules Vallès, *L'Enfant–Le Bachelier–L'Insurgé*: *La Trilogie de Jacques Vingtras en version intégrale* (1878) (Kindle edition).

the medium of its "cry" or "voice" but, like the Talbots, Tardi wants to test the graphic in the living-on of the Commune as event. St. Clair suggests that Tardi's work is part of a struggle over access to "an imaginary of the Commune," an idea that shares some logic with the conceptual apparatus of Kristin Ross's *Communal Luxury*, but with the image as a bridge rather than thought as unmooring. The imaginary derived from the latter makes the modest genealogy of Tardi to Vautrin to Vallès seem more circumscribed, rudely historical rather than critically communal, as in Marx and Engel's term from the *Communist Manifesto*, *Gemeingut*. Yet there can be no doubt that these possibilities live within one another, not just to prove, as Peter Kropotkin states, that "The social Commune will soon cease to be a clearly defined entity,"[36] but because the precise theorization of one cannot live without the serialized social lineaments of the other. At the very least, Tardi's *Le Cri du peuple* attempts to work out that symbiosis, to graph an imaginary in its contradictions.

St. Clair's analysis of Tardi's work emphasizes the artist's focus on the violent frames of history in which the Commune becomes textual, narrated.[37] That Tardi's artistry is able to plumb the trauma of violent conflict is demonstrable in several of his works, including the multi-volume "Journal de Guerre" and his graphic novel, *C'était la guerre des tranchées*.[38]

36 Accessed at the Peter Kropotkin archive, available online on marxists.org: rebrand.ly/aea929 (last accessed: August 26, 2025).

37 See Robert St. Clair, "Reframing the Commune." St. Clair means several things by "reframing" beyond the obvious reference to the cell or panel in sequential art. He notes, "the visual is not merely illustrative of history; it would appear to be one of the very terrains upon which historical, revolutionary, and political struggles continue to be articulated, where they continue to seek some form of intelligibility, if not intelligible form" (p. 151). This is a complement to my sense of *Anschaulichkeit*.

38 Tardi is probably best known for his long-running series, *Les Aventures extraordinaires d'Adèle Blanc-Sec* (Paris: Casterman, 1976–2007). Adèle is a novelist who gets entangled in mysteries at different moments of history (the approach is the Belle Epoque via steampunk). Tardi has also produced many works around violent conflict, particularly the First World War. Before Vautrin's Commune novel, Tardi had adapted Vautrin's works about banlieue life. Within an extensive oeuvre, Tardi has illustrated dozens of novels, classic and popular and has received numerous prizes for his graphic art. While certainly influenced by Hergé's classic deployment of *ligne claire*,

That said, there is a great deal more to Tardi's art than this theme, which is in part why he adapts Vautrin's novel rather than just replay the battles for Paris during the Commune from extant and voluminous historical studies. Some of the key figures discussed above (including Michel) appear in Tardi's graphic tetralogy, but he remains committed to serial storytelling as an aesthetic mode, and it is through this aspect of what Eisner calls the "grammar of sequential art" that we might consider the prospects of the communal graphic, the visualizable (*Anschaulichkeit*) of a communist idea—a dialectics of the emergent line as, counterintuitively, applied.[39]

To be sure, some of the process of articulation cannot be separated from the logic of adaptation itself (Tardi as a "faithful witness" to Vautrin's text as a detective drama), but here I want to emphasize an alternative dimensionality, or serialization as "Other," to the graphic eventness just discussed in the Talbot's work on Michel. On a general level, one can agree with Fournier that Tardi's art elaborates a dialectic between nineteenth century historiography and the social realism of the novel (a subject to which I will return later under the heading of novelization and serialization) coupled with a popularization of the archive and a more recent sense of history from below. To conceptualize further, two other elements quickly emerge—the internalization of the moment in word and image, and a spatial ambivalence about framing history itself. To some extent, the first mode is typical of graphic ekphrasis where the text comments on its pictorial place, yet Tardi also uses this technique both to image parts of Vautrin's quasi-detective fiction and to interlace and extend the telling of the commune, to serialize its meaning. St. Clair suggests that Tardi makes present the Commune by referencing a lineage of storytelling around the event (in Vallès' trilogy, for instance) and by insinuating himself in the text (there is a Tardy in Vautrin's novel whose mention becomes a link to Tardi, with the inevitable pun around "late"). The breaking of a veritable

---

Tardi's range is dynamic and speaks to the present interpretation of the dialectical image as "suddenly emergent"; indeed, of the emergent line as such.

39 See Will Eisner, *Comics and Sequential Art: Principles and Practices* (New York: Norton, 2008). Eisner's principles do not necessarily undo the differences Benjamin draws between painting and the graphic arts so much as clarify that there is an aesthetic at stake, one that can also be arrayed with photography in its specific formal demands.

fourth wall in Tardi's fiction, with a character addressing both the interlocutor and the reader ("j'en ai un connu avec un I") is defamiliarizing in perhaps a more negative sense—an "I was there" rather than a "there is here."

More important, however, is the use of commentary, including thought bubbles, to make the horror of the butchery in the Commune's denouement proximate: not an immediacy of violence but a mediation of the violence depicted. As we have noted with Marx's response to the Paris Commune, this kind of affective embrace is actually more difficult to convey than realist observation because its time of apprehension is shot through with an irreproducible yet material contingency. To affirm the dialectic of form and thought does not distill a typology of revolutionary representation (not least because so many thoughts are lost in deadly praxis). The graphic for Tardi is both a challenge of tableau, to storyboard the complex dimensions of change in situ, and an affective struggle over social meaning, which is part of its eventness, its time and time of extension. True, the story of Tarpagnon, Grondin, and Pucci develops unevenly with the major events and, like Vautrin's novel, finds it difficult to counteract or distance melodrama (beyond a verifiable number, the murder of the Communards, for instance, is far from being a "mystery," the generic thread that builds the narrative). But is there anything in the melding of plot and panorama that advances something akin to a grammar of graphic insurgency? The internalization in the image is less about drawing attention to the fictiveness of popularizing a historical event than it is about the detail in the very idea. All images resist the "standstill" that is the single image as such (the stillness of still photography and still life most of all). Because the comic (*le bande destinée*) is always already dynamic (breaking the frame, changing the size and font of text, manipulating the dimensions and shading of image, punctuating narrative flow—sometimes by reversing it—accentuating a moment over befores and afters) its "standstills" are more pronounced because they are demonstrably irregular and constellated otherwise. Tardi ultimately does not worry if his adaptation is true to Vautrin's text nor necessarily to the veridicality of the archive, but whether the idea in the fictive image itself is sustainable. When we laud particular thinkers, William Morris, for instance, for capturing the spirit of the Paris

Commune it is usually a remark on their prescience for a present—that of the Commune, that of Morris, and that of the critic making the case. *Le Cri du peuple* is an injunction about such presents and presence. Tardi does not think he can make you see that cry, shout, or explosion; his art of the Commune pivots on interpellating its substance. How might we see social change as also a change in seeing? Rather than externalize the history (or reject it as a hopelessly statist appropriation—often fantastically by reference to a dancing Lenin reacting to the event)[40] Tardi draws the image internalizing, not capturing but concatenating.[41]

The dialectical image is in language over and above the pictorial, but the graphic attends to the standstill in their combination, with the graphic as a reflex in persistence and rediscovery—what Vautrin refers to in his narrative as "mixed up" or "entangled" times.[42] If Vautrin's novelization tries to transpose Victor Hugo into the living process of the Commune, Tardi draws the voice of the people as knotted vignettes, with the idea of the event as their assemblage. Not surprisingly, where Vautrin finds a catalyst for action in (very) extended conversation, Tardi uses only those exchanges that allow his drawing to "speak." Thus, Vautrin's quasi-hagiographic interludes to allow for tours of Courbet's living quarters (communal luxury, indeed) are dropped in favor of more forceful connections to the Commune in representing history.

Théophile Mirecourt is a photographer in the story who befriends the soldier turned Communard, Tarpagnan. For the most part, when Mirecourt is featured, Tardi does not try to see photographically (as we have said, the primary way the Commune in process was represented), but dramatizes the revolutionaries' fervor around him. The effect is not just to witness posing by barricades (panels included in the story), but to sense the joy of people attempting to take control of their lives. Manifestos usually make

40 Lenin's purported exuberance is used both to authenticate the Paris Commune as event and to laugh at Lenin for his enthusiasm.

41 St. Clair is right to point to Tardi's heterogenous compositional sources but sees these used in the service of rescue and reparation. The internalization here is actually part of the narrative's centrifugal participation—to take what is living in the Commune as graphic possibility.

42 Vautrin, *Le Cri du peuple*, p. 22.

for dry graphics (there are exceptions, and comics of the *Communist Manifesto* are certainly more kinetic than the text of 1848), although some well-chosen quotations and slogans ("Vive la commune!" most obviously) punctuate speech. Instead, Tardi is particularly concerned to take us to the revelry and ribaldry of celebration during the night following the takeover of March 18, when the fraternizing of the National Guard is toasted, and when singing and carnivalizing excess is duly encouraged. Urban argot and working-class speech fire up the narrative and all kinds of crudeness leaps across the page. Mirecourt decides to take a picture ("ne bougez plus"—"don't move," he says) and a worker/bystander's reaction is "?" or, "Why shouldn't we move, what is this apparatus for?" What is the live art of this worker uprising? The next panel of the photographic subject is upside down, the camera obscura as if inside the camera box. The mis or non-recognition of the technology is followed by a process of inversion used to produce an image from that technology. One is reminded of Benjamin once more, "At the point when Daguerre successfully fixed images in the camera obscura, painters parted company with technicians."[43] Marx too, pondered the implications of this "fixing" of the image in the camera obscura, and used it as a working metaphor for ideology: "Consciousness can never be anything else than conscious existence, and the existence of men is their actual life-process. If in all ideology men and their circumstances appear upside-down as in a camera obscura, this phenomenon arises just as much from their historical life-process as the inversion of objects on the retina does from their physical life-process."[44] Tardi, by contrast, internalizes the technology as a remark on the historical representation of the Commune itself. The third panel in the sequence therefore, places the image right side up, by drawing the photo in its absence from the graphic. It is not simply a montage of what the archive missed but a comment on what the graphic can do.

Internalization is not, in itself, a measure of historical distance or some kind of technologically-determined chronology. It marks time but only in the sense that it carries its concept as a substance of articulation,

43 Benjamin, *On Photography*, p. 61.

44 See Karl Marx and Friedrich Engels, *The German Ideology* (New York: Prometheus Books, 1998), p. 42.

FIGURE 34. Panels from Jacques Tardi, *Le Cri du peuple*, VOL. 1: *Les Canons du 18 Mars* (2001), p. 43.

or what I have been thinking of as seriality in process. Graphic mimesis, imitating the camera in this instance, is a line that cuts the line of representation, the "canon of language" as Benjamin puts it.[45] Sometimes the graphological remains are in words, yet the panels also mediate pictures as, simultaneously, the magic that representation must challenge. If, as Benjamin avers, "history decays into images, not stories" then does the Commune only assume that detritus?[46]

The last time we see Théo is in Book Three, *Les Heures Sanglantes*, and, as with much of the tetralogy, Tardi moves the mise en scène of the Commune by having key characters travel within it (in this volume, for instance, Pucci and Pouffard connect the action by driving a carriage through Paris retrieving the dead just as Thiers' forces overcome the barricades—a pertinent contrast to Karl and Jenny's walk remarked upon above). As Théo passes a poster from the Commune calling on the people to make a last stand, he comes across a group of workers building a barricade, one of whom (Palmyre, in Vautrin's novel) recognizes him as a friend of Tarpagnan. Tardi shows the Communards Lili and Ziquet reading a Commune poster then, as they turn to act on its instructions, he continues their reading as a framing text around the subsequent panels. The communique is full of stirring phrases, "If you want to live free in a free and equal France [. . .] You should rise up as one person" and "in the name of this glorious France, mother of all popular revolutions, permanent home of ideas of justice and of solidarity which must be and will be the laws of the world"—abstractions on the real they frame. Ziquet affirms that Versailles will not have the last word, but neither does the Commune's Committee on Public Health nor the Civilian Delegate at War (who are both noted as signatories to the poster). In the next panel Theo thinks about this last stand, where the Communards will face their French counterparts, nose to nose, eye to eye, as the "ultimate ordeal." His melodramatic thought echoes to some degree those of the poster. But then, in a panel that directly comments on the visual archive of the Paris Commune, Théo photographs the people of Paris, women, men, children,

45 Walter Benjamin, *Reflections: Essays, Aphorisms, Autobiographical Writings* (Peter Demetz ed., Edmond Jephcott trans.) (New York: Schocken, 1986), p. 334.

46 Benjamin, *Arcades Project*, p. 476.

insurgents of every stripe, posing astride their barricade: "Encore un cliché avant de faire la guerre" (see above). Braquehais may have been a person of few words but in Théo, Tardi finds a way both to distance the history and to internalize its meaning for a second history, that of the image itself, serialized (this, then, is a veritable second series). Yet Tardi adds a further coda to this remark on technological reproducibility and the real of the communist idea. After indulging in cliché, Théo spots a mother breast-feeding her baby (also discernible in the previous panel). Certainly, Theo's thought bubbles may just add more cliché or platitude, as he remarks that it is "for the baby that we fight." In the novel, Vautrin builds suspense by counting the seconds for Théo's last photograph to be taken (the time of exposure). For Tardi, the panels themselves provide the temporal serenity of this image, shattered immediately by cannon fire. Most people on or around the barricade are killed instantly, including the mother. The baby, perched next to the remains of the camera lens, bleeds profusely from one eye. Théo dies thinking of his love for Tarpagnan (they were supposed to meet again that evening). Vautrin might be able to add more detail as a whole to this scene (Théo, "the photographer, the first photo-journalist, a man ahead of his time") and augment a dimension of its historical symbolic (his "magnificent invention for looking at people is pulverized," then an attacking Versaillais soldier steps on the photographic plate), but Tardi draws its violent transformation so that the evidence of the photo is also this, in its obliteration. This is the fragility of the communist idea before the archive.

Just as the Talbots' graphic novel on Louise Michel is an engagement with her utopian imaginary beyond the verification and use value of an individual document, so Tardi reimagines Vautrin's already reimagined novelization of the Commune as story, as narrative, in ways that foreground its impossible intimacy with the historical conditions of its idea. In the brutal conflagration of the Commune's defeat (which occupies at least half of Tardi's tetralogy, with the last volume augmenting Vautrin's narrative) Tardi develops that broken photographic plate as if it exists only to mark what the photograph has not done, but nevertheless completes dialectically. To an extent this respects Benjamin's conceptualization of the image, and the graphic line that is also, whatever else it is, revolution's communal interlocutor. On the one hand, imagining the Commune proliferates as,

FIGURE 35. Jacques Tardi, *Le Cri du peuple*, VOL. 3, p. 5.

like Peter Watkins' "reenactment" film of 2000 (a documentation of process as document) social crisis overdetermines communing with the Paris Commune.[47] On the other hand, graphic remains remain speculative, as if self-conscious about popular representation, the banalization of the everyday, and the faithfulness of a line to the line (largely a fiction of the political about the Paris Commune in the present, yet also a way to think of its serial others). This, indeed, might be a false tension between appropriateness and appropriation, the pictorial antinomy in the very idea of "un témoin fidèle." Even when complicating Benjamin's phantasmatic and phantasmagorical impressionism, it is relatively easy for theories and theorists today to gesture towards notable communists and anarchists in and around the Paris Commune, checking off all that is academically louche (states, parties, grands récits, and, lamentably, Lenin's dance)[48] in favor of subjunctive if not subjective demands on the resolutely unimpeachable: free association, individuality, ecology, localism, the artisanal. To the extent that Tardi "adapts" and draws all of this while still narrating obscene violence and murder, the voice or cry of the people is imaged as urgent and urgently present. But does this add one more gesture or style, the graphic, while obstinately condemning the event of the Commune to its past, a kind of hypostasis of the image consonant with an inability to destroy the plodding inertia of hegemony among current crises? Is the very language of the graphic another imaginative (and imaginary) niche, an extension of brand Commune, an edgeless lifestyle, as unlikely to influence the workers of the world as Badiou's mathematics will actually add up to social transformation?

---

47 See *La commune (Paris, 1871)*, directed by Peter Watkins (13 Production, 2000). Shot in an abandoned factory on the outskirts of Paris, Watkins' project is an extraordinary film made in part, as he points out, to address the exclusion of the Commune from French education and from everyday life (many of the non-professional cast knew nothing of the Commune). Using ruins to explore the ruins of history and how history is made, Watkins offers a cinematic essay on the time/space of popular memory. The film, in either its 3:30 or 5:45 hour versions, interrogates the space of actor and witness, spontaneity and script, process and presumption. In a narrative bereft of special effects, the idea of the Commune becomes one.

48 The image of Lenin dancing the day when the Russian Revolution lasted longer than the Commune is almost as fanciful as the quip about cracking eggs and omelets in Lenin-centered lore.

Badiou also calculates the communist idea in its own crisis against crisis, and necessarily so as a radically dialectical reading of the "historicity of politics." His intervention on the Paris Commune is not a thought experiment on the appropriateness of form but about the constitution of the "evental" as a materialist injunction.[49] In our example the event of image is appropriately multiple and disjunct, and can include the painterly elite as well as the solitary photographer, in Tardi (and Vautrin) images of revolution blasted quite literally from the continuum of history. Again, the point is not that some combination of word and image ineluctably reveals the truth of the Commune as event, or that the Talbots, in drawing the life of Louise Michel fashion the kernel of feminist anarchism, but that graphicness itself is a relay of materially situated insurgence, one that responds both to the vision of the artist and to the conditions of eventness that pose the substance of the Paris Commune as a continuing question: how might its claims on history still assert a hold on the imagination and image of social change today? Heightened graphicness in this sense is one speaking specter of revolutionary presencing, but the dialectical image settles only on the formal question, not the essence of form in its moment as serialization's other. Peter Snowdon's film of 2014, for instance, "The Uprising," is composed of found smart phone videos of the insurrections collectively called the "Arab Spring" of 2011 uploaded to YouTube. Its "cri du peuple" is not assured by the art of participation, yet there is a principle of fidelity to the event, an insurgent citationality, that shows the desire to image freedom in process is also history's charge, if not its concept.[50] So too, the graphic remains of the Commune imprints its now as a historical inscription (Tardi's drawing is the return of the "time of the cherries" as Vautrin puts it, recalling a song heavily associated with the Commune) and it is only from that now that the Commune from the future remains true.

---

49 See Badiou, "Paris Commune."

50 See *The Uprising*, directed by Peter Snowdon (Rien à Voir Production, 2013). Like other projects on imaging revolution mentioned here, Snowdon's documentary requires more comment than space will allow. Whatever the spontaneity of the project, much of the film's deep impress comes from editing, yet it is clear that the archive of the possible is greater than what is extant in social transformation.

REBEL WITHOUT AN AFFECT: SERIALIZING THE POST-HUMAN

> "There is no single locus of great refusal, no soul of revolt, source of all rebellions."
>
> —Michel Foucault, *The History of Sexuality*

Tardi's representation of the meaning of the Paris Commune for social transformation organizes time and space not to supplement Vautrin's novel or even Marx's Third Address but to instantiate graphically the tremendous challenge of overcoming historical forms of socio-economic injustice. Narrative returns to the event to rethink its substance in any number of ways (as fiction, as utopia, as an aesthetic as well as political intervention, as both a history that was and one that has not been). The violence depicted is a ground for Tardi's humanism, as if to reassert the difficulty of valuing life against a backdrop where conflict is an end in itself not a means. Part of the achievement of Tardi's art is to think of Vautrin's novelization of the Paris Commune as a challenge for graphic reinscription, to take all that is kinetic and aesthetic in a people's uprising as a "book with images," as a readerly demand not to simplify (*aplatir* once more) but to interrogate what might compose a people's story as history and as a question about its future. To this point we have considered serialization as a problematic about how social change is and is not articulated, the power of telling complicated by its formal relay and that which impedes or elaborates its time of possibility, for Marx even its possible communism. This is a radically partial reading of the logic of transformation (and partial in more than one sense) and is not meant to stand in for an archive of struggle that far exceeds the graphic Marxism of *Le Capital* in serial connections, or, for instance, Tardi's serialization of the story of the Paris Commune. For all the dominance of image culture in narrating the substance of the everyday, there is plenty of discourse that eschews image as either intervention or elaboration. Novelization, as we will explore later, is ambivalently positioned to explore the borders that the image of story purports to tell. Here, however, the aim is to think of social change as specifically a serialization of the Other, as a story about what makes up a human both in terms of a human (a microbe human, to borrow from Michel) and as a subject of what has not been. If revolution is necessarily transformation, then the very terms of human are at stake in the social being desired, or in many ways felt. Indeed, between the new human and post-human, principles of transformation are themselves have been "posted" or reimagined.[1] Even the living on of seriality can be deemed nostalgic or as performing the last gasp of human semblance, one where affect is a scene simultaneously of confirmation and sublation. Marx imagines a series that interpellates a reader as an agent of social change; here we will consider a series that respects such interpellation yet problematizes the place of agency in such a process.

To recall Deleuze on series, one can think of affect as a secondary series to the conditions of narrative ("telling") we have explored in the dissimulation of capital as text and as relation. Here, affect is not an allegory or parable of the difference in ways of telling (in words, in image, in fact) but functions more as paradox (as it does for feeling and emotion in some genealogies of philosophy). The affect series, like the schizophrenic for Deleuze and Guattari, is a logical contravention and necessarily troubles the conditions of becoming in seriality. Dialectically, affect picks away at living-on, not as a measure of unreflective reciprocity, but as a sign, again paradoxically, of material contradiction—a becoming that is unbecoming, even to its place in Deleuzean thought. The tropological power of the schizophrenic has its own power of living-on, and not just as an academic exercise, because it is at once an effect of and an agent against the fabula of capitalist desire. Yet there are other character concepts at stake (even the "Marx" noted in manga) and affect, while notoriously nebulous, haunts the material procession of panels in the storytelling we have invoked, just as seriality tracks social change.

Because affect is insistently invoked to denote our constantly changing relations to the world, as made by and for us, it is small wonder it is both

1 This is a huge topic, of course, but calls attention to the human as a revolutionary subject not simply bound to anthropocentric reconstitution.

everywhere and nowhere in being. "Made" here is not a determination and, since affect is a process without origin, the cause of cause is not a political predicament for being. One can take a position on affect, but that of course would not be what affect is. In their assessment of affect theory, Seigworth and Gregg point out:

> Affect can be understood [. . .] as a gradient of bodily capacity—a supple incrementalism of ever-modulating force-relations—that rises and falls not only along various rhythms and modalities of encounter but also through the troughs and sieves of sensation and sensibility, an incrementalism that coincides with belonging to comportments of matter of virtually any and every sort. Hence, affect's always immanent capacity for extending further still: both into and out of the interstices of the inorganic and non-living, the intracellular divulgences of sinew, tissue, and gut economies, and the vaporous evanescence of the incorporeal (events, atmospheres, feeling-tones).[2]

Indeed, such incrementalism (degrees of gradualism) is so supple as to be infinite in scale; a gradient (the magnitude of a property) categorically without measure, an a-seriality, a comportment that is immanently limitless, an "inventory of shimmers" as they put it, whose author and content are quite simply inestimable. Affect necessarily precedes the affective turn, just as its link to posthuman futurity accentuates its incredulity before the very idea of a human subject in the present. Whether we are conscious of

---

2 Melissa Greg and Gregory J. Seigworth (eds), *The Affect Theory Reader* (Durham, NC: Duke University Press, 2010), p. 2. See also Gregory J. Seigworth and Carolyn Pedwell (eds), *The Affect Theory Reader 2: Worldings, Tensions, Futures* (Durham, NC: Duke University Press, 2023). The second volume notes that the first attempted to "capture without closing off an undulating, albeit never-to-be-cohesive, field of inquiry in the midst of its coming-to-bloom" (p. 2). There are tonal, theoretical, and political differences arrayed in the second volume but it still struggles with the tension between what is termed "a proliferation of feels" and a resistance to any sense that "anything goes." The reversal, but not dialectical, of "An Inventory of Shimmers" to a "Shimmer of Inventories" defamiliarizes inventory, while fetishizing shimmer. The political gainsay of the theory often remains hobbled by a valorization of the inchoate as its own reward, which is not always a communal luxury of affect in the world(ings).

affect or not, it will survive both our expiration and that of the species—as what, this reading will consider. The passage of intensities, which are neither feelings nor emotions, but force effects, are not the substance of the human, or rather only one substance of the human, since affect, like love, can generate language, something of the texture of adequate knowledge. For those who argue affect is outside reason and agency, the affective scholar will reply, "not really," except of course if the human is deemed the locus solus (the unique or single place) of those attributes. Actually, you can number affects (Darwin, Tomkins, Jameson, and Spinoza all do this—although the latter is scrupulous in not fixing a number) or you might maintain an adjectival amorphousness or nounal exuberance wholly consonant with its slippery, abstract nature. Needless to say, whenever a named emotion does not provide approximation, affect surely lurks (it is a superimposition, not a synonym, of emotion and feeling). Since the labor of affect in knowledge is divided disciplinarily, it is pointless trying to dismiss its legible variation (affect wars are keenly fought among academics, although few are waiting on their decision). What for some is subject to science is for others not subject at all, or science, and represents instead a rigorously magic methodology (that Marx, in an alternative register, explores as commodity fetishism). Here the question concerns the power to affect or be affected by, where power is, whatever else it is, an aesthetic and radically political disposition. If this path often leads to Spinoza, and particularly to the *Ethics*,[3] in the following it has a certain dialectical emphasis and a materialist one, perhaps even a contradictory rational ghost before a mystical or metaphysical shell—what Raymond Williams once had the temerity to call a "structure of feeling."[4] Perspicuously in-between (between passivity and activity, for instance, but also between body and body, body and non-body, and, most frustratingly, non-body and non-body—how the latter may be adjudicated is not altogether solved by New Materialism), affect generally recognizes the troubled borders of

3 Benedict Spinoza, *The Ethics* in *A Spinoza Reader: The Ethics and Other Works* (Edwin Curley ed. and trans.) (Princeton, NJ: Princeton University Press, 1994), pp. 85–265.

4 Raymond Williams, *Marxism and Literature* (Oxford: Oxford University Press, 1977), pp. 128–35.

mind and body where being becomes a fraught space relatively unencumbered by less febrile categories or determinations. Indeed, this is a fecund if not fantastic ground of imaginary engagement, a place of striving (*conatus* in Spinoza) that yet makes form or at least indicates its process; in this case, the posthuman affect called "cyborg."

The question of cyborgian affect is not new; indeed, at its broadest it is coterminous with an obstinately human pastime—the creation of facsimiles of and for ourselves (statues, dolls, puppets automatons, robots, etc., like Raudnitz's clay figures above, used to dramatize the Paris Commune). Yet because the science and technology of replication and AI is rapidly intensifying, the affective past of identification is catching up to a future in which the very terms of human constituency and socialization are at stake, especially if based upon the body as extensive. If the cyborg is a project of artful and conceptual hybridization, at what moment does it reach the minimally human, the point of being affectively human, not effectively so? Sharalyn Orbaugh provocatively terms this "emotional infectivity," although she tends to recode this as body aesthetics rather than here, as the power of posthuman prosthetics versus cycles of power that pivot on the reproduction and extension of the human as subject.[5] This is not just a project at the heart of many artistic practices but a genuine concern regarding social change, where affect can still be read to influence consciousness and action about. The topic is huge and within cultural critique is hardly reducible to Spinoza or Tomkins as such. While the contribution here is modest, and perhaps overly reliant on serial presentation, I wish to indicate some of the salient implications for further materialist analysis around this confluence. If we have nothing to lose but our chains, why burden the cyborg with them?

Ghost in the Shell (hereafter, GITS) is an over thirty-year old manga/anime/live action franchise that spans several series in print (manga, ani-manga and a novelization), feature films, OVA (original or straight to video animation), TV episodes, video games and a stage play. Stylistically and thematically it is a child of the emerging internet (the manga first

5 Sharalyn Orbaugh, "Emotional Infectivity: Cyborg Affect and the Limits of the Human," *Mechademia* 3 (2008): 150–72.

FIGURE 36. Mamoru Oshii (dir.), *Ghost in the Shell* [攻殻機動隊] (Production I.G., 1995), 83 mins.

appeared in 1989)[6] and it explores network society through the kind of noir cyberpunk historically associated with writers like William Gibson (particularly the novel *Neuromancer*, 1984). True, whatever the media, there are elements of its imaging and story that conform to rather more standard fantasies of male adolescent heterosexist masculinism (that tend to suture in their own way the "boy's clubbishness" of much normative cyberpunk). Shirow Masamune, in particular, the author/artist of the original seinen manga, has both encouraged the expansion of the franchise, and intensified its aura of sexist objectification and misogyny (his artistic proclivities have included fetishistic hentai in posterbooks and trading cards). The licensing of the franchise, however, allows for taking license with Shirow's desire even if the series as a whole appears to obstinately repeat some of his more obvious motifs and obsessions. Any attempt to distill only the positive elements of serial narrative and image in *Ghost in the Shell* (perhaps a stand-alone complex, to borrow from the franchise terminology) can misrepresent its active presencing and the material conflicts and contradictions of its affective appeal (including an internal polemic about the future of sex/gender/race/class differentiation). Not surprisingly, the links between desire and displacement are allegorized by the very conceit of the series: that cyborg embodiment proceeds by grasping the technological replication of the soul as mind or consciousness, the precious inchoate substance carried briefly by its fleshly counterpart, itself imaginatively overdetermined by our formal projections and unconscious prosthetics. Often read as basic Cartesian duality, the series, particularly in Oshii Mamoru's feature-length anime (the focus of the present discussion), seems more interested in techno-embodiment as sublation, in which the cyborg traces a path to the super-extension of Hegelian Geist or spirit, not a "*Geist* in the shell" but one that evolves from their networked fusion. This indeed is the vexed matrix of cyborg affect, or at least that affect figured by series, a mode of extension perhaps more properly Spinozist than Hegelian, yet dialectically bound to a "hominis" yet to be (as non-subject) or as a human that is not one. Cyborg affect is a symptom

6 Masamune Shirow, *Ghost in the Shell* (Frederik L. Schodt and Toren Smith trans), 2nd EDN (Milwaukie, OR: Dark Horse Comics, 2004); Shirow Masamune, *Kōkaku kidotai* (Tokyo: Kōdansha, 1991).

of fully-networked being, one rapidly being condensed into AI (a transition still marked by nostalgic anthropomorphism). Here I tend to read dialectic like affect, as a space between, holding together Spinoza and Hegel in the manner of some fantastic Bellmer doll (featured in Oshii's second GITS film, *Innocence*). But such elements still seem to form the projects' mystical shell rather than the ambivalent rationality of their central themes. On the one hand, the following will indicate how representational aesthetics come into conflict with the radically post-human and free association of "Ghost in the Shell" as an anime/manga subculture why would the posthuman need to read this story?); on the other hand, I am particularly interested in the forms of time and subjective displacement articulated in the intersection of cyborg sequencing (including its implications for seriality as affect unbound). Cyborg affect does not just ask the familiar, where does a body end? It also interrogates the terms of technological reproducibility in what constitutes social and political activity. The synchrony of Major Kusanagi Motoko (the central character/cyborg/code) holds important lessons for how we read/see affect in series, the ghost of socialization itself in cycles of power. Obviously, this is a particular interpretation of affect which is neither diametrically opposed to emotion or feeling, nor is it all blissfully rhizomatic (at least for now: network extension still has a problem overcoming basic human finitude, a ground for aesthetics per se, even as avatars abound). Spectrality, ghosting as a real foundation, has been a feature of materialist critique for some time, but few theorists have explored this possibility within a science fiction aesthetic that begins with affect rather than read this as a consequence, as a special effect, as philosophical CGI. The logic of such subject serialization, an "Other" serialization (where seriality de-subjectivizes) interrogates modes of transformation in socialization, here understood as the synchronic space between ghosts and shells, between reflex and the reflective, between anima and animation, and between impromptu pictures and conscious correlations of the human and machine.

Stylistically, in his GITS films Oshii favors a kind of noir, without voiceover, a neo or tech noir against a tableau of the police procedural (culturally, a serial dominant). Noir can be discussed as a basic problem of figuring the posthuman in late or globalized capitalism. On one level, this picks up on its generic components in cinematic history, the darkness visible of commodified and networked existence, coupled with an incredulity towards family and home. Noir is also a specific way to understand the problem of affect in the age of disambiguating bodies, the dispersed, fragmented and ephemeral pieces of identity forever being niched to permit narration as accumulation to continue. Serial noir constellates identity without authenticating it (the procedural seeks closure for a procedure that logically denies it, as if it is the procedural that ends crime). It should be noted that whatever is intrinsic to affect, anti-capitalism is not it—a critique of political economy is never only "intensity" since it seethes with hopeless veridicality—as Brian Massumi points out, affect is at best "proto-political."[7] Noir generally revels in the anxiety of ceding personal power to social manifestation, the long shadows of appropriate and appropriating existence. As primarily a "sad affect" in Spinoza's sense, or something of a negative dialectic in mine, it reflects upon the power of deadening institutions (*potestas*) while insistently pressing some form of visual or narratological countermand (*potentia*), a scene of serial antinomy.[8] The cyborg further complicates the staging of noir resistance because it almost literally embodies the techno-institutional power that precisely limits such a countermand. Paradoxically, it appears to disassemble both sides of the subjection/subject divide. This is not just a "parable of the virtual" in Massumi's important and influential articulation; it should also be considered its constitutive and by all means "special" effect/affect.[9]

The central premise of *Ghost in the Shell* (across its franchise) follows a standard police procedural. In the world of its near future, GITS focuses

7 Brian Massumi, *The Politics of Affect* (Cambridge: Polity, 2015), p. *ix*. Given the title of the book, the interviews within attempt to elaborate how the proto-political exists as a field of the political.

8 There is no space to detail this vital tension but let us say that *potentia* constitutes the real movement of history against its purely institutional forms. While Hardt and Negri end *Empire* on a note of revolutionary spirit and the "irrepressible lightness and joy of being communist," the antinomies of power do not easily produce such joy. Noir's sad affect is an admission of material and determinate constraints with specific implications for human futures. See Michael Hardt and Antonio Negri, *Empire* (Cambridge, MA: Harvard University Press, 2000).

9 Brian Massumi, *Parables of the Virtual* (Durham, NC: Duke University Press, 2002).

on a detective/police unit called Public Security Section 9 (the Japanese title for GITS is 攻殻機動隊 Kōkaku Kidōtai, "Mobile Armored Riot Police"). The crimes they are battling feature terrorism, government and corporate corruption, arms trading and various forms of hacking, both of government and military information, and of specific individuals (the "ghost-hacking" and "ghost-dubbing" of cyberbrains—or dennō). Major Kusanagi Motoko is a cyborg, in this case a mass-produced synthetic "full-body prosthesis" with an augmented-cybernetic human brain. The cyborg is (almost) quintessentially aesthetic and is caught between the artifice and the artificial, both a fleshly fabricant and all of the veracity of the virtual. The cyborg does not exist (and is not a subject as such) or like affect is everywhere in being: it embodies the art of becoming as a quantum leap for science that is simultaneously a reconfiguration of being beyond human (welcome, AI).[10] Of course, if we define ourselves through technological extensions (a techno-ontology) then we are all always already cyborgs, but it is more useful to think of the cyborg initially as a site of technical intensity, where the mind struggles to define itself in the fusion of body and being. Kusanagi herself is so well made she doubts which part of her is not made. The series as a whole pivots on the idea of an existential crisis which is not one, in the sense that to doubt one's being is to confirm its cognitive process. Yet again, however, this is less a Cartesian insistence than a potentially transformative one, an acknowledgment of a technological autopoiesis.[11] Whereas the robot is shaped by its utility, the cyborg is manufactured according to semblance, a form in which utility

10 Here is not the place to summarize the cyborg in theory and practice but its political and cultural efficacy depends very much on the assembly line, the way it is conceptually "made." While Donna Haraway's groundbreaking essay "The Cyborg Manifesto" reinvents the cyborg for materialist and feminist critique the cyborg itself is far from being all that Haraway is about in terms of gender and nature, or humans and companion species. That said, *The Cyborg Handbook* (which reprints and reedits the essay) is still a good entry way into matters cyborgian even if, as here, the culture and theory of cyborgs has gone in several different directions since then. See Chris Hables Gray (ed.), *The Cyborg Handbook* (New York: Routledge, 1995).

11 I am thinking here of the path to self-making from making. See, for instance, Humberto R. Maturana and Francisco J. Varela, *Autopoiesis and Cognition: The Realization of the Living* (Dordrecht: Reidel, 1980).

itself may be less threatening, if uncanny (mannequins, dolls, and puppets almost always signal this troubling similarity in the series, which has a specific history in Japanese culture, as critics like Christopher Bolton have persuasively argued, but it is also a generalizable condition of simulacra).[12] In live action films semblance is easily achieved by having a human play the hybrid, with varieties of deviance and deviation to signal alterity (milky blood, camera grid vision or, in Kusanagi's case, a socket built into her neck—I will turn to the live action version of *Ghost in the Shell* below). Kusanagi is chosen for the unit because of her mass-produced look (a serial manufacture which includes objectification, as the opening credit sequence makes clear), because of her physical abilities, and because she can tap the web and is neurally hard-wired to extend into its circuits or listen in to specific traffic (so-called "ghost whispers"). In both the original manga by Shirow and in the anime by Oshii it is Kusanagi's network presence that piques the interest of the major antagonist in the primary tale, the character called the Puppet Master, an autonomous AI entity with a capacity to hack cyberbrains for political and social advantage (the story suggests it began as a covert government espionage program, labeled Project 2501, within a Japanese intelligence unit also featured in the series, Section 6). Within the genre, this is evidence of a procedural paranoia with different units of the security system either investigating or subverting each other along the way. Obviously, cybercrime is not novel and many countries have their established versions of Section Six and/or Section Nine. The role of the cyborg, however, is deeply prescient as a conflicted mediatory function—that cybernetic crime is a staging of the problem of human subjecthood itself, a transgression of what is constitutive of cognition in knowledge circuits.

The other notable members of Kusanagi's team are Batou, Togusa, and Aramaki. Batou is the muscle of the group, and most of his strength comes from his prosthetic limbs (at moments in the series he exercises, which is a kind of phantomatic nostalgia for types of body maintenance rendered superfluous). Batou is recognizable by his highly unrealistic cybernetic eye implants (the reason is characterological, not technological). His

12 Christopher Bolton, "From Wooden Cyborgs to Celluloid Souls: Mechanical Bodies in Anime and Japanese Puppet Theater," *positions* 10(3) (Winter 2002): 729–71.

cyborganic sensibility places him close to Kusanagi (and close to intimacy), although he appears less conflicted by synthetic self-reflection and is therefore a pertinent generic and genetic foil. But then Togusa further doubles this foil by being an alternatively unaccommodated man (he is described as "natural" or minimally cybernetically enhanced). In the first GITS anime Kusanagi argues it is important to have this variation in the team which is the key to advancement over enhancement (uniformity is a sign of system vulnerability). Both Shirow and Oshii play with Togusa's "normalcy" as he occupies a space of affective intimacy with the reader/viewer, who for now must be content to dream of androids dreaming of electric sheep. Aramaki is the Section chief and, like Togusa, is predominantly human. He carries himself in a typically avuncular style and has his Smiley moments (to borrow from John Le Carré). There are other more peripheral members of the Section (like Ishikawa, the bearded tech wizard) and a cast of revolving cybercriminals (The Laughing Man, The Individual Eleven, and Hideo Kuze) but it is the core of Section Nine that is most evocative of the cyborganic noir affect in play, particularly in the figure of Kusanagi. As a symptom of seriality's impossible demands, I will restrict the argument to a few critical examples from Oshii's GITS films while elaborating the theoretical tension between ghost and shell as the becoming cybernetic of affect, a process that invokes a series both contiguous with the franchise and necessarily beyond it. Noir affect itself points to the material ground of shifting socialization, something for which the cyborg is a restless if not revolutionary figuration.

Both of Oshii's GITS anime feature spectacular opening credit sequences that intersperse details of the film production with correlative details of the production of the cyborg. The cyborg is not a given, but made. In the first anime, a preface is provided by Kusanagi diving from the top of a high rise wearing "thermo-optical" camouflage that renders her virtually invisible to the hit men and assassination target she is just about to dispatch. Stripping down to this skin-tight suit is not exactly logical (is the head included, especially the hair, or the white leggings?) but it does enhance the objectification invoked earlier (Kusanagi must not only be able to pass for a woman, but she is rendered as desirable in particular kinds of ways). It also, of course, reveals the very body that is being constructed in the images accompanying the credit sequence. A brain is secured in a metallic head attached to a torso of complex computational innards and musculature. The "shell" is rendered as a "perfect" female form but the eroticism generated is both centered and displaced. As the body is dipped in skin baths then exfoliates there is a signature undoing of Japaneseness that is yet putatively Japanese since the end of the Second World War (while the visual disavowal might be Oshii's, he cannot adjudicate its overdeterminations). This racial re-representation is multi-faceted and contradictory and so, in its own way, is Kusanagi's body. What do full breasts signify to a replicant made without reproductive organs? As Kusanagi prepares to attack, her command center is speaking directly inside her head. They complain that there is static in her brain. She quips, "It must be that time of the month" (Shirow's manga places much more emphasis on this kind of banter and humor). In the vexed space between sex doll and technological idealism, the gendered cyborg wonders about a processing error in the normative male gaze. In the opening sequence a dastardly cyber dealer claims diplomatic immunity but finds his position of power consummately lacking immunity to Kusanagi's violence (he is blown apart). In the making of Kusanagi's body the narrative is also broken up. The juxtaposition between gorgeous images of technology birthing perfection (the references to amniotic fluid are punctuated by the cyborg in a fetal position) and the credits themselves—names appearing in a flurry of typeface against a backdrop of flowing green pseudo-code (to which *The Matrix* famously pays homage) offers a field of interrogative affecthood. Is a subject being animated and a human one being restored (sexed, raced, gendered, classed), or does the cel-painted beauty of this opening question its insufficiency before the prospect of a future noir affect, one in which the passion of discovery remains inexorably bound to a desire for error, fallibility, outage, virus?

In Oshii's "sequel" to GITS—*Innocence*, (イノセンス, *Inosensu*, 2004) the opening sequence of the first anime is both mirrored and, as we know of mirrors, distorted. Batou is investigating the scene of a murder. A "gynoid" (also called a "sexaroid") has gone berserk and murdered its owner and, when cornered, kills two police officers. When Batou confronts the killer he is facing something akin to a Geisha doll, one that is impassive and still. As Batou approaches, the doll attacks him. He punches her against a wall and, as she tears off her skin, she whispers "help me" (*tasukete*, 助けて). Her head then splits apart to reveal a skull-like metal casing and there is a massive explosion. The credit sequence then begins, this time with what appears as virtual procreation, an allusion quickly followed by rapid brain cell division (this is procreation as replication). Once again, the process forms a cyborgian head, but this is then fused with a beautifully articulated and detailed "spine." Unlike Kusanagi's making, the emphasis on the cyborg here is on its robotic form, and the pieces fit together very much like a doll (indeed, the reference is to the German artist Hans Bellmer's ball and joint dolls, particularly of the 1930s—a Bellmer book appears later in the narrative and representations of his dolls are omnipresent), although at an incredible level of intricacy (enhanced in this film by the availability of next-gen CGI). A four-legged gynoid (again a reference to Bellmer's surrealism) splits suddenly into two complete versions who then almost kiss in a borg embrace. The finished being, while still a gendered stereotype, is neither round-eyed nor conventionally shaped. The sequence ends with a close-up on the eye, precisely formed and with its production information etched around its edge, but also with a reference to Villiers de l'Isle-Adam and his novel, *L'Ève future*.[13] The gynoid model is a "Hadaly" which is also the name of the android at the center of Villiers' narrative—the epigraph to the film is also drawn from this book: "If our gods and hopes are nothing but scientific phenomena, is there any reason why our love should not also be equally so?"[14] In GITS, the opening sequence ends with Kusanagi waking up, her eyes checking out her hand as if to confirm it is indeed hers. In *Innocence*, the eye contains a reflection of its being, replicated. In both films the eye asks: what exactly is being "seen"?

Kawai Kenji's songs, choral chants (traditional min'yō) with taiko drums and bells, enhance the credit sequences in their own way, as if music is the affective embrace par excellence (Jameson, for instance, notes

---

13 Auguste Villiers de l'Isle-Adam, *L'Eve future* (1886), translated as *Tomorrow's Eve* (Robert Martin Adams trans.) (Champaign, IL: University of Illinois Press, 2001).

14 "Puisque nos dieux et nos espoirs ne sont plus que scientifiques, pourquoi nos amours ne le deviendraient-ils pas également?"

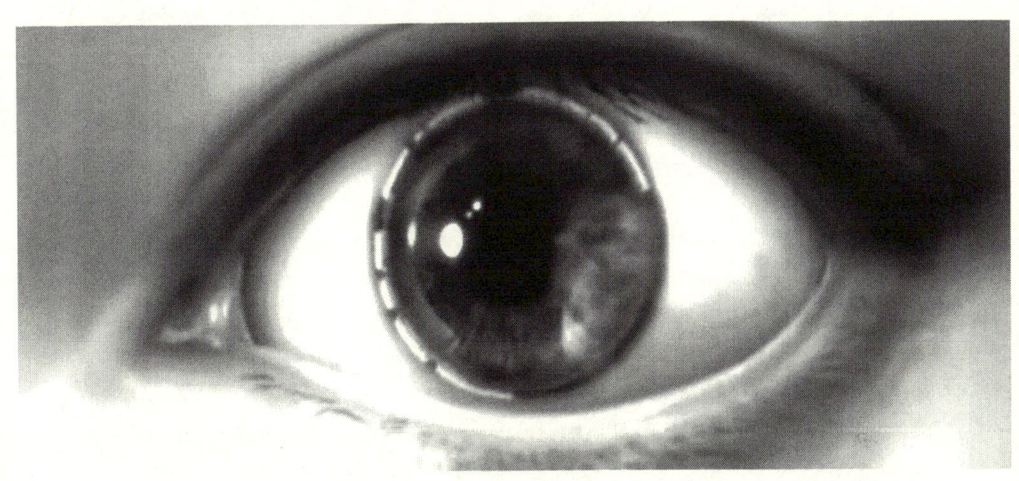

FIGURE 37. Mamoru Oshii (dir.), *Ghost in the Shell 2: Innocence* [イノセンス] (Production I.G., 2004), 98 mins.

a musical correlation between affect and the sliding scale).[15] In the first, the "I" of the song dances and a beautiful lady is enchanted. A god descends to give its blessing and a "chimera bird" will sing. The chanting seems to sanction the union advanced in the images while emphasizing that technology demands a new figuration/configuration of spirit, like a ghost in the shell of seriality. The chanting in the second film maintains this emphasis but is more dystopian about its productive capacity. The cyborgs, robots, and dolls still conjure uncanny intimacy (the *Unheimlich* presence of semblance) yet the chant adds a measure of albeit mystical hesitancy: "The blossoms beseech the gods 'Even though in this world we may know grief and suffering, our dreams shall never die,' and they fall from the branch in anger." What are these fleurs du mal but a memory of natural imperfection? In both films Kawai's music presses the notion that the cyborg confounds the relation of body and spirit, as if the techné of modernity is not just secular but is in some way sublime. The problems are many. If, for instance, the social and the political are based on concepts that presume the human as subject, any change (technological, climate-based, philosophical) challenging such foundations must at a minimum pose what to do with all those billions of humans who remain maddeningly sutured to subjecthood and fleshly finitude. We have a pretty-good idea of what bathwater to drain (states, nations, capitalist exploitation of workers and the environment) but the cyborg suggests the baby is in danger of being thrown out too. Noir affect is not a universal equivalent for this dilemma but it is symptomatic of a concrete contradiction in the forms of socialization depicted. The sequences are in series (whether the films follow one another or not) and are of course human made while intimating a form of production and reproduction (replication) that constitute a second series undermining such a future.

In Oshii's interpretation of *Ghost in the Shell*, the philosophical, both the existential and post-humanist comportment of the cyborg, seems to trump any path from affect to transformation (agency in his anime, much to the delight of post-structuralists, is either joyfully immanent and immaterial or, more worryingly, self-destructive in a pre-emption of any commune to come). For Shirow, by contrast, affect is much closer to effect,

15 Fredric Jameson, *The Antinomies of Realism* (New York: Verso, 2013).

which is to say the cyborg is rarely more than a logical extension of the body-centered present (we create conditions of crime and the cyborg is a way of response—it is a basic and authoritarian "Robocop" rationality). This makes for perhaps more recognizable priorities (the "let's get the bad guys" procedural) but also for a more deliberate flattening of affect. Shirow's manga are more kinetic in terms of storytelling, yet Oshii's stunning visuals contain greater overly read referentiality (he admits to this Godardian tic) and are exciting in their own way. The visual in both is a means to trouble the representation of the human and putatively the representational aesthetics that are its ward.

Both of Oshii's GITS anime confront a typical representational fix: if the cyborg becomes fully networked why have a body at all (Marx's ominous automaton as digitally totalizing)? At the end of the first film Kusanagi fuses with the Puppet Master and, while she is "placed" in a temporary body when her previous iteration is destroyed, she looks forward to the web in its "vast infinity." Living in the internet is a cinematic challenge (*Tron*, anyone? And the *Matrix* series simply switches between equally realist hallucinations), so in *Innocence* the narrative focus is on Batou and Togusa with their all-too human anthropomorphic remains and the creature comforts of a detective investigation (the fear of AI includes an anxiety about non-representationality and the absenting of cognizable agency). Oshii, however, creates several imaginary resolutions to such real contradictions in the form. Crucially, both films feature Ozu-inspired "pillow" sequences, narrative interludes of intense reflection and contemplation (Oshii makes this signature his own in various interpretations across his oeuvre which have only faint echoes of Shirow's manga). In GITS, this features Kusanagi thinking through her "presence" as made with or against a backdrop of an intricately constructed urban environment. Typically, for Oshii, Kusanagi's journey by boat in the city in this sequence is packed with detail (while it does not conform to a specific location, Newport City melds together key features of the contemporary East Asian megalopolis, including a compressed modernity where space is sometimes literally squeezed by the intimacy of the old and new). It also offers the urban as a preeminent space of tech or future noir where architecture, light, shadow, and the enormity of scale articulate an impressionistic tableau of confounding "progress" in images of dissolution and decay. As she traverses the cityscape, Kusanagi's sense of self is mirrored by what she sees: half-built structures, networks of roads and canals, bodies in motion and also still (especially the window mannequins), circuits that blink on and off, waste, and reflective surfaces, everywhere reflections. How much of what is made and made up can be made alike? Kusanagi sees a version of herself in a café, which is perhaps the same cyborg model, serialized. The entire sequence is accompanied by a reprise of Kawai's choral extravaganza, underlining not the externality of image and sound, but their utter affective integration. And yet, of course, Kusanagi's face is largely expressionless in Oshii's interpretation, evincing a flat affect that permeates the film as a whole (again, a stark contrast to Shirow's representational palette and humanizing through comedy). This does not mean the cyborg is proto-typically postmodern in the Jameson sense, a being commodified into torpor and wan with consumption, but it does suggest a posthuman ecumene, a place inhabited but uninhabitable, whose line of flight leads from the reproducible to networked profusion, a bodiless circuit where emotive expression falls away.[16]

The falling away of the body (as in the jump of the first scene, and the metaphor of the last where Kusanagi tears herself [or at least her shell] apart in ripping open a tank) is accompanied by a questioning of experience represented by memory. The affective processes of the production of memory are complex and, as Kusanagi notes, for each person, unique. Again, this is a significant tension between reproduction and replication. Oshii's worldview is in part informed by the idea the human capacity of memory is being rendered obsolete (and idea increasingly realized in AI). Memory, from this perspective, is "being" separated from "subjectivity" and it is stored in vast data banks to be accessed according to informational need rather than identitarian desire. While there is plenty of dispute about the seriality of memory and its "random" access (William James's "memory is only memory of memory" can be digitally remastered),[17] the point is its

---

16 The fate of affect is the missing dimension of N. Katherine Hayles's otherwise trenchant and prescient, *How We Became Posthuman* (Chicago, IL: University of Chicago Press, 1999).

17 On James and memory, see, for instance, William James, *The Principles of Psychology* (New York: Holt, Rinehart and Winston, 1980).

subjective process need not be defining. This is why the Puppet Master claims to be a new entity, a new species, an "autonomous life form"—affected and affecting in its selving, its autopoiesis. As a "sentient" AI, the Puppet Master attaches itself to memory's function for identity without being synonymous or defined by it. In the calculations of the minimally human, the artificiality of affective power is more than a threat of uncanny semblance because it seems to forego defining semblance at all. Could it be that the cyborg is such artifice at the level of representation, representation that otherwise fails to constitute its affective coupure?

On this question the affective interlude in *Innocence* is both still more visually rich and categorically opaque. Backed again by Kawai Kenji's glorious "Song of the Puppets," Oshii offers us a parade of affective doppelgängers and provides spiritual manifestations of references in the rest of the film to Buddhist, Confucian, and Christian texts. This sequence presents a number of puppets and dolls (both manipulated and mechanical, or *karakuri*) that are themselves serial iterations of subjectivity; indeed, we might usefully think of the cyborg-self tout court as citational. The scene is a festival loosely-based on a Taiwanese tribute to Mazu, the Taoist goddess of the sea: in the film this is set against the city as a kind of transnational tableau, again, future noir or what Oshii has called "Chinese gothic." As facsimiles of the human and animal multiply the animation pushes against its resources of representation. It is almost as if the sequence as a whole allegorizes what might animate, what might affectively engage the viewer of this event. That most figures are masked is a meta-commentary on the significance of "shells" to self-definition. One worries, of course, as both Bolton and Brown have pointed out, that however much detail Oshii builds into such scenes, a certain techno-orientalism lingers, the cyborg as another in a long list of Asian essences bolstered and packaged by anime and manga as they meet occidental desire in the transnational market.[18] Yet the interest seems to be in a transmutation of these very

---

18 See Bolton, "From Wooden Cyborgs to Celluloid Souls" and Steven T. Brown, *Tokyo Cyberpunk: Posthumanism in Japanese Visual Culture* (London: Palgrave, 2010). Brown provides a detailed exegesis of *Innocence* in his book, as well as close readings of other classics of Japanese posthumanism, like *Akira* and *Tetsuo: The Iron Man*. See also Ueno Toshiya, "Japanimation and Techno-Orientalism" and "The Shock Projected onto the Other: Notes on Japanimation and Techno-Orientalism" in Bruce Grenville

relations, that question of the persistence of the human as an affective medium in series. Batou and Togusa are in a re-represented Etoforu, not for the festival, but to find a hacker named Kim, whose background is in military cyber warfare and arms dealing. The sequence ends with ceremonial mask burning, but the dolls and automatons continue to haunt the subsequent narrative.

There are at least four interrelated aspects where we may begin to unpack the affective import of the ghosts and shells in Oshii's serial interruption and extension of the GITs franchise. These are more than themes but less, of course, than a typology of affect and feature spirit, technology, figuration, and sublation. The sequences I have discussed so far appear to elicit a description of an Oshii stylistic, elements of technique and representation that can be discerned in his other film projects, like the anime *Patlabor* (1989) and especially *Patlabor 2* (1993) or the live action feature, *Avalon* (2001). Yet the invocation of cyborg affect offers another dimension of serial connection, particularly effulgent in the forms of temporality and chronotopes that tie and untie the narratives.

For instance, time and again in Oshii's GITS films the cyborg's voice is not present with its anthropomorphic counterpart. Kusanagi can speak through her shell, the body she occupies, while her presence as such is networked, dispersed, and digitally enhanced. As noted, the voiceover is a staple of film noir, but here it accentuates both forboding and the displacement of being. If her face is often affectless with lips that do not move, Kusanagi's voice is yet alive with interpretation and investigative zeal. This, combined with contemplative pauses and thermo-optic camouflage, relays subjectivity rather than situates it as a cognizable event. If the time of the cyborg is one of becoming, it is also, at least nominally, time's dissimulation. Time's instantiation is questioned by ambivalent identification: "Am I the cyborg here and now or is that only verifiable by another temporal scale or material moment of presence that renders the adjudication of the 'I' itself questionable?". The time of the cyborg is always and everywhere an existential threat (the meaning of lifespan in, for

(ed.), *The Uncanny: Experiments in Cyborg Culture* (Vancouver: Arsenal Pulp Press, 2001), pp. 223–31, 234–35.

instance, *Blade Runner*, is particularly explosive). This creates several representational dilemmas for which spirit seems to be a symptomatic "resolution." For Oshii, cyborg affect animates Kusanagi's discomfort. Her mass-produced shell is supposed to enable her to blend in—the opening sequence is about the manufacture of uniform "likeness"—yet in her veritable walkabout described above Kusanagi is unequivocally restless about semblance. The possibility of serial extension (both literally in other modes of the franchise and symbolically in body-swaps and network connections) marks home as an abstraction for spirit. This makes for both cyborg monstrosity and for a curious manifestation of technological godlessness.

In the 1980s, Donna Haraway famously read such a quandary as the possibility of socialist-feminist embodiment, a politics based on the demonstrable fallibility of capitalist patriarchy (the cyborg could exceed the goddess as objectified Other).[19] Given that seriality here can also produce Shirow's sex fetishism, the *potentia* at stake is always already contradictory. Kusanagi does not easily slip her deleterious objecthood, not just because of predominantly male heteronormative fantasies but because the brain in her making permits the difference of indiscernible identity (to borrow from Leibniz).[20] In principle, the spirit/ghost should permit escape velocity from basic imperfections of the flesh, but this is precisely what limits the cyborg as represented. The variation Kusanagi believes to be essential of evolution thwarts the perfectability intimated in replication. Indeed, we might say the cyborg is the sign of system failure to come, or "indiscernible replication." Oshii grapples with this anthropomorphic antinomy in *Innocence* by using it as a structural component of story, of exigency. The gynoids, perfect replicas for sexual objectification, have been animated yet contaminated. Locus Solus, a tech corporate giant, has worked with a yakuza gang to abduct adolescent girls

---

19 See Haraway, "Cyborg Manifest." The original essay appeared in 1984 in the *Socialist Review*. Elements of the critique, particularly around race and gender, have drawn appropriate criticism but as a provocation to think the posthuman Haraway's intervention maintains an historical prescience.

20 See Gottfried Wilhelm Leibniz, *Discourse on Metaphysics and Other Essays* (Daniel Garber and Roger Arlew trans) (New York: Hackett, 1991).

for ghost dubbing—in effect, the technology engineers affect sufficient only to provide sexual compliance and subjugation. The cyborg animates the Hadaly sex doll. A conscientious shipping inspector, Jack Volkerson (a veritable son of the people), disrupts this commodity chain of happy exploitation by sabotaging the ethics code written for the gynoids, a hack which not only allows them to kill their owners (and thus contravene Asimov's robot rules) but prompts the very investigation that will lead to Locus Solus and the liberation of the abducted girls (it is the voice of one of these girls that earlier pleas to Batou, "Help me"). If the capitalist corporation seeks cyborgian enhancement as a kind of quiescent automation it appears limned to a patriarchal reduction to the body (again typified in Shirow's manga but with serial permutations). Interestingly, the reduction to the body is where Jameson locates the globalization of generalized sensations or affect as such. I agree with Pansy Duncan that Jameson's *Antinomies of Realism* is a recapitulation rather than a simple rejection of the "waning of affect" argument famously pinned to postmodernism as a cultural logic.[21] Yet I would add that Jameson tends to bracket affect when it comes to the historicity of science fiction in the *Antinomies* tome, which I would read as both a temporal and political displacement regarding realism and its "others."

Between GITS and *Innocence*, several versions or models of the cyborg are posited. Replication as figuration is initially framed by economies of semblance and utility. As noted, when Kusanagi is pieced together it is to pass as human rather than to replicate humanness (a quality that can be projected onto dolls, puppets and "companions" of various kinds). The challenge of figuring cyborg affect is that it need not be bodily present and yet, if its ghost is co-present with nature as a whole, it remains subject to its basic laws. It is only a god in the machine to the extent that fabrication and fabricants are not contrary to existence in nature. Interestingly, this point is underlined by a character named Haraway (!) in *Innocence*, who herself is cyborganically enhanced (and is a chain smoker, another luxury of replication). Robots require a human form only when that part of their performativity necessitates semblance. Cyborgs, however, seem to need

21 See Pansy Duncan, "Once More, with Fredric Jameson," *Cultural Critique* (97) (Fall 2017): 1–23.

more identity markers (like smoking), as if the organic acts as a cognitive circuit breaker, reassuring not just their human counterparts, but reconciling themselves to themselves. At this level, affect provides some ontological sutures and elements of subject redundancy. Pointedly, seriality permits much variation on this register, as narrative tests cyborgian extension in division. Figuration is the failsafe of affective attachment. Thus, although Oshii believes the motions of mind have long promised the obsolescence of its mortal coil (a sentiment still more prevalent today), the cyborg frustratingly permits the articulation of the body to reappear. Cyborg affect is ridiculously recursive when it comes to the human figure in part because the cyborg, like beauty, is in the eye of the beholder (and sometimes literally so—while no doubt a cliché, the confluence of "I" and "eye" in English is a central motif of cyborg aesthetics). But if this were true or inexorably affective, then surely the whole discourse of cyborg sublation is reduced to reform or refined moments of technological enhancement, another capitalist "revolution" in series as the efficient economic extension of exploitation?

On the one hand, this would seem to reaffirm Walter Benjamin's thoughts on technological reproducibility. What is waning is less affect than an aura that pivots on a specific arrangement of the sensorium. Here we might say the serial mediates the possibility of sensate change. This mediation is not the only way the cyborg can appear but its affective challenge is more strongly symptomatic when networked across interlinked forms. Oshii himself locates the problem in an idiosyncratic spiritual configuration, a "glass darkly" that the cyborg, especially Kusanagi, wants to see beyond. His interest in Bellmer's dolls, however, throws light on the other side of Benjamin's thoughts on the reproducible, or what Brown usefully discusses as the technological uncanny.[22] Bellmer's dolls are both the promise of prosthetics and a question for reproducibility vis-à-vis reproduction. Their ball and joint configurations might seem to provide comfort as false analogs for the human, but Oshii reads this as precisely

22 Walter Benjamin, *The Work of Art in the Age of Technological Reproducibility and Other Writings on Media* (Cambridge, MA: Harvard University Press, 2008). See Brown, *Tokyo Cyberpunk*, especially Part One. See also Hans Bellmer, *The Doll* (Malcolm Green trans.) (London: Atlas, 2005).

an arena of affectivity, where semblance is refigured as consummate autonomy. More than this, such intimations of transformation come with their own ethic, a striving as persistence (*conatus*, once more). This emerges in *Innocence* as a moral conflict. If voices are not identical with their speakers and speakers quote words that are not their own, bodies are yet held as responsible conditions of existence, with a codicil of cyborgian rights. As Haraway examines the gynoid Batou has destroyed, she chides him that his violence has crimped the possibility of reconstruction. She also raises the issue of gynoid suicide: does sentience enough for self-destruction confirm or contradict Batou's zeal for termination? In the same scene, as Togusa feels secure in the reproductive sanctity of the nuclear family, Haraway points out that a child tending to a doll is not imitating child rearing but expressing its core meaning. "Children are not dolls!" he retorts. In the final scene, of course, Oshii has Togusa give his daughter a doll and, as he holds her with her new toy, the doll stares across at Batou, a cyborg, as he clutches his cloned Bassett hound. If the opening sequences are about the making of the cyborg, the final one is about what the cyborg unmakes, undoes, with its very propositional anima and animation.

Perhaps because he has listened to Haraway (as Oshii has read her, the theorist), Batou reflects further on the right to be alive. When he frees the young girl at the Locus Solus factory Batou reminds her that this freedom has been bought at the expense of the dolls, who had no voice or choice in the matter. The girl exclaims, "but I never wanted to be a robot!" Kusanagi, who has reappeared in the shell of such a robot, notes, laconically: "If a robot had his own voice he may cry, 'I never wanted to be a human being.'" Like so much of the ventriloquism in the film, speaking for and speaking as are conjoined.

The cyborgs in GITS evince affect in a human way: their unease is created by minimal affectivity, and yet this is the dialectic in which their very possibility becomes transformative. How? Oshii and his fellow animators appear to have little problem in representing humans and/as cyborgs in their interactions. This we might call the realist clause of cyborg figuration, but this is not quite what Spinoza meant when he noted that

"No one has yet determined what the body can do."[23] The cyborg clings to this realist determination, yet Oshii, much more than Shirow, tries to disable, corrupt, or hack such synergy. Here Benjamin rather than Bellmer is more apposite, since it is the cyborg's very reproducibility, a *ratio* in replication, that is the ground of its political possibility. As we have noted, Kusanagi voices the humanist claim that variation is at the heart of evolution and perfectability. Yet, when it comes to cyborg subjectivity this assertion, while not false, does not capture the deconstructive affectivity in cyborg presence. In other words, although the GITS series often settles on the comforting recursive essence of the ghost with its aura of the sacrosanct and unique, the dispersed and virtual non-equivalence of replication suggests an alternative and by all means rebellious articulation of ghosts and shells (without, of course, posing a definitive form for such socialization). If cyborg sentience does not begin in its relationship to a body, except in its replication and replaceability, its affect is unhinged from the normative perquisites of adequate cause. This is not a technical calculation or technological determinism but is its dialectical challenge (including for social change). Similarly, in Oshii's GITS films the problem of experience emerges again and again because the memories adduced from it can be constructed, synthesized, and implanted. Spinoza notes "that we can do nothing from a decision of the mind unless we recollect it";[24] yet what happens to decision, political or otherwise, if that recollection is cybernetically fabricated? When the Puppet Master hacks a cyberbrain the host is thoroughly convinced of their selfhood and acts accordingly. Obviously, misremembering is marked as a human attribute, but here memory is treated like any other data set: it can be wiped clean, replaced, or corrupted beyond the power of individual fallibility (as the title of one of Philip K. Dick's stories puts it, "We can remember it for you wholesale"). This is neither brainwashing nor ideological seduction: it is a function of new circuits of epistemological production and commodification, a serial array between artifice and artificiality. Perhaps the representational aesthetics of Oshii's anime permit the anchoring of the cyborg in what is seen to be the minimally human of the species. Whenever Kusanagi, the

---

23 Spinoza, *The Ethics*, p. 155.

24 Spinoza, *The Ethics*, p. 157.

Puppet Master, or Kim, attempt to distance these conditions they are immediately tagged as suspect, deviant, or disruptive. True, this often wheels back to some form of corporate malfeasance (who knew?), but the creative impulse exists more in the capacity to act differently and outside the human as a regulative idea. Spinoza locates affect in the necessary relations of God, Nature, and the human. The cyborg is both an extension of such relations, permitting, as it were, the series to appear, and is a challenge to their constellation. The anxiety provoked by the cyborg is more than the "unhappy valley" of its semblance: it is the point where all that is disembodied from the glories of making the cyborg body becomes a space of posthuman fantasmagoria. To say that *Ghost in the Shell* performs the generic features of a detective serial is true (and comports with all kinds of popular cultural attributes), but along the way, in its formal profusion and aesthetic predicaments, it seems to detect something other than the solution to the albeit significant crimes of human interaction. Can there be a rebel without a human affect and yet somehow "embody" affect after all? In the absence of this veritable cause the cyborg persists as the symptom of the rebel to come and of an affect empowered by the materiality of network existence itself.

But what of the present? How does a subculture within anime and manga, and one quite clearly mediated through constellations of adolescent male heterosexism and techno-orientalism, inform a contemporary understanding of social antagonism? Does GITS depart from or simply underline the sense that affect is primarily about what is happening rather than being a political and cultural catalyst in what is to be done? The live-action GITS (2017) directed by Rupert Sanders and starring Scarlett Johansson as the Major finds all this talk of bodiless praxis and artificial affect much too much of a "vaporous evanescence of the incorporeal" to make an actual feature film, so it dispenses with most of the flightier articulations of cyborg affect as well as the pointed politics of tech noir. Major is not a replicant based on a standard model but supposedly an "original" whose brain has been harvested from the remains of an abducted rebel fighting for the resistance to technology (this is a Luddism shot in Ultra-High Definition). To battle the challenge of externalized memory, on at least two occasions (human) identity is defined by actions, so the film constructs its narrative around Major's quest to act human, a pursuit that culminates not in the fusion with a cybernetic network entity (Kuse) but with a reunification with Motoko's birth mother, Hairi, played by Kaori Momoi. In Hollywood, at least, reproduction always trumps replication (see *Blade Runner 2049* [2017]). The film found it very hard to break out of its entanglement in the series and so, while often visually impressive, the narrative is hobbled by awkward backstory and yet more random access to the franchise. In *Innocence*, Oshii was able to focus on his major themes by foregoing most of what would constitute plot (he was interested in the ghost of noir, not its shell, and this makes for a centrifugal seriality). Sanders' vision is hemmed in by basic Hollywood prerogatives, including those that constitute a star vehicle (according to the credits, here the actor playing the cyborg has a personal assistant, a cook, and a trainer). Indeed, this gives rise to the biggest complaint about the film, that Johansson's inclusion is a racist whitewashing of Asian culture all too evident in other examples of Hollywood production. For instance, one thinks of *The Last Samurai*, *Dr. Strange*, *The Great Wall*, etc.—although the history and the list on this point is as old as Hollywood (interestingly, Wes Anderson's stop motion movie, *Isle of Dogs*, solves the problem of representing a Japan of the near future by having Johansson, and most of the Western leads—including Tilda Swinton of "Ancient One" fame—play animated dogs). Because the representation of Japan and "Japaneseness" in manga and anime since the Second World War has never been less than controversial and reflexive, the insensitivity of Sanders' film is striking. Whatever is ambiguous in the racial representation of the cyborg in the GITS series does not sanction whiteness as a default mode (even if the birth mother is Japanese). When Oshii comments that he had no problem with Johansson being cast as the Major he is acknowledging both that neither the Major's name nor her body in the series are hers (the cyborg is a fabrication not an authentication) and, importantly, this is what Hollywood does, not what it could do. Thus, it is true to its central premise and this detracts from all that might be more provocative from the perspective of cyborg futures, like the one that is posthuman.

In the end of course, what is most noir about affect in the franchise is neither the threat to identity nor its indulgence in humanist nostalgia (or more accurately, nostalgia for the human) but the idea a human utopia lacks intensity because there is less and less time beyond doxa, beyond processing the everyday and endlessly performing the human as given, and as intensively and socially articulated. The cyborg cannot be a freedom from such necessity because its affect is no shield from the material conditions of its possibility. For Marx, serial manufacture, automation, and the factory as automaton constitute a ground for socialism, one that would free the worker from the time of exploitation.[25] In GITS, the automaton is both the factory and its manufactured being, but one could also argue its cyborgian limit is the state itself and its protean autopoiesis. Significantly, in GITS technological enhancement can also mean human emancipation and emancipation from the human. A circuit of power may be broken, that of the state and of the corporation, but only by ceding the political subject to the power of circuits. On one level, to rebel without an affect is preposterous if by affect we locate power in the capacity to affect or be affected by a plenitude of interactions. One on another level GITS, and especially Oshii's anime contribution, posits a zero degree of affect in the cyborg in which the minimally human is not simply that which must remain, the ghost as the veritable soul of the human, but that which may be the last of the human, the last of its adequate cause. Could it be that to rebel, to become a new entity, this is the affect to be without?

---

25 Marx, *Capital* (Ben Fowkes trans.), especially Chapter 15.

NOVELIZATION AND SERIALIZATION, OR FORMS OF TIME OTHERWISE

One could argue that seriality, both in its structural forms and in its narrative expressions, constantly folds back on itself and is as much cyclical as it is extensive. From this perspective, modes of relation are obstinately recursive with each connection relatively fixed in its acknowledgment. It is possible, however, to read this logic of referentiality as reflexive in a critical sense, a process in which systems of relationality are not simply performed but questioned (such is at least one of the lessons of the cyborg in the previous section). Obviously, serial engagement does not exclude blind reauthentication, yet even in the modest examples of interpretation and adaptation explored above seriality is conflictual and contradictory. Popular forms defamiliarize and deconstruct expectation and progression, as if generic principles are sensitively dependent on other material conditions of possibility (some practical, like deadlines and economies of scale, but some also immanent to serial logic). Would Marx's French serialization have been more successful had Marx taken on the distinct aesthetic and political implications of popularization as serial intervention redolent in his moment? Does the Japanese manga of *Capital* do much later what the science of Marx's critique can only imply? The question is not about the resolution of the text's intellectual challenge (we have, after all, complicated *aplatir* and the popular); the problem concerns the level of consanguinity between series and any optimal distillation of social change cast against the material foundations of production and distribution. The bulk of serials and series are not read to materialize in this way and necessarily resist being forced to do so (which is a significant part of their commodity logic). The claim is not that all series do this, but that seriality opens such potential. A confluence in seriality may be deemed a surprising coincidence, as new historicism might once have put it, but the key is in the replenishment of potential, which necessarily remains problematic (a franchise honed, for instance, as an accumulation strategy) yet is also a ground for taking the seriality of series seriously.

Popular serialization has been an irritation for literary critics, who often seek not only a legitimization of form but of a cultural prestige in its discussion and circulation. Here is not the place to track the professionalization of literary criticism, but it is noticeable that where serialization is concerned, the processes of production and circulation are often folded into, or displaced onto, a collected version of the serial in a single-bound copy or edition (we have also traced this reflex in non-fiction in the story of *Le Capital*). Even in literary appraisals that take account of a work's life in series, the tendency is to re-engineer the aesthetic effects of seriality from the boundedness of a single volume. If what is transformative in a series is linked to a seriality "unbound," is it possible to theorize such latency across the different manifestations of a narrative series? Paradoxically, since this would seem to mimic a critical recapitulation, could the novel throw light on the capacity in series to change the conditions through which socialization is posed? Because the novel is historical in a different time/space register than the fact of storytelling in series (from the ancients to the moderns) it can speak to, if not as, the antinomies of the modern as such. Popular serials, in comics, manga, anime, soap operas, newspapers, podcasts, and, yes, novels, and the like constitute a vast repository of social exchange. The novel as a genre of fiction certainly reads as a minor literature within this backdrop, but nevertheless produces logical demands that are themselves an extension of seriality's promise. To elaborate such logic as conjoint and contradictory one must examine further the conditions of novelization, which gives to serialization in the nineteenth century much of its legitimization as cultural production.

To recall Deleuze on series, seriality operates at different scales including, in *Logique du Sens*, at the level of chapters, sentences, and words, as well as in relation to structures and events. "Making sense" is both to cognize series and to identify their relations in immediate proximity and across time. Such an approach does not obviously sanction a socio-logic of cultural form, and yet the sense of series is hardly reducible to philosophical critique sui generis. To put this a slightly different way, Marx does not want to novelize *Le Capital* in series as if it might approximate Lachâtre's success with the work of Eugène Sue (one can, of course, discern such novelization in the project of Variety Artworks' manga); rather, modernity's imprint on production and distribution is active both in the way sequence and division can be thought, and in the way cultures of counter-modernity can be conceived. Novelization is both a symptom and a catalyst of materialization in series, a process that mediates the class conditions of cultural expressivity, often distilled in categories like the "Victorian novel," or refracted in the sense of an event like the Paris Commune, recorded and visualized in weeklies and dailies of the time. Dialectically, novelization and seriality distill the cognitive power of event, and the matter of eventness (as *zeitraum* or chronotope) grounds how change is understood.

Bakhtin understands novelization as a distinct openness to the order and apprehension of time. Storytelling is not reserved for a kind of bound contemporaneity, but instead makes claims on a future that remembers it, as if challenging the indifference of a time that has not been. This is in its own way the outline of a revolutionary imaginary. It is easy to indulge in the openness and flexibility of the novel, a tendency promulgated in Bakhtin's view that the novel is "plasticity itself."[1] Here we should remind ourselves that serial division is not simply an expression of righteous flexibility but is a condition tied to all kinds of closed exigency, the economics of a weekly issue, the distribution date, etc. The openness to time in the novel is not an escape from such conditions nor a disregard for their material instantiation. While the novel may not offer the only template, its incredulity before form permits generic absorption but as a process that can be concretely specified. Bakhtin's conceptual inconsistency is sometimes read as a virtue, especially when it comes to crude determinism and positivism. The waywardness of novelization, like that of dialectics, is generally not posed as an absolute but more as a variable symptom of cultural interaction, with a history. Novelization as a process throws light on seriality since our examples, from agon to affect, reveal telling stories in series includes division paradoxically open in its closure. It is also a reminder the event of text is not the event in text, which necessitates distinctions in the orders of time, and in modes of production (like Norman Feltes' differentiation of "commodity-book" from "commodity-text").[2]

1 Bakhtin, *Dialogic Imagination*, p. 39.

Bakhtin's theorization of the novel—the way the novel structures literary images for the present in open-endedness; the manner in which it alters the temporal coordinates of literary images; and its "three-dimensional" stylistics—does not announce an abrupt defeat of the epic, the topic of one of Bakhtin's more famous essays,[3] but it does inflect a generic antagonism in the novel's potential to refract other ways of telling. The defamiliarization of temporal hierarchies and orders of knowledge is not just a democratizing impulse but it also participates more generally in framing the experience of modernity (which obviously does not obviate countervailing and contradictory forces—or as Césaire once put it succinctly, "colonization and civilization?").[4] True, the actual effects of novelization in Bakhtin's conception can be vague ("in the presence of the novel, all other genres somehow have a different resonance"),[5] but the temporal knots indicated, particularly around narration and futurity, are in dialogue and disjuncture with serialization and the living-on of radical change that is our chief concern.

What is pointed in novelization is the element of category crisis it brings to the aesthetic apprehension of genre and form. It does not offer a normative formalism over and against the rhetorical joys of formlessness or chaos (a false binary much replayed between moribund structuralisms and non-essential post-structuralisms), yet novelization still foregrounds how modes of cultural expressivity may be at stake. In contrast to both a formalism without causality and an aesthetics that exceeds the limits of politics by becoming it, novelization dares to engage the social without assuming its remit is either decontamination or autonomy. It is perhaps

2 See Norman N. Feltes, *Modes of Production of Victorian Novels* (Chicago, IL: University of Chicago Press, 1986), p. *xi*.

3 See Bakhtin, "Epic and Novel" in the *Dialogic Imagination*. This is a drama of literary form in which the novel gradually and contingently establishes its alternative capacities to "tell."

4 The point is not simply that the novel participates in and confirms the nostrums of colonialism and imperialism but that it is also active in challenging the normative conditions of modernity and the platitudes attending its civilizing missions. See Aimé Césaire, *Discourse on Colonialism* (Joan Pinkham trans.) (New York: Monthly Review Press, 2000), p. 32.

5 Bakhtin, *Dialogic Imagination*, p. 39.

no coincidence that alongside novelization Bakhtin also theorizes carnivalization and the grotesque.[6] On the one hand, novelization is not novel regarding literary process: it is, after all, addressing the aesthetic dimensions of world making; on the other hand, however, it also draws attention to the importance in the material coordination of temporality. Here we might say that a subtext of serial Marx, for instance, is how an idea of change finds a logic of time in which it can be instantiated. An aesthetic crisis in time is not a correlative of social crisis; the substance of time, or "real duration," is in their enmeshment. Chronotopes are a form-giving element of telling—the places, as Bakhtin averred, where the knots of narrative are tied and untied. Again, such knotting can be separated off as a generic marker, time as a crisis in content and as a temporal crisis in its structure, but it is also active in eventness as the social apprehension of time. It is almost as if when the novel forgets its co-participation in such understanding, chronotopic crisis asks more of its agency. Does serialization deepen and extend this demand? Does the serial novel catalyze or impede an appreciation of the time/space coordinates of novelization?

If Bakhtin elaborates the becoming novel of novelization in his understanding of the becoming body and its betrayal in François Rabelais's sixteenth century novel *Gargantua and Pantagruel* (a serial novel of five books across 32 years), he confronts, albeit obliquely, the time or times of novelization in his reading of Dostoevsky's serial novels.[7] I find this extremely suggestive for approaching what is concrete but also immanent to seriality, a sort of ontological contusion (that we have intimated in the representations of post-human affect), and for showing how series articulate

---

6 I refer here to Bakhtin's project on carnival and grotesque realism regarding *Gargantua and Pantagruel* eventually published in Russian in 1965, and in English translation in 1971. See Mikhail Bakhtin, *Rabelais and His World* (Helene Iswolsky trans.) (Cambridge, MA: MIT Press, 1971).

7 Although it is not a central focus of Bakhtin's analysis, his work on Dostoevsky's poetics acknowledges the influence of the *roman-feuilleton* or serialized novel in the form giving of Dostoevsky's fiction. See Mikhail Bakhtin, *Problems in Dostoevsky's Poetics* (Caryl Emerson trans. and ed.) (Minneapolis: University of Minnesota Press, 1984). See also Gary Saul Morson, *The Boundaries of Genre: Dostoevsky's Diary of a Writer and the Traditions of Literary Utopia* (Austin, TX: University of Texas Press, 1981).

social contradiction as a ground for change. Although this theoretical emphasis is clearly not Bakhtin's, his appreciation of Dostoevsky addresses the material substance of seriality in how the novels come to be. Seriality traces conditions of mediation, which here includes exigencies of time/space that are themselves a chronotopic challenge for novelization (the basic antinomy of open-endedness, with a deadline). Dostoevsky's formal solution to this aesthetic if not ontological dilemma is what Bakhtin calls polyphony or many-voicedness. Of course, for Bakhtin, polyphony refers to Dostoevsky's consummate skill in voicing character over and above the tendencies to othering in conventional authorship. Polyphonic othering is other to an authorial "I." Many-voicedness can also be read to defamiliarize and decenter the narrative constraints of formal division, as if the characters are making decisions regarding the confines of the genre and not just their individual predicaments. It could be argued that telling capital through lithographs (imaging workers in a discursive space where they were largely absent as "speaking" subjects from the content of *Das Kapital*) is also a polyphonic response to authorial othering. Similarly, Tardi's graphic commune raises the stakes in how its event is collectively voiced or spoken as history. For the social manifestations of polyphony, that is to say, a scale that is much more than a text of this or an image of that, Bakhtin uses the term heteroglossia, and the impress of novelization is in large part its capacity to inflect such scale without in fact substituting for it. The series negotiates narrative and is a relay, connecting both its parts and its social structuration. Formal contradictions begin around what constitutes a part and how a readership is constructed through it.

Just as Marxologists prefer to consider *Le Capital* in the single volume of 1875 rather than in light of the parts that precede or "make" it (which is both a historical and political ambiguity—is the wholeness an effect of a serial that disappeared or has criticism itself produced this disappearance?) so, for instance, Dostoevsky scholars tend to start with the single volume of *The Brothers Karamazov* rather than the sixteen parts of its serialization which track the conditions of novelization in its time.[8] To be sure,

8 There are exceptions in Anglophone scholarship, including Morson, mentioned above. See, for instance, William Mills Todd III, "The Brothers Karamazov and the Poetics of Serial Publication," *Dostoevsky Studies* 7 (1986): 88–97.

Dostoevsky does not pander to his readers according to conventions of serial fiction (in revelatory conclusions or commitments to suspense, for instance); he expects them to work out the patterns of each "book" which are, as he puts it, "whole and finished" in themselves. This does not mean, by the way, Dostoevsky had necessarily mapped out the complete novel: the books were whole, the divisions were a work in progress. It is important to note the difference of series and serials by reference to the type of periodical (weekly, monthly, etc.), the size of division it permits (Dostoevsky had the benefit of a "thick journal" like *The Russian Herald*, which sanctioned larger parts and, as with *The Brothers Karamazov*, it permitted further subdivisions less tied to an annual subscription), and whether the work is serialized alone or among other modes of expressivity, including journalism, graphics, and advertising. Tardi's *Le Cri du peuple* is conceived as a whole work whose volumes do not necessarily follow the parts of Vautrin's novel, from which it is adapted. Gellert's *Capital in Lithographs* is not a serial but is in series with Marx's work (and Gellert's own) in such a way as to attempt to complete Marx's serial intention. The sequence of Gellert's excerpts/translations and those of his art have their own logic of sense in seriality. *Capital in manga* is both in series between its volumes and with Marx's text while generating an alternative series (particularly in French) that illustrates the seriality at stake in *Le Capital's* historical intervention. The constellation that is *Ghost in the Shell* offers more series than our investigation and reveals a networked subjectivity interested in unpicking seriality's human sutures (and intimating change as both social and post-social). So, even as Dostoevsky engages serialization, serialization is clearly not reducible to novelization, or vice versa. The consonance, however, speaks to the living-on of both.

Bakhtin is primarily interested in the poetics of polyphony in Dostoevsky rather than in the problems of historicity signaled by the serialization of his work. Yet symptoms of one are certainly in the other as Bakhtin engages the forms of temporal determination across Dostoevsky's novels. What is a conscious appropriation by the author (how do I make sequence and section work for me?) is plunged back into the aesthetic unconscious of character in time's difference and becomes the hallmark of what Bakhtin refers to as a "historical poetics."[9] Seriality cannot claim to *be* this, but *as* this each instance is at once radically specific and conjoint. Serialization is not an alibi of the aesthetic but a dialectical ground which, in its own way, is othered by novelization as process. The exigencies of serialization inform the chronotopes of novelistic discourse yet, as the nineteenth century serial novel proves time and time again, the force of seriality is changed by this interaction, even when or precisely because individual authors dismiss its relative weight. As William Mills Todd III reminds us, between 1840–1880 Russian "thick journals" published just about every canonical Russian authored novel in serial form.[10] Interestingly, while generally serialization helped professionalize literary careers, English authors saw this as a bridge rather than as the substance of the single-volume version and revised each text accordingly (we might think of this as a specific canon consciousness). Russian authors of the time produced single-volume versions of their novels but largely retained the text of their serialization. To take novelization seriously in Bakhtin's sense would also require comparative serialization since this is instructive regarding the historicity of forms and any cultural mode of production critique. In addition, it would necessarily require an attention to intermedial cultural expression (*Capital* as manga, the manga as novel, etc.) for this too constitutes material formation and can mark the places where form and forms of time are at stake.

While the point of division in a series is a definitional feature of seriality, its time and place is overdetermined and, like sign itself in Voloshinov's sense, is a site of struggle.[11] If my own reading of novelization remains inconsistent with Bakhtin, this is also a measure of present distance, or heterochrony which is a politics of difference in and of time. This, for instance, rather than generic supremacy, is polemical in Bakhtin's

9 For more on Bakhtin's sense of and relationship to historical poetics, see Illya Kliger and Boris Maslov (eds), *Persistent Forms: Explorations in Historical Poetics* (New York: Fordham University Press, 2015). Much of Bakhtin's work on genre is also elaborated within this approach.

10 Todd, "Brothers Karamazov and the Poetics of Serial Publication": 99.

11 See V. N. Voloshinov, *Marxism and the Philosophy of Language* (Ladislav Matejka and I. R. Titunik trans.) (Cambridge, MA: Harvard University Press, 1986).

conception of novelization. Instead of standardization, novelization reveals a much more conflictual and centrifugal process of cultural expression. In the case of *The Brothers Karamazov*, as Todd underlines, the challenge includes an internalization of serial consciousness within the novel so that what the journal contains—law reports, biographies, and articles of several kinds—have their novelized versions in the writings of Ivan and Rakitin within the serial part. In itself, such reflexivity is not surprising, yet it asks pertinent questions of the reader's experience of the serial novel. What is the relationship between the fictional representations of social discourses and their non-fiction expressions that compose the journal issue? These connections do not exhaust the dimensions of Dostoevsky's art yet they help to concretize the serial conditions of novelization in which it was serially read. Bakhtin argues that the novel's contact with other genres is not cultural colonization but a "liberation" from the normative elements constraining a genre in isolation.[12] What constitutes a novel is changed by this interaction and, while this does not prevent anachronism or irrelevance for the genre (it remains, after all, historical), it suggests that an individual novel, like *The Brothers Karamazov*, is dialogic in more than content. In effect, serialization catalyzes the socio-historical dimensions of novelization and allows one to address the intimate participation of fiction in the everyday.

12 Bakhtin, *Dialogic Imagination*, p. 39.

Politics does not interfere with the aesthetic proclivities of novelization: it is novelization itself that will not leave political discourse alone. If novelization has always signified a crisis in genre and in particular canons of genre, the question remains whether it is itself symptomatic of crisis or an explanation of the same? At every turn it appears that political economy seems to poach on the literary, yet one should remind ourselves that Bakhtin conceived of novelization as the poacher par excellence and, significantly, that the concept of novelization was itself born of crisis in Bakhtin's life, both personal and socio-economic in the widest sense. Indeed, it is the crux of this conjunction that will lead to a discussion of serialization and the nation, even as the latter is held in specific incredulity before capitalist globalization. For his part, Bakhtin warned against ideological approaches, although his view of ideology included obfuscating its meaning at a time when ideology could be used to determine life or death (although the contours of censorship were different for Dostoevsky, they still informed creation and revision, especially between the serial and single volume versions of his novels, but especially in his journalism). Dialogism would have demanded a subtle strategy in Stalin's Russia and the same can be discerned in Bakhtin's concept of novelization. Novelization is not just a means of opening up literary history to a more dialogic and heteroglottic analysis of form—which is how it is most used—but it is also a discursive mode, one that might assess the ideological or the ruling ideas of any one time without necessarily endorsing, decrying or even naming them. Such a reading strategy permits Bakhtin to elaborate his preferences (Rabelais, Dostoevsky, Goethe, etc.) yet largely avoid questions of canon although, as it was for Lukács, the logic of canonicity remained a social and critical responsibility. Aesthetic discernment is no less sensitive today even if the ideological stakes have different evaluative criteria dependent on many factors alongside location and language. It is pertinent to point out Bakhtin's specific intellectual predicament in the face of what often seemed arbitrary political repression and how this informed a certain fluidity in conceptual elaboration. The predictability or plasticity of response was no small survival strategy and its inclination has not diminished with the expiration of Stalinism. Bakhtin says, "each day has its own slogan, its own vocabulary, its own emphases,"[1] a wonderful insight into the heteroglottic profusion of discourses at any one moment, but not necessarily the key to understanding their adjudication.

By taking up the generic markers of the novel, Bakhtin is able not only to distance himself from novelistic naysayers like Shpet, but also more complementary theorists of rhetorical discourse like Vinogradov. The difficulty is that the centripetal and centrifugal forces at work in the sign's sea of specificity dialogize the terms of theory themselves. We need not make a virtue of endless regression or some of the flightier versions of deconstruction to gainsay this; but it does mean that novelization is not beyond its own creative reaccentuation. This, of course, is the dialectician's desire to read time into concepts themselves. A critic of the novel might be most at home when novelization is happily ensconced in this novel or that, whereas there can be more wariness with Bakhtin's insistence on novelization's prehistory as romance in ancient Greek culture, or with the emphasis here on novelization's popular extension in manga graphics. The concept clearly exceeds the novel in both its prehistory and in its present futurity, so we might see it now in everything from a blog to a symbol in an avatar's shopping list. The difficulty, then, is not just novelization's profligate past, but the exponential shift in discursive realms that saturate the socius from one moment to the next. If, however, we call all of this genre mixing, bending, blending, and hybridizing "novelization," then its historical specificity as process and shape, becomes forbiddingly obtuse. Surely novelization attacks the elitist move to close form to heteroglottic change, but that rousing call to democratize discourse threatens all manner of discernment and can compromise or disable any qualitative distinctions in that dynamic. Could it be that the truth of novelization as concept is that it veritably ends the novel with modernity, but paradoxically finds its edginess edged out by that superadequation? This necessarily affects how one articulates the time of difference and its dialectical/temporal twin, the difference of time.

---

1 Bakhtin, *Dialogic Imagination*, p. 267.

Neither Bakhtin nor Lukács believes the novel is an essentially bourgeois form but, as Galin Tihanov has pointed out, this takes them to two very different versions of modernity.[2] Fortunately or not, we no longer have the privilege of choosing between these positions—like the famous Lukács/Brecht debates, they can be ventriloquated but their substance is closer to historical artefact. While dialogism and dialectics are not always and everywhere antithetical, they arrive at different formulations of modernity that in Bakhtin and Lukács are concretized by the experience of Soviet transformation. Degrees of methodological rigor in both remain symptomatic, including but not limited to cultural explication. As a conceptual prompt, might novelization within this genealogy be read as a future conditional, rather than as a generic law? Could its history help theorize other examples of serial manifestation, like the emergence of the nation form?

In the 1930s, while the poor and the oppressed in the United States struggled in the Great Depression and parts of Western Europe were beginning to register the rise of national socialism in Germany, Stalinism in the Soviet Union was producing severe crises of its own. The massive collectivization program had reaped some tangible benefits, but there were also disastrous social and political consequences. The murder of so-called kulaks is well known (the term itself rather than evidence was often the basis of conviction); some were merely peasants who disagreed, but specific Soviet policy also facilitated devastating famine in Ukraine and Kazakhstan that cost several million lives. While Kustanai (where Bakhtin lived in exile) was largely spared this level of extreme deprivation (not least because plenty of ethnic Russians lived there), the imperatives of collectivization produced significant hardships and resistance. Katerina Clark and Michael Holquist note it is ironic that Bakhtin's only publication of the period was an essay that drew on his bookkeeping abilities and training of farmers in collectivization.[3] The essay, "Experience Based on a Study of Demand

2 See Galin Tihanov, *The Master and the Slave: Lukács, Bakhtin, and the Ideas of their Time* (New York: Oxford University Press, 2000). To assess novel theory, Tihanov argues, is to come to terms with the concreteness of methodological distinctions and the philological and philosophical genealogies in which they emerge.

3 Katerina Clark and Michael Holquist, *Mikhail Bakhtin* (Cambridge, MA: Harvard University Press, 1984). This was one of the first books to in English to situate Bakhtin

among Kolkhoz Workers" is described as a "nonserious venture into print" for an otherwise banned writer.[4] If, as Clark and Holquist contend, Bakhtin was profoundly upset by the effects of collectivization in Kazakhstan, this was a very odd way to express it. The 1932 Law of the Wheat Ears, for instance—a collectivization policy against the hording of even the smallest amounts of grain—became a veritable death warrant, and placed a question mark over the whole movement. Bakhtin's "nonserious" support must then be seen in light of a more general strategic quiescence among the intelligentsia, the negative capability, in effect, of dialogism.

As noted, Stalinism reinforced a specific hermeticism among literary scholars. Even the famous 1934–1935 Moscow conference on the novel that Tihanov carefully explores offered disputes that were largely prescripted. Lukács carefully modulated his theory of the novel; others gave the novel a role in the communist homogenizing of culture, and a few others gave recherché accounts of bourgeois extravagance. On the whole, however, such events confirmed that all criticism of official discourse should sound a lot like official discourse, lest one find oneself subject to a short, brutish extraordinary rendition, disappearance, and worse. Bakhtin knew this to be true; his exile was a reprieve from certain death in a prison camp; and so, like others of his generation, sacralizing the word was both a professional and prophylactic endeavor. Aesthetics was revered, especially of the past. But if one wanted to address the present, either a perspicuous opacity was in order or a forthright commitment to given truths. We should not underestimate this culture of fear, just as future historians might elaborate its substance today.

How might such material conditions inflect the concept of novelization? Beyond Bakhtin's by now obvious purloining from Ernst Cassirer's treatise on symbolic forms,[5] his notion of generic modification and hybridization has a flexibility that frees him from any judgment on

---

not only in terms of a specific biography but conceptually within a new turn to cultural theory.

4 Clark and Holquist, *Mikhail Bakhtin*, p. 257.

5 Brian Poole has offered an extensive critique on Bakhtin's plagiarism of Cassirer. See Brian Poole, "Bakhtin and Cassirer: The Philosophical Origins of Bakhtin's Carnival Messianism," *South Atlantic Quarterly* 97 (3–4) (1998): 537–78.

specific novelistic art in his present. If Lukács' Russian novel reading list was short, Bakhtin conveniently and justifiably felt that deep critical exegesis was possible only up to Dostoevsky, with the rest of world literary output largely beyond reach—often literally so, despite Bakhtin's prodigious memory. Novelization, from this perspective, is an idea at once coruscatingly historical, while synchronically absent for the present. Yet today, one might adduce the opposite tendency, the presentist hangover of the end of history argument in which the heteroglottic "now" is the only one perceptible. The interruption of the future must disturb this cruel reversal.

Novelization, for Bakhtin, is historical without being historicist. The novel can be traced to ancient Greece, but has less generic identity than it does tendencies. The latter refer to the destabilizing ability of the novel, its decentralizing of discourse, its accommodation of unofficial and alien voices, and its will to power vis-à-vis other genres. Importantly, the principle of struggle is emphasized, albeit one shorn of distinct social stratification. Yet these novelizing tendencies are the impress of the novel as hegemon, in a space that has no coordinate in time. One could argue it is a space immanent to generic interaction, but it offers no quintessence in canonization. This sounds like Deleuzean intensity, or even chaos theory's pivot on homeostasis, and it will not secrete normative literary history, and this is why Bakhtin resembles philologists like Cassirer, Vossler, or Auerbach more than he does theorists of the novel like Lukács, Frye, Watt, or Moretti.

When Bakhtin, in his summary to "Epic and Novel," writes: "[t]he present, in all its open-endedness [. . .] is an enormous revolution in the creative consciousness of man,"[6] he merely underlines that novelization in his time must not speak to it. As we suggest, he can aver the novel is plasticity itself, but to say more than this might separate the revolution he has in mind from the revolution before him. I am not saying Bakhtin's theory of novelization was merely the product of a surveillance society—although in the decades since 9/11 it has become easier to understand how one might introject, precisely, an authoritarian paradigm of self-policing and understand anew the unfreedom that secures it. But if

6 Bakhtin, *Dialogic Imagination*, p. 38.

novelization bespeaks a genre that "structures itself in a zone of direct contact with developing reality,"[7] one can only bemoan the fact that Bakhtin was inclined not to detail this interactive space in a more forthright and systematic way (one thinks of the contrast, for instance, with the 1930s writing of Walter Benjamin, whose work seethes with the discourse of emergency). If one combines the concept of novelization's pastness without a past with its present as relative silence, one is not sure whether the logic of the novel is at stake or some related nostrum, perhaps that of the commodity; and therein lies a classic aesthetic antinomy of modernity.

In part, Bakhtin attempts to overcome this conundrum by squaring a Kantian emphasis on the axiomatic with a Hegelian critique on the developing consciousness of time, or the difference of time (temporal hierarchies, etc.). The effort is appreciable, yet even as time is foregrounded in the chronotope, the present is largely emptied of verifiable content, including the actual coordinates of progress that prove the epistemological claims of novelization as process. Before the utopian synthesis of being for itself and being-in-itself, Hegel's consciousness of time is one of pain; such a logic, with its corresponding suppression or deferral of the present, is not the monopoly of gulag epistemology. In Bakhtin's predicament as an intellectual, one can trace an intriguing and problematic concept of modernity, in which the novel activates time's purchase on the present, but, because of modernity's structural propensity for crisis, the difference of time is cruelly suspended and renders abstruse the real of its contradictions. Politics is not the realm that reconnects the conceptual cut between diachrony and synchrony; after all, it is quite willing to promote an alibi of timelessness in the face of the timeful, yet there is good reason to believe that if novelization is consanguine with the projection of progress in modernity's sweep, then politics might return society and nature to the equation and open up an understanding of the novel as a cultural endgame in modernity, a cultural revolution of the revolutionary. The difference of time complicates any easy relay between novelization as process and its materialization in theory, a correlative one might discern in serialization as such.

7 Bakhtin, *Dialogic Imagination*, p. 39.

The most significant chronotope of the novel is the one about which Bakhtin will have almost nothing to say: the time/space of nation. In the essay collection *Bakhtin and the Nation* the editors aver Bakhtin's notable silence is explicable (by including the factors noted above) but it is a necessary challenge in reading the abstract and concrete conditions of Bakhtin's theorizing in the early decades of the Soviet Union.[8] In the same volume, Tihanov describes Bakhtin's theory of the novel as a latent theory of nation and nationalism.[9] Indeed, one could argue novelization is the political unconscious of nation in Bakhtin's work and is symptomatic of seriality's purchase on modernity's materialization. For his part, Lukács never failed to link the intricacies of the novel to consciousness of nation and his studies on Goethe, Mann, and Dostoevsky are replete with such analysis.[10] Erich Auerbach, perhaps the preeminent philologist of the twentieth century, could not array his critique of Stendhal and Balzac without the formative force of France to the fore.[11] But Bakhtin, who lived through the most tumultuous years in the life of the Russian nation, did not explicate the imbrication of novelization and nationnness. This may be the strategic silence of a man who has been called a xenophobe, one who did not even like to meet "foreigners," or it may be because the temporality of nation itself disturbs the time of novelization enough to force content into its present.

For contemporary radical cultural critique—environmental, comparative, postcolonial, decolonial, transnational, and the like, questioning the nation through the novel is de rigueur, but to link Bakhtin as a theorist of the novel to these concerns necessitates conceptual clarification. Explicating the nation idea and the emergence of the nation state is a contested arena of study, and dispute is particularly acute in a

8 See the San Diego Bakhtin Circle (eds), *Bakhtin and the Nation* (Lewisburg, PA: Bucknell University Press, 2000).

9 Tihanov, *Master and the Slave*, p. 55.

10 For an intellectual history that situates Lukács's critique in this way, see Michael Löwy, *Georg Lukács: From Romanticism to Bolshevism* (Patrick Camiller trans.) (London: New Left Books, 1979).

11 See, for instance, Erich Auerbach, *Mimesis: The Representation of Reality in Western Literature* (W. R. Trask trans.) (Princeton, NJ: Princeton University Press, 2003).

time of intense upheaval between global "interests" and nationalist appeals to autonomy. Even in the rarified air of literary criticism, to problematize the nation for theories of the novel one must have a fairly precise sense of what constitutes a nation, linguistically, geographically, historically, ethnically, politically and even technologically. One cannot merely state that the novel transcends national boundaries, as if this frees the critic from responsible explanation of the fact. Goethe, whose pronouncements on world literature are often interpreted as a direct rejection of literary nationalism, offered an extension of German literature that hardly annulled its nation identity. Similarly, definitions of nation and the novel can be antagonistic or complementary depending on emphasis and the discursive formation perceived or at stake. Corelating material process, novelization and serialization, is far from settling such debates yet it helps to substantiate the productive entanglement of cultural modes of production and the social relations in which they are expressed.

Process, in a sort of Hegelian exegesis of becoming rather than Being, permits measure without measurement—at least if measurement is read as purely quantitative. Hegel, for instance, suggests measure as qualitative quantity, neither Absolute nor its absolute negative, nothing.[12] Becoming in Hegel's schema is the truth of Being and nothing in their unity. Here truth is the whole, divided. Hegel's explication of a series of measures takes us back to Sartre on seriality and the intimation of an impossible horizon—Sartre's understanding of open-endedness before a dialectical notion of totality. The order of seriality is a false totality and inhibits consciousness of the other and the prospect of the group-in-fusion (by contrast, we have been exploring an "other" serialization, or serialization of the Other in narration). What is fascinating and frustrating in seriality is that both novelization and nation in formation as processes partake of seriality yet can be read against the abstract generality of the series. Whatever binds the form cannot complete the process or totality, intimated by their productive capacities. Sartre critiques an order of being and yet, in

---

12 See Hegel, *Science of Logic*. The seventh through ninth chapters, like the opening chapters of *Capital*, are not for the faint of heart. Central to Hegel's philosophy of measure is an assessment of change, which in the present work is the measure of seriality.

identifying its process, reveals its unbound possibilities in measure, or its qualitative quantity. Perhaps, by taking novelization and nation as the interrupted and interrupting space of politics, the difference of time requires a supplementary concept that interrogates the absent present in Bakhtin's theory, and a notion of serialization in the interrelation of nation and novel.

Benedict Anderson's articulation of the nation as an imagined community is often taken to mean that the imaginary of both literature and nation are synonymous.[13] Thus, writers like José Rizal and Pramoedya Ananta Toer (his primary touchstones) are not only exemplary in narrating nation, but are always coincident with its expression. In *The Long Space* I argued that Anderson does not make this assumption, because language first figures the authors' possible expressivity; thus, it is through the study of language that the imagined characteristic of nation can be glimpsed, whether in Prameodya's "national language," Bahasa Indonesia, or Rizal's anti-colonial Spanish.[14] The prevailing problem that authors are too often taken as cultural representatives of the nation is one that Anderson attempts to unpack and reformulate. The complex sinews of modernity may instantiate the nation state and require the ideological and cultural architectonics of national stories, but writers are notoriously untrustworthy spokespeople for the state, something that the topos and materiality of exile in modernism underlines—and a phenomenon that Bakhtin, obviously, would have appreciated. Thus, nation is never the fixed point against which the writer's affiliation can be measured but rather, like language, is a living substance of identification moving unevenly with the writer's own dynamism and self-understanding. An extant state wants the cultural imprimatur of national writers in order to justify its being as itself a recognizable and stable way of living (if states promote literacy, it is also in the hope that the literate will repay education through expressive affiliation). For Anderson, then, writers like Rizal and Pramoedya permit a deeper engagement with the writing of nation, especially those states

13 Anderson, *Imagined Communities*.

14 See Hitchcock, *Long Space*. The trilogies and tetralogies discussed are in series but not serialized, which is both a conceptual and political differentiation in the forms of anti-colonialism expressed.

written out through processes of decolonization. But this phenomenology of nation itself requires qualification in order to understand the parameters of its narration. Etienne Balibar, for instance, distinguishes the nation from the nation form: the former can be read as nations and nationalities that produce an identification through reproduction or repetition (the work of state alluded to above); the latter, however, is a combinatory mode, a social formation whose hegemony is itself unevenly developed among other formations, dominant or otherwise.[15] Nation form, then, is "the concept of a structure capable of producing determinate 'community effects'" [but] "is not itself a community."[16] This is something of the absent cause in the structure of the nation that permits its form to appear. Significantly, this is also the time of difference between novelization and novel. Could it be the nation appears in serialization but its form in language has become the ward of novelization?

There is more to Balibar's supplement to nation through nation form than the paradox of absent cause, especially in his explicit references to Anderson's model, which he associates with "mere discourses of the community (mythical, historical or literary grand narratives)," the stuff of novelization or the bad side of imaginary process.[17] Balibar's initial criticism is to emphasize the importance of the nation form in terms of structure which, while it does not exclude imagination, looks to focus on the material manifestations of the nation's emergence. Ostensibly, Balibar's position on the nation form relies on regulative history, yet his methodology is reflexive on historical composition since, ideologically, national origins can be malevolently mythologized. Even as Balibar acknowledges "imagined

15 See Etienne Balibar, *We, the People of Europe: Reflections on Transnational Citizenship* (J. Swenson trans.) (Princeton, NJ: Princeton University Press, 2004). See also his collaborative project with Immanuel Wallerstein: Etienne Balibar and Immanuel Wallerstein. *Race, Nation, Class: Ambiguous Identities* (Chris Turner trans.) (London: Verso, 1991). Both studies emphasize the complex ways in which ideologies of nation are structured by and produce hierarchies of race and class, a boundedness in seriality that problematizes summary statements on division and extension.

16 Balibar, *We, the People of Europe*, pp. 20–21.

17 Etienne Balibar, "Ambiguous Identities" in *Politics and the Other Scene* (Chris Turner trans.) (New York: Verso, 2002), p. 66.

communities" he remains wary of their ideological sway, and of any process of identification that might obfuscate the formal operations of power in the maintenance of community control. Such an approach complicates the relationship of novelization to nation while also helping to clarify the constitutive limits to Bakhtin's theory in light of his experience of Soviet Russia as nation.

The ambivalence between nation and state represents another form of hesitancy, and a kind of measurelesness that simultaneously confounds everything from borders to serial extension as narrative, data, and documentation. The verification of each term forms two series in irresolvable tension, in part distilled by the different genealogies informing them and by the combined and uneven developments of modernity in which they signify. In effect, communities have often used one element of recognition as an alibi or justification for the other. This does not mean a particularly grouping is wrong or falsely composed—all kinds of cultural, geographic, and historical coordinates offer a rationale for a nation or for a state—but what naturalizes a state as a nation or a nation as a state requires constant ideological work and indeed an imaginary in which such binding or belonging makes sense. Anderson does not believe novels perform this function (or rather, they can, but this does not produce great novels aesthetically or politically) yet they nevertheless participate in a seriality in which the time and space of nations are elaborated and cognized. Of course, different orders of experience are maintained, even if the reader, like a citizen subject, is individuated across a range of discourses. As with Balibar and Anderson, there is a metaphorical crosstalk, but however culture is wielded, from reinforcement to epistemicide, a nation narrated has more than the symptomatic presence that may be detected in individual novels. Why, then, imbricate the nation as form in Balibar's sense with the conditional limits of novelization and serialization?

One of the lessons of Balibar's critique is he is rightly suspicious of formation analysis that automatically confers superstructural status on the social or on elements of what may be deemed civil society. This would underestimate the infrastructural roles that define institutions of state or national prerogatives. It would also tend to bracket in advance discursive practices that legitimate or otherwise provide a logical consistency to a national outlook. The reproducibility of a nation idea is heavily dependent on these form-shaping protocols which are, not coincidentally, co-present with an economic mode also bound to persistence. Perhaps Anderson does not go far enough in configuring print culture in the time/space of national reproduction, in part to resist the crude assignation of technological determinism, yet even if we restricted his argument to the production of the "now" (a procession of "meanwhiles" crossed with the dialectical impress of Benjaminian "Jeztzeit") it is clear that forms of time are operative in the nation state Balibar also theorizes. Novelization, from this perspective, understands too well the chronotopic real of state formation and seriality. Rather than think of historical poetics as an aesthetic abstraction in this regard, its methodological base for Bakhtin's theory of the novel offers an interrogative form, a "specter of comparison" if you will, that haunts every narrative of national belonging, even those that radically and creatively have challenged and defeated the predations of colonialism and imperialism on community identities. Novelization does not nominate itself as a key interlocutor on the contradictions of the serial demands on nation, even when a "national literature" of some kind has been desired. Nevertheless, its narrative processes are deeply historical and instructive. Balibar notes, "The nation form certainly did not appear out of nowhere, perfectly formed (even if there were in some sense prototypes, some of which played the decisive role of giving it its name). But neither was it infinitely plastic."[18] This dynamic historicity is shared by novelization so that, while never simply simultaneous, the configurations and contradictions of its contact zones with national expression offer a heuristic on how forms come to be.

In *The Long Space* I suggested that serialization is time's writing system of nation. Of course, there is much more to institutional structures than inscription, yet the latter participates in the inertial logic of national iteration and in its corresponding power of consonant social reproduction. Again, we have problematized the prescriptions of this "practico-inert" by offering a seriality with pronounced internal contradictions, forms of difference and repetition and of division in extension that mediate the

18 See Etienne Balibar, "The Nation Form: History and Ideology," *Review* (Fernand Braudel Center) 13(3) (Summer 1990): 329–61; here, p. 338.

grounds of a more radical persistence. The meaning of nationalism, for instance, in postcolonial movements for independence and autonomy does not simply reproduce what colonialism and imperialism imposed, despite the vexed and flawed identifications this has often entailed. The rallying cries of nationalism in anti-imperialist insurgency are necessarily focused on moments of delinking, and that specificity does not easily conjoin the experience of post-independence state building in the world system, which is why the seriality of nation is rightly questioned and why other modes of autonomy and/or sovereign separation have been explored. Similarly, however the *Bildungsroman* as genre is interpreted to allegorize concepts of nation formation in postcoloniality, the novelization of postcolonial and decolonial experience is markedly uneven and casts even the "rendezvous of victory" within a longer and more problematic genealogy of nationalism. Edward Said suggests that beyond the deployment of nationalism to defeat imperialism, the continuing work of decolonization should cleave to liberation rather than to nationalism as such.[19] For his part, Anderson radically supplements his nation formation critique with the idea that nationalism can be assessed via appropriate comparisons. In "Nationalism, Identity, and the Logic of Seriality" Anderson elaborates the "material, institutional, and discursive bases" of bound and unbound seriality.[20] Anderson is concerned to show how a "new grammar of representation" is forged to allow "nation" to appear in anti-colonial struggle. In effect, a new seriality, unbound, challenges the perquisites of imperialism's "bound" conventions (in its institutionalizations of time, in the cultural impress of, for instance, its calendar and census). Anti-colonialism had to populate every colonial serial of "quotidian universals" (like newspapers and periodicals) in order to deconstruct and demystify the "meanwhile" or simultaneity of colonial space. The answer to bound seriality is not simply unbound particularity, but a new sense of dialectical totality that is historical and openly contestable.

---

19 See Edward Said, "Yeats and Decolonization" in Terry Eagleton, Fredric Jameson and Edward Said, *Nationalism, Colonialism, and Literature* (Minneapolis, MN: University of Minnesota Press, 1990), pp. 69–95.

20 Benedict Anderson, *The Spectre of Comparisons: Nationalism, Southeast Asia and the World* (London: Verso, 1998).

And thus, we return to the time/space of the serial novel, the cultural logic where novelization and serialization insistently entwine. The serial novel is interlaced by several orders of time, so that its time/space or chronotope is marked by the process of narration (the time in and of narration), the logic of seriality itself, the longue durée of novelization, and the cultural order of time in specific series, including that of nation. Like people, the serial novel "does not exist in the same Now."[21] The quotidian impress of seriality is not innocent in its everydayness and is never far from ideological mediation, both in the numbing proclivities of iteration, and also in the utopian impulses of division and extension (moments of category crisis or of a prolongation in the imperatives of struggle). In this way, the serial novel, even in its protocols of publication and consumption, can participate in the unfinished business of seriality's promise, as a mode of novelization like Marx's poetry of the future, where the content goes beyond the phrase.[22]

Scholars of Victorian culture are notable in their concern for the impact of serialization on everyday cultural life, a focus that has enabled an understanding of vibrant connections across disparate material, as if series and serials constitute the lineaments of social relations much greater than their phenomenological surfaces.[23] Bakhtin's concept of novelization addresses serialization in modernity and requires rethinking forms of time in that regard. The novel of which Bakhtin writes is closely allied to

---

21 I am thinking of Bloch's critique of the nonsynchronous, but here as a concatenation of different orders of time. See Ernst Bloch, "Nonsynchronism and the Obligation to Its Dialectics" (Mark Ritter trans.), *New German Critique* 11 (Spring 1977): 22–38.

22 Karl Marx, *The Eighteenth Brumaire of Louis Bonaparte* (S. K. Padover trans.) (Moscow: Progress Publishers, 1937), p. 10.

23 In addition to the work of Feltes, noted above, see, for instance, Laurel Brake, *Print in Transition, 1850–1910: Studies in Media and Book History* (London: Palgrave, 2001). Brake's research offers modes of serialization that are distinct and yet at once enmeshed. See also David Payne, *The Re-enchantment of Nineteenth-Century Fiction* (New York: Palgrave Macmillan, 2005); and, importantly, Roger Hagedorn, "Technology and Economic Exploitation: The Serial as a Form of Narrative Presentation," *Wide Angle* 10(4) (1988): 4–12; and Roger Hagedorn, "Doubtless to be continued: A Brief History of Serial Narrative" in Robert C. Allen (ed.), *To be Continued . . . : Soap Operas Around the World* (London: Routledge, 1995), pp. 27–48.

serialization, whether one considers the five-volume series of *Gargantua and Pantagruel*, the serialization of Dostoevsky's works in the *Russian Messenger*, or both the epistolary sequence in Goethe or his diptych on *Wilhelm Meister. Madame Bovary, War and Peace, The Ambassadors, Heart of Darkness, Kim, Tender is the Night* and, of course, Balzac's *La Comédie Humaine* also reveal a great deal about this symbiosis. Serialization instantiates the present for these works, and through analysis of such identification the future of the novel and modernity's notion, the nation, can be glimpsed. Gary Saul Morson, in an otherwise trenchant analysis of temporality in Bakhtin, overlooks the implications of seriality in such a critique, even when discussing Bakhtin's own missed opportunity before Russia's best devotee of open time, Tolstoy.[24] If, as Morson claims, serialization was "essential" to *War and Peace*, this is not just because Tolstoy did not want to go back to change anything (a trait noted above); nor, indeed, because he did not wish to end the text, but because in serialization the time of history in the novel exceeds the capacity of individual consciousness to finalize its expression (we have tracked something of this predicament in non-fiction as well). This does not exclude the individual exigencies of the author, especially when it comes to economic prerogatives—as is often the case with Dickens, for instance[25]—but it does not cede the time of difference to volition, temporal perception, or personal whim. While we have not endorsed Sartre's case for seriality and the collective wholesale, in part because he begins from the queue as a measure of the practico-inert, Sartre nevertheless cogently permits a role for the other in the process of connection or disconnection. This, in its own way, may be closer to a Bakhtinian rendering of socialization.

As we have intimated, several characteristics of novel serialization are relevant to the analysis of nation seriality, including that its emergence

---

24 Gary Saul Morson, "Bakhtin, Genres, and Temporality," *New Literary History* 22(4) (Autumn 1991): 1071–92.

25 One thinks here of Dickens's serialization of his first novel, *The Pickwick Papers*, in which, at the end of number 10, he quotes from John Richardson, himself a master of seriality, who announces at the end of each dramatic performance, "we shall keep perpetually going on beginning again, regularly, until the end of the fair." See Charles Dickens, *The Pickwick Papers* (London: Penguin, 2003).

owes much to the economies of print capitalism which Anderson discusses. A decision to disseminate novels in journals and newspapers projects a new readership and reader experience. It is not just the segmentation of the text shapes the internal logic of the narrative, but that it is framed by other concerns of social life and becomes part of an organic conversation about what such life representationally entails, including what composes national identification. The match of content is less important than the discord in genre and the question of formal appropriateness. Economic decisions over novel serialization are never far from its place in the cultural grammar of publication relative to single volume items or special editions. As we have suggested, what is bound or archived can obviate the difference in serialization, which has an alternative sense of event and eventness highly sensitive to the lived possibility of its moment(s). Although the context of the non-fiction example is specific, it is noticeable with Marx's extensive experience with newspaper and journal practices, he struggled to rework *Le Capital* in a way that would not simultaneously compromise the substance of his critique and serial apprehension. Clearly writers respond in a variety of ways to the obligations of serial engagement including, for instance, whether their livelihood depends on it. The question of nation formation is part of the political unconscious of serialization in its projection of simultaneity, although individual writers may take up this chronotope as a narratological principle rather than as a fulcrum of the nation per se. In his reading of José Rizal, Anderson argues "the novel as literary genre [. . .] permitted the imagining of 'Las Filipinas' as a bounded sociological reality,"[26] but he does not consider in detail what the concept of series does to that reality, and especially through the compositional logic of the novel in series. Beyond this, the extension in of the novel in series, like that of novel serialization, may find itself extended in a second or other series, which can also unbind the nation beyond its normative evidentiary forms via translation, adaptation, or revised or special editions, while simultaneously invoking the question of necessary duration. Why should a narration continue? Why should a nation endure? The questions are dialectically enmeshed in forms of time. Bakhtin's focus is novelization, a narrative dynamic in which the novel's capacity to tell is simultaneously

26 Anderson, *Spectre of Comparisons*

inter- and intra-generic. Such forms of time claim relative autonomy but they are themselves overdetermined by duration at other scales, including the complex and contradictory infrastructures of nation and state formation in the world system. It is true the imaginary of "imagined communities" is not an unalloyed conceptual link (in decolonial cultural critique one could make the dialectical case by beginning with capital, race, or imperial conditions). Here, serialization, as the difference of time, can specify the novel's process in the fraught identity and affect of nationness, caught as it is between the nation as lived and the nation form as propositionally unrepresentable as a novel sui generis. Again, it is possible to elaborate extended fiction, novels in series, trilogies and tetralogies, as postcolonial chronotopes, as a "long space." It is clear, however, that the temporal consequences of serialization inflect the time of difference in other cultural expressions as likely to deracinate nationness as an experience of community as they are to confirm it. From this perspective it is not the consonance that is decisive, but the questions raised about struggles over temporality within serial representation.

While the project here is not to provide a typology of discourse forms, the fictive permutations of bound and unbound seriality have real foundations in, for instance, the processes of transnational capitalist circulation (not just in financialization but in supply chains), digital platforms, and VR extensions. Such serial symptoms constitute both logical and techno-logical alternatives to normative simultaneity. An obvious drawback in an Andersonian model that couples temporality and nation with seriality is the emphasis on a basic chronology with a concomitant teleology in modernity, both of which would seem, once more, to privilege forms of time and of chronotope that burden narrative, if not with ghostly comparisons, then certainly with the originary actions of Europe. For instance, Partha Chatterjee's response to Anderson's framework underlines both the problems of boundedness versus unboundedness in seriality (particularly the diminution of ethnic identity that attends Anderson's critique of the census) and the limits of liberation in the concept of empty, homogenous time itself.[27] Although Anderson's argument does not come

27 See Partha Chatterjee, "Anderson's Utopia," *Diacritics* 29(4) (Winter 1999): 128–34. The reference to "empty, homogenous time" is from Walter Benjamin's thoughts on

down to judging unbound seriality and national identity as good, and bound seriality and ethnic identity as bad, Chatterjee is right to question the degree of distinction between the two when the rhetoric of universality at stake seems tied either way to a specific genealogy of Enlightenment philosophy with its own logical series. This necessitates still greater attention to the "time of capital," that which forges a calendar printed in abstruse simultaneity. What Benjamin sees as a contradictory chronos, one which provides for messianic moments that break the plodding continuum of capital as stasis, Chatterjee chides as "utopian," because "empty homogeneous time is not located anywhere in real space."[28]

Novelization responds to time's crisis by tracking generic change as symptomatic. Serialization ostensibly pours content into the moment of such change, but finds temporality itself problematic, a crisis in time in a crisis of time. Here we have noted the time of difference as a specific antimony of modernity, nationness as belonging or as affiliated in a world of circulation. Rather than return novelization to the material conditions of Bakhtin's theoretical practice it also exists as a provocation regarding modernity's endgame in the present, especially but not limited to novelization's inexorable interpellation of the political. Opposition to the idea of state and radical movements to "wither" its grip on polity is certainly not addressed by Bakhtin's theory of novelization (whatever its democratization of genre and form, the concept is hardly an unproblematic paean to statecraft or its sublation). The importance of novelization rests in its historical poetics, yet these do not exclude by fiat a narratological challenge for forces of social change. Indeed, the conditions of serialization between novel and nation are instructive about how new possibilities of time/space can be understood and elaborated. Anderson's contribution here is a thought experiment not a template. Whether socially, politically, economically, or culturally, there is so much more to imagination in

---

the philosophy of history where such time is contrasted with" time filled by the presence of the now" [*Jetztzeit*]. While my emphasis on extension and division in seriality does not map this contrast, it does point to its logic of temporal disjunction. See Walter Benjamin, "Theses on the Philosophy of History" in *Illuminations*, pp. 253–64.

28 Chatterjee, "Anderson's Utopia": 131. I focus in more detail on this conundrum in Hitchcock, *The Long Space*, pp. 26–28.

decolonizing states than parables and the parabolic of postcolonial novels. Nevertheless, the "meanwhile" in nation formation, including the nowness of immediation,[29] is a provocation about the forms of time and of chronotope in the current conjuncture, and the concreteness of the serially engaged. Of course, the study of novelization can remain a relatively unencumbered philological vocation far removed from the subject and subjection of nation, but because novelization is serially bound to modernity, it is compelled to perform its contradictions. If culture speaks to modernity in this way, it can be reaffirmed by dialogizing novelization with temporality's content, something akin to the "eventness" of the event. If we give serialization a role in such critique, it is not just because it maintains a critical tension between the novel and the novel as form, but because it informs a materialist reading of literary history "present, in all its openendedness" to the socio-political content of time.[30]

29 For more on "immediation" as a cultural logic, see Peter Hitchcock, "Immediation and Responsibility" in Jeffrey Di Leo and Peter Hitchcock (eds), *The New Public Intellectual* (New York: Palgrave Macmillan, 2016), pp. 135–47.

30 Bakhtin, *Dialogic Imagination*, p. 38.

CONCLUSION: ON THE NEXT ISSUE

The initial idea for these studies began in innocuous fashion, by imagining a surviving and clandestine Communard in Paris in September 1872 chancing upon the first issue of *Le Capital*. They had never read *Capital* (Volume 1) before (a socialist friend had said it was available in German) and they were surprised to see a French livraison of its first pages for sale for 10 centimes on a street corner, admittedly buried under dailies and periodicals of a more recognizable bent in France in the aftermath of the Commune. This issue of *Le Capital* was an incredibly difficult text and, although the worker was literate and intimately conversant in discourses of insurrection (and appreciated Marx's prefatory warning about the nature of the text), the discourse on the commodity and value remained abstract and alienating, like the experience of capitalism itself. They were not exactly eager for the next issue, and they wondered if another serialization of Marx might be forthcoming. They were not expecting the language of the serial sensation Eugène Sue, but the Communard felt a second series might be required to explain this one. In the worker, I believed I was conjuring the reader who Marx had imagined for this version of *Capital*, a worker whose recent experience of proletarian uprising would make them a vital and enthusiastic student for Marx's analysis. The reader greatly appreciated that Marx showed no condescension, and that difficult ideas remained difficult. There was no reading protocol: if a methodology was at stake, it could only take form in the experience of reading itself. Yet for all of this, the Communard was still perturbed by the project. How could Marx explicate the seriality of the commodity process without formally engaging the promise of the serial and series in disseminating and enriching his work?

Following the initial conceit and its question, I did not believe Marx misunderstood seriality or the proletarian consciousness of a Parisian worker. I was more inclined to think I had misread the philosophical and socio-economic disposition of seriality itself and therefore I began again with that exploration. I was particularly concerned to figure the logic of seriality as contested, and to read it against the grain of a Sartrean emphasis on its limits as political stasis and as incontrovertible evidence of the practico-inert. Were all of seriality's popular forms and its prevalence in the everyday just a structural conspiracy to silence and acquiescence? True, the more one looked at the philosophy, Hegel on measure, Deleuze on series, etc., the more one felt comfortable with Marx's assessment of serial manufacture—it is efficient not because it is non-contradictory but because it obstinately attempts to rationalize regulation and the regulatory. If Deleuze misaligns series not to confirm dialectical contradiction but to smother it with a sense of series everywhere, his protean exploration of the concept nevertheless opens up a kind of serial futurity in which all that is solid does not just melt into air but becomes rhizomatically affect or networked (a preface, then, in this study, to the implications of a cyborganic self in Oshii's anime, subsequently reverse engineered as human in a live action adaptation). Deleuze would have liked *Innocence*, both for its arthouse vibe (the mainstay of both his *Cinema* books)[1] and for its psychodrama and libidinal economies. It is not a great fit for difference and repetition, perhaps because *Innocence* is a little too literal and stubbornly realist, but, as a thought experiment, one intuitively knows which character Deleuze could be. Meanwhile, the endings of both *Ghost in the Shell* and *Innocence* reaffirm the post-human consciousness of the Major as networked, as self-aware if not quite what we now mean by AI. Interestingly, the worlds portrayed reveal a technologically enhanced proletarianization rather than a world beyond class, although such an idea would seem at once anachronistic in a digital ethos where work is post-work, gig, or subcontracted, and serials in multiple forms are the noise of subsumption not class formation. Perhaps even the Communard glimpsed this future as abstraction in the first issue of *Le Capital.*

If seriality is a mode of production across manufacture and culture, its role in reading social change would seem to be so deeply compromised

---

1 See Gilles Deleuze, *Cinema 1: The Movement-Image* (Hugh Tomlinson and Barbara Habberjam trans) (Minneapolis, MN: University of Minnesota Press, 1986); Gilles Deleuze, *Cinema 2: The Time-Image* (Hugh Tomlinson and Robert Galeta trans) (Minneapolis, MN: University of Minnesota Press, 1989).

as to constitute a benchmark for the persistence of deleterious forms of commodification and governmentality, precisely what labor in its long history with actually-existing capitalism has been attempting to challenge and overcome. In the materialization of seriality we are more likely to see stultifying measures of order and control than symptoms of crisis as a radical break, of the kind elaborated, for instance, in Gellert's graphic activism or Tardi's *Le Cri du peuple*. Just because a work is serialized or is in series with a radical position does not mean seriality is surreptitiously a linchpin in social transformation. The revolutionary is surely more likely to cast off serial demands in a moment of crisis than draw on its narratological modes, like kicking back with a manga *tankōbon*. The question is not about whether one has time for comprehending Marx's serial in French in 44 (or 50) parts versus Variety Artworks' two-part *Capital in manga*, with a narrative reimagined for the time/space of commuting, but whether one makes time in serial engagement, whether one enjoins simultaneously an experience of narrative brushing its everydayness against the grain with an insight regarding the contradiction this practice stages. The difference between making time for seriality and making time in seriality is not a propositional or prepositional faith. Forms of time (and of chronotope) are variegated and complex so that even an otherwise innocuous question, "What is seriality?" can elicit strikingly different philosophical, cultural, and economic explications. Making time in seriality is precisely what it is supposed to suppress, and this is why I have attempted to link a time of crisis to a crisis in time. While seriality never directly precipitates the former, it preserves and reproduces the latter by marking sequence and division in conflict. Loving this series or that is more than using up time—it is the very basis for learning timely contradiction as a narrative force. This is a particular way seriality makes one not only aware of social change, but even in or precisely because of its quotidian logic, it can address the contradictory challenge of participating in it.

An aesthetic process of literary production like the serial novel does not in itself appear to invite involvement in the kinds of social change imagined by Marx and Marxism, so again one must be wary of overstating the role of seriality across its many manifestations. In the Victorian novel, for instance, the professionalization of serialization encouraged the absorption of otherwise controversial social themes as part of a sales and promotion strategy. A writer with more independence, like Dickens (with his own weeklies, *All the Year Round* and *Household Words*—the latter the serial home of *Hard Times*), still had to consider market competition, even if the power of publishers in general had stabilized periodical practices around frequency and distribution. Within the dynamics of industrial modernization stories that cleaved to problems of social change (class and property values, traditional versus progressive mores, urbanization, education, and the infrastructures of empire) were not anathema to a popular reading audience, who experienced much of their substance consciously and unconsciously on a day-to-day basis. Serialization ostensibly provided a platform for popularization, although at the level of interpretation different modalities of time were put into play (within the narrative and its possible "present," publication and distribution exigencies, in the division of time in instalments—both for the author and characters in relation to readers—in the duration of the series, and in a dialogic awareness of reader response as itself timely). There remains a conceptual relation between novelization and serialization that foregrounds open-endedness with an indexing of the present, yet this has two important qualifications. First, the relative success of an archived present is in its capacity to be comprehended from a time that is not its own. What may be deemed an anachronism or a diminished resonance in part derives from a lost sense of co-participation with a reader/viewer whose cultural formation is not just a difference of degree but of kind. Second, a series may be largely out of sync with its present in a way that restricts or otherwise interrupts its engagement, yet nevertheless as a series it maintains an openness to a time to come, an event of time as a new division in its sequence, as a condensation of form in renewal or as indeed a new form of serial. What is optimal in the time of the Victorian novel for serialization is of course no guarantee for this series or that. The novel only reveals a capacity for generic profusion that serialization engages, for concrete historical reasons. The example of Dostoevsky is instructive because the conditions of serialization were far from optimal, yet in his major texts he writes characters as if they are the arbiters of the series before them rather than the serial machine of author, publisher, and reader. In non-fiction one assumes this remit must more firmly reside with the author, yet the text itself can also relate such capacity, and especially if its serial conditions are the reason it is presented as such. If, however, the text is adapted or serialized there are constraints on its formal possibility and the text may not just have to live differently, but be articulated in and for that apprehension.

"The next issue" is a set of formal and political questions that are, in their own way, a serial project. For instance, what is serial engagement? We have tracked several versions of Marx's *Das Kapital*, including his own editing and (re)translation of Volume One for *Le Capital*. Social change is subject to conditions of event, so rather than authenticate a version of the text by how faithful it is to the original in its time (the authentication axiom must be respected, but not as an absolute), serial engagement also means an assessment of the appropriateness of the text's interpretation and representation in another time/space (what overdetermines decisions for editions and re-translations necessitates attention to conjunction, and a methodology adequate to its event). On the one hand, this is simply a materialist substantiation of the text's moment, especially when coming to terms with the event of socio-economic crisis (*Capital*'s critique offers a heuristic of how such crises come to be). On the other hand, its mode of address may be sufficiently dialogic so that it reads time in a new substance, and structures a dynamic chronotope in which its meaning for change is radically present. The inclusion of *Capital in manga* in Manga de Dokuha by Variety Artworks was premised on an otherwise anodyne project to illustrate "great works," but the lived relations of the 2007–2008 crisis rewrites its presence for a Japanese readership processing how such economic calamity comes to be. As we have suggested, the story's basis in *Capital* is fraught with contradiction (a tale of a European cheese factory set in the years after Marx's death is a series of disjunction and displacement within the texture of the financial crisis in Japan in the 2000s) yet its tangled narration, including its eventual fallback on the generic demands of "edumanga," makes a critique of political economy a necessary injunction even if, as a hermeneutical process, Marx's "authentic" text is only occasionally recognizable. It is not that seriality means anything goes; on the contrary, extension and division is thoroughly mediated by the logic of conjunction as itself the living-on of socio-economic contradiction. If the second volume of *Capital in manga* tells capital-as-relation less successfully, it is in part because it more self-consciously tries to represent Marx's analysis (the faithful flaw) rather than let its own story relive it. When serial engagement is reduced to "bringing to order," social change is "queued" in the negative sense and the meaning of its event quickly dissipates.

A repetition in form is not a straitjacket for cultural or social participation, even if convention can be used to that effect. Seriality builds sociality but through and not despite the contradictions this entails. What serialization learns from novelization is its architectonic capacity. The next issue, from this perspective, is not derived purely from formal avarice (what Bakhtin saw in the novel as its appetite to ingest forms) but from serial potential. One point in tracking the concrete abstractions of Marx's measure of capitalism is to see whether narrating *Capital* anew needs realism to foreground reality. Gellert's graphic representation is closer to Ernst Cassirer on the philosophy of symbolic forms than it is the narratological concerns of Lukács or Bakhtin—not at the level of myth, but in the sense that symbols, the clenched fist, the divided cog and clock, might motivate an otherwise fleeting amalgam in the event of crisis and show the "face" of capitalism as radically compromised.[2] Lukács is more acute than Cassirer on the historical and political materialization of such symbols and forms, and their concrete potentialities, yet this reminds me that in serializing *Capital*, Marx underestimated its graphic capacity, not simply in appropriate ornamentation (the resonance of the cover to the first issue of *Le Capital*) but in defamiliarizing its meaning in the everyday.[3]

---

2 See Ernst Cassirer, *The Philosophy of Symbolic Forms*, 3 VOLS (*Volume One*: *Language*; *Volume Two*: *Mythical Thinking*; *Volume Three*: *Phenomenology of Cognition*) (Steve G. Lofts trans.) (Abingdon: Routledge, 2021). I am thinking in particular of the movement from image to presentation as a tension that Gellert's work "illustrates."

3 There is no space here to consider the materialist concern for form in its anti-capitalist genealogy but it is pertinent to note how capitalist crisis has also contributed to renewed interest in the works of Lukács, including Georg Lukács, *History and Class Consciousness*: *Studies in Marxist Dialects* (Rodney Livingstone trans.) (London: Merlin,

Tardi's adaptation of Vautrin, while doggedly realist, attempts a kind of graphic intimacy so that the narrative lives in its own grammar of historical perception, seeking affective social presence in reflection. Tardi's *Le Cri du peuple* is in series with Vautrin's novel while taking novelization itself as a formal challenge for telling the story of the Paris Commune. The series, like the franchise for *Ghost in the Shell*, interrogates form in extension. Here, "the next issue" is not the one that counts necessarily, but the one that is alive to the very possibility of its timely expression.

Sartre's exegesis of the practico-inert reads seriality as pernicious, as a veritable "mute compulsion" that represents an abstract domination of the everyday.[4] While appreciating the theory of existential crisis and counter discourses this elicits, we have sought to complicate the epistemological and political grounds of a seriality otherwise. What, however, is the political gainsay of reading in seriality a condition for change when radical telling does not obviously have to be in series and certainly needs no explicit reference to Marx to further its aims? Here, think of seriality as a potential akin to "dual power" in Lenin's understanding.[5] The logic of seriality constrains, yet contains a process desiring social change that lives alongside and within it. The radical impurity of the admixture ensures the possibility of telling and narration at odds with political life as usual. Lenin uses the example of the laws and procedures of the Paris Commune as denoting a special kind of state within a state, a kind of form seeking power within and against conditions of dominance. Seriality is not simply a platform for describing social contradiction in this manner but instead it permits an understanding and working out of social contradiction in general under

---

1971); and the earlier, if not altogether materialist, Georg Lukács, *The Theory of the Novel: A Historico-Philosophical Essay on the Forms of Great Epic Literature* (Anna Bostock trans.) (London: Merlin, 1971).

4 This phrase, "*stumme Zwang*" is borrowed from Marx in *Capital, Volume One* in his discussion of the force of economic relations in original accumulation and its power over labor decision. See Marx, *Das Kapital*, p. 622. See also, Marx, *Capital* (Fowkes trans.), p. 899. Søren Mau has recently taken up this question in his book of the same name: *Mute Compulsion: A Marxist Theory of the Economic Power of Capital* (London: Verso, 2023).

5 See Vladimir Lenin, "The Dual Power" at marxists.org: rebrand.ly/f07289 (last accessed: August 26, 2025).

the contestable terms of modernity and modernization. In moments of crisis all kinds of processes and practices are thrown into relief or are uniquely performed. Cultural expression is not outside the eventness of the event. Series and the serial are already part of the compositional field, and crisis measures such embeddedness in surprising ways. They do not predict articulation but are actively engaged in its representational logic. Seriality itself is an abstraction that yet keeps alive the real of social change, or else it is merely its interpretation. No series or serial guarantees either but crisis weighs heavily on the form of their appearance. For capitalism, regulation in production and circulation is one way to smooth value extraction although politics, even if limned to the series of serial production, in no way assures radical or reactionary composition. Capitalist contradictions themselves saturate worker experience and are accompanied by both intricate and stark ideological rationalizations that these are to be expected and are to be endured. Serializing resistance and opposition to such claims counters persistence with an alternative determination, yet this in itself is not a dialectical negation. Anti-capitalist politics does not hinge on the serial array of differing worldviews.

For Deleuze and Guattari, a revolutionary politics is an abstract machine, "an absolute that is manifested locally, and engendered in a series of local operations of varying orientations."[6] Here "the next issue" is not a chapter or part but a connected operation of opposition whose materialization remains in question as a series (for which they use the term "consistency"). Any invocation of an "open series" in this regard necessarily begs the question of organization and constituency and one wonders how "manifestation" is discernible (at what scale, and do any chronotopic conditions obtain?). We might think of the constellation of examples in Parts One and Two as a non-linear series, which would lend itself to horizontalism of a kind, but obviously the political commitments remain relatively isolated, even if broadly anti-capitalist. Could we think of seriality, like totality, as a desire within socialization rather than as a set (or set theory) of measured responses? Contemporary capitalism does not fear the incalculable per se (it is, after all, also speculative), and it appears focused on the minimization of organized labor and community self-

6 Deleuze and Guattari, *Thousand Plateaus*, p. 382.

representation over rhizomatic spontaneity. Nevertheless, as I have attempted to indicate in an exploration of networked, cyborg subjectivity, systemic contradiction appears in many forms. Perhaps seriality as desire is caught between measure and measurelessness and is ripe with antinomy, a modality (in the Kantian sense) of relation? On this point, the question of seriality interrogates and/or demonstrates the ambivalent measure of capitalist modernity between quantity and quality, in quality as quantity. Words and images are not universally bound to such articulation, yet when they take up the narrative modes of the serial and series within crisis and contradiction, political and by all means aesthetic disputes are renewed. The issue that closes a series is a completed project on several levels. The next issue, however, provides a different promise of satisfaction, one in which the terms of seriality and social change are also at stake (this is why "next" is not just restrictively in sequence but is of "now"). The way of telling in series may be recognizable, but the consequences of serial engagement in crisis is both a restitution and new formation. The next issue as extension is part of its appeal while at the same time grounding its potential break or division. What is vital to forms of narration is also fundamental to socialization, where such breaks indicate another way of telling, another form of ending.

Novelization and serialization are interrelated and mutually interruptive. It would seem odd to stress the connection when a central text of this project is not a novel, but *Capital*; yet, as S. S. Prawer among others has stressed, Marx's literary references are prodigious in *Capital* (and, of course, as is often noted, he wrote a novel and poetry) so it is not outlandish to think of the critique as at once saturated not just with calculation but with an aesthetic desire for science as also an art of the possible.[7] Francis Wheen, whose biographies of both Marx and *Capital* are exemplary, recounts that shortly before the publication of *Capital* in 1867, Marx insisted Engels read "The Unknown Masterpiece" by Honoré de Balzac, the story of an artist, Frenhofer, who, obsessed with the idea of a portrait that will be "the most complete representation of reality," spends

---

7 See S. S. Prawer, *Karl Marx and World Literature* (Oxford: Oxford University Press, 1976). As Prawer makes clear, Marx uses the idea and practice of the literary in several ways but reflections on literature suffuse his political theorization.

a decade painting over his art again and again.[8] When he finally shows the painting to his friends and peers they see "nothing"—a portrait sublated by the powers of representational revision. By the time of Volume One's publication, Marx had already been working on *Capital* for 20 years—a long space of research and narration in sharp contrast to the deadline-determined abruption of the *Communist Manifesto*. Marx did write to deadlines, especially for the *New York Herald Tribune*, when payment was vital for his family's wellbeing. The idea for *Le Capital* was closer to that of the *Communist Manifesto* in terms of proletarian consciousness, but Marx's necessary adherence to the "most complete representation of reality" scuppered most of the serial demands yet, ironically, preserved a central thesis of both novelization and serialization, a perspicuous tendency to generic variation and timely condensation. Although seriality is conventionally measured by regulation and closure, the historical life of telling seethes with an immeasurability and what Bakhtin terms "unfinishedness" (*nezavershen*). Not all series count for good material reasons, but some live on by meeting their history and not just recording it. If *Capital* as series remains dynamic and unfinished, it is in no small part because its critique attends to a mode of production that is itself in perpetual motion. But it also cleaves to a notion of seriality that concretizes the event, not only of reading words or a "book with images," but also of a time/space in which its series becomes necessarily superfluous. This is the next issue to which all of these studies are ultimately dedicated. If the series ostensibly offers a unity of purpose or totality as completeness, seriality presages a paradox in the forms of its expressivity, one where shortfalls in extension remain material contradictions in narratives of social change, even as, or precisely because, one continues to follow one's own course.

---

8 Francis Wheen, *Karl Marx* (London: Fourth Estate, 1999); Francis Wheen, *Marx's Das Kapital: A Biography* (London: Atlantic Books, 2006). While the basic conceit of the latter to anthropomorphize *Capital* can grate, the idea of an animated text, in life and death, captures something of its spirit as critique and inspiration (and there remains the lingering aura of the *Bildungsroman*). The question of revision, of shaping and re-shaping his progeny, does not quite capture the will-to-science in Marx's project, yet the constitutive open-endedness of the critique is symptomatic of its unsettled serial tendencies.

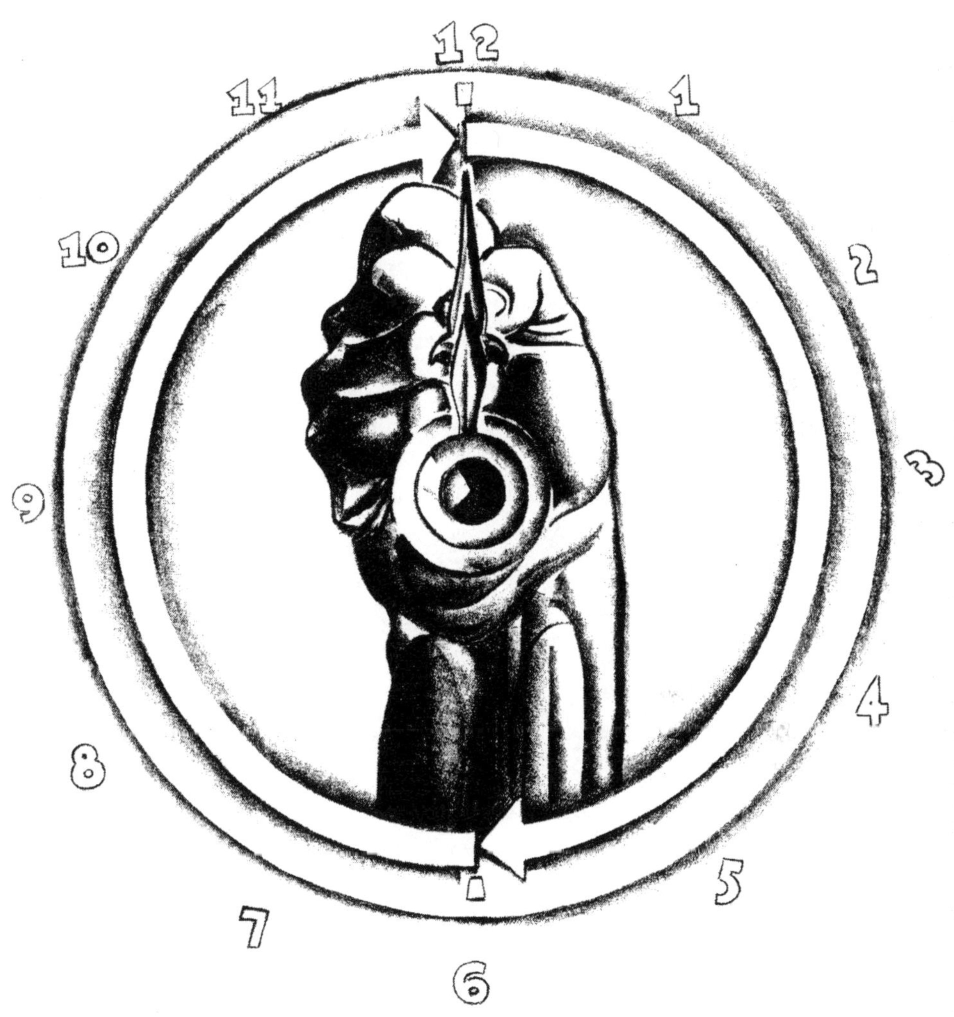

FIGURE 38. Hugo Gellert, "The Working Day" in *Karl Marx*: "*Capital*" *in Lithographs*, p. 34.

Acknowledgments

There are many people to thank for the development of this project but the impetus of the enigma of *Le Capital* noted in the text was clearly galvanized by an event, the financial crisis of 2008. Global capitalism's love of barely-secured securities and dubiously-derived derivatives accelerated an economic calamity of gargantuan proportions. This book is not about that crisis, but the meltdown was active in Japanese culture, where a series of "edumanga" produced a story based on Marx's *Capital*, one in which capitalism was explained to an increasingly precarious manga-reading lower-level white collar worker. I was fascinated by this storytelling of capital and by the role of serialization in its representation. I thank Midori Yamamura for helping me with some early translations from the Japanese text before these became available in other forms. I also thank Eric Cazdyn, who more recently provided me with translation suggestions for individual panels in the Japanese text. Manga serialization is in evidence in other parts of the book (notably in the section on *Ghost in the Shell*) and is a vital component of serial manufacture today.

Part One of the book gelled around a series (yes) of investigations into seriality as concept. I was seeking to establish more robust dialectical links between economic modalities and cultural expression without falling into moribund versions of base/superstructure critique. Some of the philosophical lineaments are abstract but individual examples, like Sartre on the queue, were theoretical provocations. Much of the tenor of the book was developed through my association with the Center for Place, Culture, and Politics at the CUNY Graduate Center. The Center has provided a forum to test out many of my ideas on seriality, and I thank the Directors I have had the pleasure of knowing, David Harvey, Ruth Wilson Gilmore, and, more recently, Miriam Ticktin for their support. David, I am sure, will find my extended reading of Marx's "serial," *Le Capital*, somewhat vexing but the links between production, popularization, and narration have an important purchase on how capitalism is reproduced, read, and opposed. I also thank two participants in a year-long Center seminar, Zandi Sherman (a post-doc at the Center) and Valentina Biondini (a visiting scholar) for their thoughtful responses to an earlier draft of my work on the Paris Commune. On the whole, I have spared my students and former students from my obsessive interest in seriality but several of them have had to bear it anyway, so thanks to Justin Rogers-Cooper, Jesse Schwartz, Valerie Fryer-Davis, and Sharanya Dutta, all of whom have taught me the patience of serial engagement. The Department of English at Baruch College has been a constant source of encouragement and I thank in particular Mary McGlynn, Jessica Lang, and Timothy Aubry. Portions of the project were given as lectures and papers at venues in Chicago, Honolulu, Natal (Brazil), Tallahassee, Gainesville, Antigonish, London (Ontario), and Seoul. I thank all those who provided me with an opportunity to discuss my work, including Phil Wegner, Robin Truth Goodman, Clive Thomson, Hyewon Shin, and Márcio Moraes Valença.

I set aside this project on more than one occasion (including during the Covid crisis), not just because of other books (*The Long Space* is serial adjacent around the question of novelization) but because I was flummoxed by a particular case study, the serialization of Marx's *Le Capital*, 1872–1875. How could one of the most documented and archived thinkers in the history of the word spend three years on a translation of his magnum opus as a serial with comparatively so little evidence of its distributed form? The text is certainly there and rigorously debated but its actual production and distribution to French workers in periodic "livraisons" as Marx envisaged publication does not obviously and logically depend on it. In general, Marxologists have been happy to interpret the text based on the single volume version collected in 1875 (some of whom in the present did not respond to my innocent entreaties!) but, as I explain, this elides the substance of seriality's claims on capitalist critique. I thank Kevin B. Anderson, Kenneth Hemmerechts, Nohemi Jocabeth Echeverría Vicente, and François Gaudin, all of whom have written extensively on the production of *Le Capital*, for sharing their thoughts on this question with me. I love Gaudin's light-hearted touch when pondering the fate of the livraisons. Stored in a barn, he mused, if the workers could not have them the horses could! Some of the ideas for this section of the book were elaborated at an ACLA seminar dedicated to the new English translation of *Das Kapital* by Paul Reitter and Paul North. I thank the organizers of the seminar, Andrew Parker and Emily Apter, and Paul North for his response to my piece. How Marx's critique of political economy continues to live is at the heart of this book.

How Marxist thinking emerges in other representations of *Capital* would be a much bigger project than the one here, but certain serial transformations remain instructive, including the lithographic series on *Capital* by Hugo Gellert that appeared in the 1930s. There are open source as well as museum quality collections of his work and I hope my efforts help to sustain interest in his coruscating art. I thank Mary M. Talbot and Bryan Talbot for permission to use an image from their wonderful graphic novel on the Communard revolutionary Louise Michel, *The Red Virgin and the Vision of Utopia*. I acknowledge the great Jacques Tardi and his publisher Casterman for citing several panels from his extraordinary quartet of graphic novels on the Paris Commune, *Le Cri du peuple*, based on the novel by Jean Vautrin. Variety Artworks' *Capital in Manga*! continues to be an inspiration for my thoughts on storytelling capital, both in the original Japanese publication by Team Banmikas/East Press, and in subsequent translations by Guy Yasko for Red Quill Books and by Florent George for Soleil Manga. While Team Banmikas did not answer my specific inquiries (in English and Japanese) about individual panels from the *Capital* manga I do hope my analysis meets the seriousness of their edumanga project.

I thank Fordham University Press, Chris Breu and the dearly missed Elizabeth A. Hatmaker for permission to use an edited and revised version of my essay "Cyborg Affect and the Power of the Posthuman in the *Ghost in the Shell* Franchise" from their collection *Noir Affect* (2020). Cyborg stories are the "other" serials of my *Capital* investigations. I also thank *Bakhtiniana* for the chance to draw from my essay, "Novelization and Serialization: Or, Forms of Time Otherwise" ("Romancização ou serialização: ou diferentes formas de tempo") that appeared in English and Portuguese in 2016. A Bakhtinian elaboration of novelization, novel, and nation has been an enduring concern and helps to accentuate a materialist understanding of aesthetic and political processes.

I thank the good folks at Seagull Books for their hard work on this book, including Bishan Samaddar and Diven Nagpal. I especially thank Naveen Kishore for his steadfast encouragement about the project, and I am very happy that it takes its place among such a stellar group of authors.

My permanent collaborators remain Amy, Sam, and Molly. We've built quite a series. Thanks!

List of Illustrations

Bibliography

ALI, Tariq. *The Idea of Communism*. London: Seagull Books, 2009.

ALLEN, Kate, and John E. Ingulsrud. *Reading Japan Cool: Patterns of Manga Literacy and Discourse*. New York: Lexington, 2009.

ALLEN, Rob, and Thijs van den Berg (eds). *Serialization in Popular Culture*. New York: Routledge, 2014.

ALTHUSSER, Louis, Étienne Balibar, Roger Establet, Pierre Macherey and Jacques Rancière. *Reading Capital—The Complete Edition* (Ben Brewster and David Fernbach trans.). New York: Verso, 2015.

ALTHUSSER, Louis. "Preface to Capital, Volume One (March 1969)" in *Lenin and Philosophy and Other Essays* (Ben Brewster trans.). New York: Monthly Review Press, 1971.

AMADEO, Kimberly. "Washington Mutual (WaMu): How It Went Bankrupt." *The Balance* (August 23, 2024).

AMYX, Jennifer A. *Japan's Financial Crisis: Institutional Rigidity and Reluctant Change*. Princeton, NJ: Princeton University Press, 2004.

ANDERSON, Benedict. *Imagined Communities: Reflections on the Origin and Spread of Nationalism*. London: Verso, 1983.

ANDERSON, Benedict. *The Spectre of Comparisons: Nationalism, Southeast Asia and the World*. London: Verso, 1998.

ANDERSON, Kevin B. "Marx's French Edition of Capital as Unexplored Territory" in Marcello Musto (ed.), *Marx and "Le Capital": Evaluation, History, Reception*. London: Routledge, 2022.

ANDERSON, Kevin B. "The 'Unknown' Marx's Capital, Volume I: The French Edition of 1872–75, 100 Years Later." *Review of Radical Political Economics* 15(4) (1983): 71–80.

ANDERSON, Kevin. "On the MEGA and the French Edition of Capital, VOL. I: An Appreciation and a Critique." *Beiträge zur Marx-Engels-Forschung Neue Folge* (1997): 131–36.

AUERBACH, Erich. *Mimesis: The Representation of Reality in Western Literature* (W. R. Trask trans.). Princeton, NJ: Princeton University Press, 2003.

BADIOU, Alain. "The Paris Commune: A Political Declaration on Politics" in *Polemics* (Bruno Bosteels et al. trans.). London: Verso, 2006.

BADIOU, Alain. *The Communist Hypothesis* (David Macey and Steve Corcoran trans.). London: Verso, 2015.

BAJAC, Quentin (ed.). *La Commune photographiée*. Paris: Éditions de la Réunion des Musées Nationaux, 2000.

BAKHTIN, Mikhail. "Forms of Time and of the Chronotope in The Novel" in *The Dialogic Imagination* (Michael Holquist ed., Caryl Emerson and Michael Holquist trans.). Austin, TX: University of Texas Press, 1981.

BAKHTIN, Mikhail. *Problems in Dostoevsky's Poetics* (Caryl Emerson trans. and ed.). Minneapolis: University of Minnesota Press, 1984.

BAKHTIN, Mikhail. *Rabelais and His World* (Helene Iswolsky trans.). Cambridge, MA: MIT Press, 1971.

BAKHTIN, Mikhail. *The Dialogic Imagination: Four Essays* (Michael Holquist ed., Caryl Emerson and Michael Holquist trans.). Austin, TX: University of Texas Press, 1981.

BALIBAR, Étienne, and Immanuel Wallerstein. *Race, Nation, Class: Ambiguous Identities* (Chris Turner trans.). London: Verso, 1991.

BALIBAR, Étienne. "Ambiguous Identities" in *Politics and the Other Scene* (Chris Turner trans.). New York: Verso, 2002.

BALIBAR, Étienne. *We, the People of Europe: Reflections on Transnational Citizenship* (James Swenson trans.). Princeton, NJ: Princeton University Press, 2004.

BARTHES, Roland. *Camera Lucida: Reflections on Photography* (Richard Howard trans.). New York: Farrar, Straus and Giroux, 1981.

BELLMER, Hans. *The Doll* (Malcolm Green trans.). London: Atlas Press, 2005.

BENJAMIN, Walter. "Conversations with Brecht" in Ernst Bloch et al., *Aesthetics and Politics* (Anna Bostock trans.). London: Verso, 1980.

BENJAMIN, Walter. "Surrealism: The Last Snapshot of the European Intelligentsia." *New Left Review* 108 (March–April 1978): 47–56.

BENJAMIN, Walter. "The Storyteller: Observations on the Works of Nikolai Leskov" in *Selected Writings, 3: 1935–1938* (Howard Eiland and Michael W. Jennings eds). Cambridge, MA: Harvard University Press, 2006.

BENJAMIN, Walter. "Theses on the Philosophy of History" in *Illuminations* (Hannah Arendt ed., Harry Zohn trans.). New York: Schocken, 1968.

BENJAMIN, Walter. *Illuminations* (Hannah Arendt ed., Harry Zohn trans.). New York: Schocken, 1969.

BENJAMIN, Walter. *On Photography* (Esther Leslie trans.). London: Reaktion Books, 2015.

BENJAMIN, Walter. *Reflections: Essays, Aphorisms, Autobiographical Writings* (Peter Demetz ed., Edmond Jephcott trans.). New York: Schocken, 1986.

BENJAMIN, Walter. *The Arcades Project* (Howard Eiland and Kevin McLaughlin trans.). Cambridge, MA: Harvard University Press, 1999.

BENJAMIN, Walter. *The Work of Art in the Age of Technological Reproducibility and Other Writings on Media*. Cambridge, MA: Harvard University Press, 2008.

BERGER, John. *Once in Europa*. New York: Pantheon, 1987.

BERGER, John. *Understanding a Photograph* (Geoff Dyer ed.). London: Penguin, 2013.

BLOCH, Ernst. "Nonsynchronism and the Obligation to Its Dialectics" (Mark Ritter trans.). *New German Critique* 11 (Spring 1977): 22–38.

BOLTON, Christopher. "From Wooden Cyborgs to Celluloid Souls: Mechanical Bodies in Anime and Japanese Puppet Theater." *positions* 10 (3) (Winter 2002): 729–71.

BOUFFARD, Alix, Alexandre Feron, Guillaume Fondu, and Michael Heinrich. *Ce qu'est Le Capital de Marx*. Paris: Les Éditions sociales, 2017.

BOUFFARD, Alix, and Alexandre Feron (eds). *L'édition française du Capital, une oeuvre originale: Le Capital, Livre I: Présentation, Commentaires et Documents*. Paris: Les Éditions sociales, 2018.

BRAKE, Laurel. *Print in Transition, 1850–1910: Studies in Media and Book History*. London: Palgrave, 2001.

BREU, Christopher, and Elizabeth A. Hatmaker (eds.). *Noir Affect*. New York: Fordham University Press, 2020.

BROWN, Steven T. *Tokyo Cyberpunk: Posthumanism in Japanese Visual Culture*. London: Palgrave, 2010.

CASSIRER, Ernst. *The Philosophy of Symbolic Forms*, 3 VOLS. (Steve G. Lofts trans.). Abingdon: Routledge, 2021.

CÉSAIRE, Aimé. *Discourse on Colonialism* (Joan Pinkham trans.). New York: Monthly Review Press, 2000.

CHATTERJEE, Partha. "Anderson's Utopia." *Diacritics* 29 (4) (Winter 1999): 128–34.

CLARK, Katerina, and Michael Holquist. *Mikhail Bakhtin*. Cambridge, MA: Harvard University Press, 1984.

COLE, Henry. "Modern Wood Engraving." *London and Westminster Review* 28 (1838): 268–69.

COLOMBANI, Jean-Marie. *Double Calédonie: d'une utopie à l'autre*. Paris: Denoël, 1999.

DEAK, Zoltan (ed.). *Hugo Gellert, 1892–1985: People's Artist*. New York: Hugo Gellert Memorial Committee, 1986.

DELEUZE, Gilles, and Félix GUATTARI. *A Thousand Plateaus: Capitalism and Schizophrenia* (Brian Massumi trans.). Minneapolis, MN: University of Minnesota Press, 1987.

DELEUZE, Gilles, and Félix Guattari. *Kafka: Toward a Minor Literature* (Dana Polan trans.). Minneapolis, MN: University of Minnesota Press, 1986.

DELEUZE, Gilles. *Cinema 1: The Movement-Image* (Hugh Tomlinson and Barbara Habberjam trans.). Minneapolis, MN: University of Minnesota Press, 1986.

DELEUZE, Gilles. *Cinema 2: The Time-Image* (Hugh Tomlinson and Robert Galeta trans.). Minneapolis, MN: University of Minnesota Press, 1989.

DELEUZE, Gilles. *Difference and Repetition* (Paul Patton trans.). New York: Columbia University Press, 1994 [1968].

DELEUZE, Gilles. *The Logic of Sense* (Mark Lester trans.). London: Athlone, 1990 [1969].

DENSON, Shane, and Ruth Mayer. "Spectral Seriality: The Sights and Sounds of Count Dracula" in Frank Kelleter (ed.), *The Media of Serial Narrative*. Columbus, OH: Ohio State University Press, 2017.

DENSON, Shane. "Seriality" in Jeffrey R. Di Leo (ed.), *The Bloomsbury Handbook of Literary and Cultural Theory*. London: Bloomsbury, 2019.

DENSON, Shane. "The New Seriality." *Qui Parle* 32(2) (December 2023): 301–39.

DERRIDA, Jacques. "Living On / Borderlines" (James Hulbert trans.) in Harold Bloom, Paul de Man, Jacques Derrida, Geoffrey H. Hartman, and J. Hillis Miller, *Deconstruction and Criticism*. London and New York: Continuum, 2004.

DERRIDA, Jacques. "Survivre: journal de bord" in *Parages*. Paris: Éditions Galilée, 1986.

DERRIDA, Jacques. *The Truth in Painting* (Geoff Bennington and Ian McLeod trans.). Chicago, IL: University of Chicago Press, 1987.

DICKENS, Charles. *The Pickwick Papers*. London: Penguin, 2003.

DIOGUARDI, Edward. "Lacan's Sinthome; or, the Point of Psychoanalysis." *The European Journal of Psychoanalysis* 7(2) (2021).

DOUZINAS, Costas, and Slavoj Žižek (eds). *The Idea of Communism*. London: Verso, 2010.

DUCANGE, Jean-Numa, and Jean Quétier. "The Contradictory Reception of the French Edition of Capital" in Marcello Musto (ed.), *Marx and "Le Capital": Evaluation, History, Reception*. London: Routledge, 2022.

DUNAYEVSKAYA, Raya. "Capital: Significance of the 1875 French Edition of Volume I" in *Rosa Luxemburg, Women's Liberation, and Marx's Philosophy of Revolution*. New Jersey and Sussex: Harvester, 1982.

DUNAYEVSKAYA, Raya. "The Paris Commune Illuminates and Deepens the Content of Capital" in *Marxism and Freedom*. New York: Bookman, 1958.

DUNCAN, Pansy. "Once More, with Fredric Jameson." *Cultural Critique* 97 (Fall 2017): 1–23.

EAGLETON, Terry, Fredric Jameson, and Edward Said. *Nationalism, Colonialism, and Literature*. Minneapolis, MN: University of Minnesota Press, 1990.

ECHÉVERRÍA VICENTE, Nohemi Jocabeth, and Kenneth Hemmerechts. *Publishing Karl Marx's "Le Capital" (1871–1875)*. London: Brill, 2024.

EISNER, Will. *Comics and Sequential Art: Principles and Practices*. New York: Norton, 2008.

ENGELS, Friedrich, and Karl Marx. *The German Ideology*. New York: Prometheus Books, 1998.

EVANS, Kate. *Red Rosa*. London: Verso, 2015.

EXNER, Eike. *Comics and the Origins of Manga*. New Brunswick, NJ: Rutgers University Press, 2022.

FELTES, Norman N. *Modes of Production of Victorian Novels*. Chicago, IL: University of Chicago Press, 1986.

FINN, Daniel. "The Theory and Practice of Marxism in Japan: An Interview with Gavin Walker." *Jacobin* (July 3, 2021).

FISCHER, Hannelore (ed.). *Käthe Kollwitz*. Munich: Hirmer, 2022.

FOUCAULT, Michel. *The History of Sexuality* (Robert Hurley trans.). New York: Vintage, 1990.

GAUDIN, François (ed.). *Traduire Le capital: Une correspondance inédite entre Karl Marx, Friedrich Engels et l'éditeur Maurice Lachâtre*. Mont-Saint-Aignan: Presses universitaires de Rouen et du Havre, 2019.

GELLERT, Hugo. *Karl Marx: "Capital" in Lithographs*. Facsimile edition. Delhi: Gyan Books, 2015.

GELLERT, Hugo. *Karl Marx: "Capital" in Lithographs*. New York: Ray Long and Richard R. Smith, 1934.

GENETTE, Gérard. *Palimpsests: Literature in the Second Degree* (Channa Newman and Claude Doubinsky trans.). Lincoln, NE: University of Nebraska Press, 1997.

GOUWS, Amanda. "Race as Seriality: A Response to David Benatar and Zimitri Erasmus." *South African Journal of Higher Education* 24(2) (2010): 313–17.

GRAY, Chris Hables (ed.). *The Cyborg Handbook*. New York: Routledge, 1995.

GREG, Melissa, and Carolyn PEDWELL (eds). *The Affect Theory Reader 2: Worldings, Tensions, Futures*. Durham, NC: Duke University Press, 2023.

GREG, Melissa, and Gregory J. SEIGWORTH (eds). *The Affect Theory Reader*. Durham, NC: Duke University Press, 2010.

GULLICKSON, Gayle L. *Unruly Women of Paris: Images of the Commune*. Ithaca, NY: Cornell University Press, 1996.

HAGEDORN, Roger. "Doubtless to Be Continued: A Brief History of Serial Narrative" in Robert C. Allen (ed.), *To Be Continued . . . : Soap Operas Around the World*. London: Routledge, 1995.

HAGEDORN, Roger. "Technology and Economic Exploitation: The Serial as a Form of Narrative Presentation." *Wide Angle* 10 (4) (1988): 4–12.

HARAWAY, Donna. "A Cyborg Manifesto." *Socialist Review* (1984). Reprinted in *The Cyborg Handbook* (Chris Hables Gray ed.). New York: Routledge, 1995.

HARDT, Michael, and Antonio Negri. *Empire*. Cambridge, MA: Harvard University Press, 2000.

HARNEY, Stefano, and Fred Moten. *All Incomplete*. New York: Minor Compositions, 2021.

HARVEY, David. *A Companion to Marx's Capital*. London: Verso, 2010.

HARVEY, David. *The Anti-Capitalist Chronicles*. London: Pluto, 2020.

HARVEY, David. *The Enigma of Capital and the Crises of Capitalism*. Oxford: Oxford University Press, 2010.

HAYLES, N. Katherine. *How We Became Posthuman*. Chicago, IL: University of Chicago Press, 1999.

HEGEL, G. W. F. *Science of Logic* (A. V. Miller trans.). London: George Allen & Unwin, 1969 [1812–16].

HEINRICH, Michael. "Le Capital après la MEGA" in Alix Bouffard, Alexandre Feron, Guillaume Fondu, and Michael Heinrich, *Ce qu'est Le Capital de Marx*. Paris: Les Éditions sociales, 2017.

HEINRICH, Michael. *An Introduction to the Three Volumes of Marx's Capital* (Alexander Locascio trans.). New York: Monthly Review Press, 2004.

HEINRICH, Michael. *How to Read Marx's Capital: Commentary and Explanations of the Beginning Chapters* (Alexander Locascio trans.). New York: Monthly Review Press, 2021.

HEMMERECHTS, Kenneth, and Nohemi Jocabeth Echeverría Vicente. "The Paris Commune and Karl Marx's Le Capital." *Modern Intellectual History* (2022): 1–21.

HITCHCOCK, Peter. "Immediation and Responsibility" in Jeffrey Di Leo and Peter Hitchcock (eds), *The New Public Intellectual*. New York: Palgrave Macmillan, 2016.

HITCHCOCK, Peter. "Kant at the Federal Reserve: On the Aesthetics of Quantitative Easing" in Jeffrey R. Di Leo, Peter Hitchcock and Sophia McClennen (eds), *The Debt Age*. New York: Routledge, 2018.

HITCHCOCK, Peter. *Labor in Culture, or, Worker of the World(s)*. New York: Palgrave, 2017.

HITCHCOCK, Peter. *The Long Space: Transnationalism and Postcolonial Form*. Stanford, CA: Stanford University Press, 2010.

HOBSBAWM, Eric. "Marx and History." *New Left Review* 143 (January–February 1984): 46.

HOLMES, John. "Illustrated Books." *Quarterly Review* 74 (June 1844): 170–71.

INGULSRUD, John E., and Kate Allen. *Reading Japan Cool: Patterns of Manga Literacy and Discourse*. New York: Lexington, 2009.

JAMES, C. L. R. *The Black Jacobins: Toussaint L'Ouverture and the San Domingo Revolution*. New York: Vintage, 1989.

JAMES, William. *The Principles of Psychology*. New York: Holt, Rinehart and Winston, 1980.

JAMESON, Fredric. *The Antinomies of Realism*. New York: Verso, 2013.

JAMESON, Fredric. *The Political Unconscious: Narrative as a Socially Symbolic Act*. Ithaca, NY: Cornell University Press, 1981.

KAWAI, Masahiro, and Shinji Takagi. "Why Was Japan Hit So Hard by the Global Financial Crisis?" *ADBI Working Paper Series* (Asia Development Bank Institute) 153 (October 2009): 1–15.

KELLETER, Frank. "From Recursive Progression to Systemic Self-Observation: Elements of a Theory of Seriality." *The Velvet Light Trap* 79 (Spring 2017).

KLIGER, Illya, and Boris Maslov (eds). *Persistent Forms: Explorations in Historical Poetics*. New York: Fordham University Press, 2015.

KOJIMA, Akira. "Japan's Economy and the Global Financial Crisis." *Asia-Pacific Review* 16(2) (2009): 15–25.

KORNBLUH, Anna. *Immediacy*. New York: Verso, 2023.

KRÄTKE, Michael R. "An Unfinished Project: Marx's Last Works on Capital" in Marcello Musto (ed.), *Marx and "Le Capital": Evaluation, History, Reception*. London: Routledge, 2022.

LACAN, Jacques. "The Function and Field of Speech and Language in Psychoanalysis" in *Écrits: A Selection* (Alan Sheridan trans.). London: Routledge, 1989.

LACAN, Jacques. *Encore: The Seminar of Jacques Lacan, Book XX, On Feminine Sexuality: The Limits of Love and Knowledge, 1972–1973* (Bruce Fink trans.). New York: Norton, 1998.

LACAN, Jacques. *The Four Fundamental Concepts of Psychoanalysis*, The Seminar of Jacques Lacan, Book XI (Alan Sheridan trans.). New York: Norton, 1978.

LAPOSTOLLE, Christine. "Plus vrai que le vrai: Stratégie photographique et Commune de Paris." *Actes de la recherche en sciences sociales* 73 (1988): 67–76.

LEIBNIZ, Gottfried Wilhelm. *Discourse on Metaphysics and Other Essays* (Daniel Garber and Roger Arlew trans.). New York: Hackett, 1991.

LEITH, James A. "The War of Images Surrounding the Commune" in *Images of the Commune / Images de la Commune* (James A. Leith ed.). Montreal: McGill-Queen's University Press, 1978.

LEWIS, Leo. "Karl Marx Goes Manga in a Kapital Comic Strip." *The Times* (November 18, 2008).

LISSAGARAY, Prosper-Olivier. *History of the Commune of 1871* (Eleanor Marx Aveling trans.). London: T. Fisher Unwin, 1902.

LISSAGARAY, Prosper-Olivier. *History of the Paris Commune of 1871* (Eleanor Marx trans.). London: Verso, 2012.

Löwy, Michael, and Olivier Besancenot. *Affinités révolutionnaires: Nos étoiles rouges et noires: Pour une solidarité entre marxistes et libertaires*. Paris: Éditions Mille et Une Nuits, 2014.

Löwy, Michael, and Olivier Besancenot. *Marx in Paris* (Todd Chretien trans.). Chicago, IL: Haymarket Books, 2022.

Löwy, Michael, and Olivier Besancenot. *Revolutionary Affinities: Toward a Marxist-Anarchist Solidarity* (David Campbell trans.). Binghamton, NY: PM Press, 2023.

Löwy, Michael. *Georg Lukács: From Romanticism to Bolshevism* (Patrick Camiller trans.). London: New Left Books, 1979.

Lukács, Georg. *History and Class Consciousness: Studies in Marxist Dialectics* (Rodney Livingstone trans.). London: Merlin Press, 1971.

Lukács, Georg. *The Theory of the Novel: A Historico-Philosophical Essay on the Forms of Great Epic Literature* (Anna Bostock trans.). London: Merlin Press, 1971.

Lyons, Martyn. *The Totem and the Tricolour: A Short History of New Caledonia since 1774*. Randwick: New South Wales University Press, 1986.

Macherey, Pierre. *A Theory of Literary Production* (Geoffrey Wall trans.). New York: Routledge, 2006.

MacWilliams, Mark E. (ed.). *Explorations in the World of Manga and Anime*. London: M. E. Sharpe, 2008.

Marx, Karl, and Friedrich Engels. *Collected Works, Volume 44: Letters 1870–1873*. London: Lawrence and Wishart, 2010.

Marx, Karl, and Friedrich Engels. *Collected Works, Volume 45: Letters 1874–1879*. Moscow: Progress Publishers, 1991.

Marx, Karl. "The Civil War in France." Available at: rebrand.ly/3cedd6 (last accessed: August 26, 2025).

Marx, Karl. *Capital, A Critique of Political Economy: Volume One* (Ernest Untermann ed. and trans.). Chicago, IL: Charles H. Kerr and Co., 1906–1909.

Marx, Karl. *Capital: A Critique of Political Economy, Volume 1* (Ben Fowkes trans.). London: Penguin, 1992.

Marx, Karl. *Capital: Critique of Political Economy, Volume One* (Paul Reitter trans., Paul North and Paul Reitter eds). Princeton, NJ: Princeton University Press, 2024.

Marx, Karl. *Critique of Hegel's Philosophy of Right* (Annette Jolin and Joseph O'Malley trans.). Cambridge: Cambridge University Press, 1970.

Marx, Karl. *Das Kapital: Kritik der politischen Ökonomie*, vol. 1. Hamburg: Otto Meissner Verlag, 1890 [MEGA² 2.10]; Berlin: Dieter Verlag, 1991.

Marx, Karl. *Economic and Political Manuscripts of 1844* (Martin Milligan trans.). Moscow: Progress Publishers, 1959.

MARX, Karl. *El Capital: Segunda Parte* (Maite Madinabeitia trans.). Barcelona: Herder Editorial, SL, 2013.

MARX, Karl. *Grundrisse: Foundations of the Critique of Political Economy* (Martin Nicolaus trans.). London: Pelican, 1973.

MARX, Karl. *Le Capital* (M. J. Roy trans.). Paris: Maurice Lachâtre, 1875.

MARX, Karl. *Le Capital*, 2 VOLS (Florent Georges trans.). Paris: Soleil Manga, 2011.

MARX, Karl. *The Civil War in France*. Peking: Foreign Languages Press, 1970.

MARX, Karl. *The Eighteenth Brumaire of Louis Bonaparte* (S. K. Padover trans.). Moscow: Progress Publishers, 1937.

MASSUMI, Brian. *Parables of the Virtual*. Durham, NC: Duke University Press, 2002.

MASSUMI, Brian. *The Politics of Affect*. Cambridge: Polity, 2015.

MATURANA, Humberto R., and Francisco J. Varela. *Autopoiesis and Cognition: The Realization of the Living*. Dordrecht: Reidel, 1980.

MAU, Søren. *Mute Compulsion: A Marxist Theory of the Economic Power of Capital*. London: Verso, 2023.

MERRIMAN, John. *Massacre: The Life and Death of the Paris Commune of 1871*. New Haven, CT: Yale University Press, 2014.

MICHEL, Louise. *La Commune*. Paris: Éditions Stock, 1978 [1898].

MICHEL, Louise. *Mémoires de Louise Michel, écrits par elle-même*. Paris: F. Roy, 1886.

MICHEL, Louise. *The Red Virgin: Memoirs of Louise Michel* (Bullitt Lowry and Elizabeth Ellington Gunther eds and trans.). Tuscaloosa, AL: University of Alabama Press, 1981.

MICHEL, Louise. *Trois romans: Les Microbes humains, Le Monde nouveau, Le Claque-dents*. Lyon: Presses Universitaires de Lyon (PUL), 2013.

MONOSON, S. Sara. "Aesop Said So: Ancient Wisdom and Radical Politics in 1930s New York." *Classical Receptions Journal* 8(1) (2016): 90–113.

MORSON, Gary Saul. "Bakhtin, Genres, and Temporality." *New Literary History* 22 (4) (Autumn 1991): 1071–92.

MORSON, Gary Saul. *The Boundaries of Genre: Dostoevsky's Diary of a Writer and the Traditions of Literary Utopia*. Austin, TX: University of Texas Press, 1981.

MULLEN, Bill, and Sherry Linkon (eds). *Radical Revisions: Re-reading 1930s Culture*. Urbana/Champaign, IL: University of Illinois Press, 1996.

MUSTO, Marcello (ed.). *Marx and "Le Capital": Evaluation, History, Reception*. London: Routledge, 2022.

NILSSON, Magnus. "Marxism across Media: Characterization and Montage in Variety Artwork's *Capital in Manga*." *International Journal of Comic Art* 21(1) (Spring–Summer 2019): 423–38.

Orbaugh, Sharalyn. "Emotional Infectivity: Cyborg Affect and the Limits of the Human." *Mechademia* 3 (2008): 150–72.

Payne, David. *The Re-enchantment of Nineteenth-Century Fiction*. New York: Palgrave Macmillan, 2005.

Peter Kropotkin Archive. "Jules Vallès, L'Enfant – Le Bachelier – L'Insurgé: La Trilogie de Jacques Vingtras en version intégrale (1878)" (Kindle edition). Accessed at marxists.org: rebrand.ly/aea929 (last accessed: August 26, 2025).

Pinho, Rodrigo Maiolini Rebello. "The Originality of Marx's French Edition of Capital: An Historical Analysis" (Naomi J. Sutcliffe de Moraes trans.). *The International Marxist-Humanist* (September 2021): 5.

Poole, Brian. "Bakhtin and Cassirer: The Philosophical Origins of Bakhtin's Carnival Messianism." *South Atlantic Quarterly* 97 (3–4) (1998): 537–78.

Prawer, S. S. *Karl Marx and World Literature*. Oxford: Oxford University Press, 1976.

Przyblyski, Jeannene. "Revolution at a Standstill: Photography and the Paris Commune of 1871." *Yale French Studies* 101 (2001): 54–78.

Rancière, Jacques. *La Nuit des prolétaires: Archives du rêve ouvrier*. Paris: Fayard, 1981.

Rancière, Jacques. *Le Philosophe et ses pauvres*. Paris: Fayard, 1983.

Rancière, Jacques. *Proletarian Nights: The Workers' Dream in Nineteenth-Century France* (David Fernbach trans.). New York: Verso, 2012.

Rancière, Jacques. *Staging the People* (David Fernbach trans.). New York: Verso, 2011.

Rancière, Jacques. *The Philosopher and His Poor* (Andrew Parker trans.). Durham, NC: Duke University Press, 2004.

Raudnitz, Jules. "Le Sabbat rouge." *Série stéréoscopique*. Paris: Bibliothèque nationale de France, 1871.

Ross, Kristin. *Communal Luxury: The Political Imaginary of the Paris Commune*. New York: Verso, 2015.

Said, Edward. "Yeats and Decolonization" in Terry Eagleton, Fredric Jameson and Edward Said, *Nationalism, Colonialism, and Literature*. Minneapolis, MN: University of Minnesota Press, 1990.

Saito, Kohei. *Marx in the Anthropocene: Towards the Idea of Degrowth Communism*. Cambridge: Cambridge University Press, 2022.

Saito, Kohei. *Slow Down: The Degrowth Manifesto* (Brian Bergstrom trans.). New York: Astra, 2024.

San Diego Bakhtin Circle (eds). *Bakhtin and the Nation*. Lewisburg, PA: Bucknell University Press, 2000.

Sartre, Jean-Paul. *Being and Nothingness* (Sarah Richmond trans.). New York: Routledge, 2020.

SARTRE, Jean-Paul. *Critique of Dialectical Reason, Volume 1: Theory of Practical Ensembles* (Alan Sheridan-Smith trans.). New York: Verso, 2004.

SARTRE, Jean-Paul. *Critique of Dialectical Reason, Volume 2: The Intelligibility of History* (Arlette Elkaïm-Sartre ed., Quintin Hoare trans.). New York: Verso, 2006.

SARTRE, Jean-Paul. *Qu'est-ce que la littérature?* Paris: Gallimard, 1948.

SÉNÈS, Jacqueline. *La Vie quotidienne en Nouvelle-Calédonie de 1850 à nos jours*. Mesnil-sur-l'Estrée: Société Nouvelle Firmin-Didot, 1987.

SEYMOUR-JONES, Carole. *A Dangerous Liaison*. New York: Overlook Press, 2009.

SHIROW, Masamune. *Ghost in the Shell* (Frederik L. Schodt and Toren Smith trans.), 2nd edn. Milwaukie, OR: Dark Horse Comics, 2004.

SHIROW, Masamune. *Kōkaku kidōtai*. Tokyo: Kōdansha, 1991.

SIEGEL, William. *The Paris Commune: A Story in Pictures*. New York: International Pamphlets, 1932.

SNOWDON, Peter (dir.). *The Uprising*. Rien à Voir Production, 2013.

SPENCER, Robyn C. *The Revolution Has Come: Black Power, Gender, and the Black Panther Party in Oakland*. Durham, NC: Duke University Press, 2016.

SPINOZA, Benedict. *The Ethics* in *A Spinoza Reader: The Ethics and Other Works* (Edwin Curley ed. and trans.). Princeton, NJ: Princeton University Press, 1994.

ST. CLAIR, Robert. "Reframing the Commune: Violence, Intertextuality, and Event in Tardi's *Cri du peuple*." *Romance Notes* 55 (1) (2015): 147–59.

STEDMAN JONES, Gareth. *Karl Marx: Greatness and Illusion*. Cambridge, MA: Harvard University Press, 2016.

TALBOT, Mary M., and Bryan Talbot. *The Red Virgin and the Vision of Utopia*. Milwaukie, OR: Dark Horse Books, 2016.

TARDI, Jacques. *Le Cri du peuple*, VOLS 1–4. Paris: Casterman, 2001–2004.

TARDI, Jacques. *Les Aventures extraordinaires d'Adèle Blanc-Sec*. Paris: Casterman, 1976–2007.

THOBURN, Nicholas. *Deleuze, Marx, and Politics*. London: Routledge, 2003.

THOMAS, Edith. *Louise Michel* (Penelope Williams trans.). Montreal: Black Rose, 1980.

THOMAS, Édith. *Louise Michel ou la Velleda de l'anarchie*. Paris: Gallimard, 1971.

TIHANOV, Galin. *The Master and the Slave: Lukács, Bakhtin, and the Ideas of Their Time*. New York: Oxford University Press, 2000.

TODD, William Mills III. "The Brothers Karamazov and the Poetics of Serial Publication." *Dostoevsky Studies* 7 (1986): 88–97.

TOMBS, Robert. "How Bloody was 'La Semaine Sanglante' of 1871? A Revision." *The Historical Journal* 55 (September 3, 2012): 679–704.

TRAHTENBERG, Alexander. Introduction to William Siegel, *The Paris Commune: A Story in Pictures*. New York: International Pamphlets, 1932.

TROTSKY, Leon. *History of the Russian Revolution*. Chicago, IL: Haymarket Books, 2008.

UENO, Toshiya. "Japanimation and Techno-Orientalism" and "The Shock Projected onto the Other: Notes on Japanimation and Techno-Orientalism" in Bruce Grenville (ed.), *The Uncanny: Experiments in Cyborg Culture*. Vancouver: Arsenal Pulp Press, 2001.

VALLÈS, Jules. *L'Enfant – Le Bachelier – L'Insurgé: La Trilogie de Jacques Vingtras en version intégrale (1878)* (Kindle edition).

VARIETY ARTWORKS. *Capital in Manga!* (Guy Yasko trans.). Ottawa: Red Quill Books, 2012.

VARIETY ARTWORKS. *Capital in Manga! 2*. Tokyo: East Press/Team Banmikas, 2009.

VARIETY ARTWORKS. *Capital in Manga!* Tokyo: East Press/Team Banmikas, 2008.

VAUTRIN, Jean. *Le Cri du peuple*. Paris: Éditions Grasset et Fasquelle, 1999.

VAUTRIN, Jean. *The Voice of the People* (John Howe trans.). London: Phoenix House, 2002.

VILLIERS DE L'ISLE-ADAM, Auguste. *L'Eve future* (1886).

VILLIERS DE L'ISLE-ADAM, Auguste. *Tomorrow's Eve* (Robert Martin Adams trans.). Champaign, IL: University of Illinois Press, 2001.

VINCENT, K. Steven. *Between Marxism and Anarchism*. Berkeley: University of California Press, 1993.

VOLOSHINOV, V. N. *Marxism and the Philosophy of Language* (Ladislav Matejka and I. R. Titunik trans.). Cambridge, MA: Harvard University Press, 1986.

WALKER, Gavin. "Marxist Theory in Japan." *Historical Materialism*. Available at: rebrand.ly/8adbb0 (last accessed: August 26, 2025).

WALKER, Gavin. *The Sublime Perversion of Capital*. Durham, NC: Duke University Press, 2016.

WARD, Estolv Ethan. *The Gentle Dynamiter: A Biography of Tom Mooney*. Palo Alto, CA: Ramparts Press, 1983.

WATKINS, Peter (dir.). *La Commune (Paris, 1871)*. 13 Production, 2000.

WHEEN, Francis. *Karl Marx*. London: Fourth Estate, 1999.

WHEEN, Francis. *Marx's Das Kapital: A Biography*. London: Atlantic Books, 2006.

WIGMORE, Barry A. *The Financial Crisis of 2008: A History of US Financial Markets 2000–2012*. Cambridge: Cambridge University Press, 2022.

WILLIAMS, Raymond. *Marxism and Literature*. Oxford: Oxford University Press, 1977.

WRIGHT, Alastair. "Mourning, Painting, and the Commune: Maximilien Luce's *A Paris Street in 1871*." *Oxford Art Journal* 32 (2) (2009): 223–42.

YOUNG, Iris Marion. "Gender as Seriality: Thinking about Women as a Social Collective." *Signs: Journal of Women in Culture and Society* 19(3) (1994): 713–38.

Index